11261665

D1523393

The Directors Guild of America
Oral History Series

David H. Shepard, General Editor

1. Byron Haskin. 1984.
2. Worthington Miner. 1985.
3. Curtis Bernhardt/Henry Koster.
4. King Vidor.
5. David Butler.
6. Stuart Heisler.

Worthington Miner, drawing by Jo Mielziner, 1928.

A Directors Guild of America Oral History

WORTHINGTON MINER

Interviewed by
Franklin J. Schaffner

The Directors Guild of
America and
The Scarecrow Press, Inc.
Metuchen, N.J., and London
1985

Library of Congress Cataloging in Publication Data

Miner, Worthington, d. 1982.
  Worthington Miner.

  (The Directors Guild of America oral history series)
  Includes indexes.
  1. Miner, Worthington, d. 1982. 2. Television
producers and directors--United States--Biography.
3. Television producers and directors--United States--
Interviews. I. Schaffner, Franklin J. II. Title.
III. Series.
PN1992.4.M56A38 1985   791.45'0233'0924 [B] 84-22184
ISBN 0-8108-1757-8

PN
1992.4
M56
A38
1985

TABLE OF CONTENTS

FOREWORD

Worthington Miner was a pioneer and survivor by nature and a man of the theatre by discipline. We wanted to interview him for the Directors Guild of America because he had come to television when it was a new and untried medium, ultimately to create such distinguished shows as Studio One. Through prodigious effort Miner not only established program patterns which defined the entire "golden age" of live broadcasting, but also originated basic production procedures and divisions of responsibility which prevail in television practice to this day. Along the way Tony Miner provided inspiration, guidance and opportunity for many young directors who are now better-known than their mentor, having cut broad swaths of achievement across the large and small screen as well as the stage. Frankin J. Schaffner, director of Patton, Islands in the Stream, The Boys from Brazil and Yes, Giorgio, is one of the distinguished achievers Miner recognized and helped.

The rewards of reading this book exceed by far the mere discovery of information. Worthington Miner allows free access to his incredibly wide-ranging mind which not only witnessed and shaped but also reflected upon seminal events which redefined art and communication in the twentieth century. Miner shows us how to conquer changes in technology and circumstance by looking ahead with enthusiasm rather than back with nostalgia. He shows us afresh the precision and beauty that spoken English can achieve. (In editing this work I more than once went to unabridged dictionaries to discover that usages which first seemed wrong were arcane but precisely correct.)

It was difficult to persuade Mr. Miner to begin this work of reminiscence, but when he saw its potential as his testament of values, he devoted more and more effort and enthusiasm to its improvement. The first draft was a verbatim transcript of a series of audiotaped interviews. It displayed many of the fine qualities of the final product, but also disclosed the fragmentary and halting nature of the search for events long unrecalled. Miner decided to use this draft as the rough basis for a new composition entirely of his own devising, an autobiography in the form of an interview. This was shaped and modified in long telephone sessions which he dictated and we discussed while a tape recorder took everything down. An edited transcript of these calls became the second draft. Thereafter, Miner revised the book in longhand, his poor eyes struggling with microscopic writing under intense light. Franklin Schaffner, who was involved at the first stages of the project, re-entered at the end to work with Tony on a significant clarification and revision of the text, which was substantially in finished form three months before Worthington Miner died on December 11, 1982.

For important contributions to the long evolution of this text, we are grateful to Robert Saudek, Paris K.C. Barclay, Adele Field, Ann Lewis Hamilton, George Wallach, and to Margaret, Peter and Mary, the children of Fran and Tony Miner.

--- David Shepard

PREFACE

As the reader will discover in these memoirs, my father Tony Miner came to feel strongly in his old age that fortune had played a great role in his life. Born in 1900, he called himself "a child of the century," lucky enough to come of age in the ebullient and vital theatrical world of the twenties. And then, at the end of the thirties, when he was searching for a new direction, lucky enough that the century presented him with a completely new challenge -- television. In the 1960s and 1970s, as an educator, Tony devoted his talent and energy to the American Academy of Dramatic Arts.

At the very end of his life, fortune again gave him a chance to work productively -- on these memoirs. He died in 1982, and by 1979, realizing that there was little more work he would have the strength to do, his mind turned toward summing up his life and experience. He would have liked to produce a standard, formal autobiography, but not only did the task seem quite formidable, he wondered if others would really after all be interested. It meant an enormous amount to him that the Directors Guild of America, especially through David Shepard, asked him to review his career in the form of an oral history and assured him that there would be people who would want to read what he had to say. The Guild not only arranged for two interviewers (and Tony's family is particularly grateful to Franklin Schaffner for his sensitivity and kindness), but also encouraged Tony to edit and add to the original transcripts to provide a fuller account of his life.

Subjectively, this kind of interest obviously would raise anyone's spirits. But more important, objectively, these oral history projects are extremely valuable. Usually memories are entirely lost when a person dies. Tony, curiously, rarely even spoke of his early days in television. Perhaps he thought that no one would care about this "old news," but at any rate the effect was that the information he possessed would not even have been remembered by his family; it would have disappeared upon his death. And there are few other sources for the history he lived through, especially for the early years of television, and most especially for the creative aspects of the medium. It is difficult, in the light of what television has become, to recall the excitement, versatility, and energy that it provoked at its outset. Even the visual record is almost entirely erased. And so, to understand the early development of this uniquely influential force in our lives, we must capture the memories of those who were there. We all benefit when an institution such as the Guild sets out to record the past in this way. Otherwise so much experience and accomplishment may be wasted and forgotten.

--- Margaret Miner

WORTHINGTON
MINER

SCHAFFNER: Tony, finding myself cast in the role of an Interlocutor, I am stunned to discover that, despite our four years together on Studio One, what I had known about you is pitifully small against this monumental stack of notes I have been handed by the Directors Guild to guide my questioning. Where shall we start?

MINER: How best have you known me up to now?

SCHAFFNER: As a part, a most important part, of those early days. To the people watching, Milton Berle was "Mr. Television." For those of us on the inside, that title belonged with far greater justice to you.

MINER: The measure of that compliment depends on how good we really were -- all of us, any of us. It's a searching question.

SCHAFFNER: Good! That gives us a starting point. Your name is so closely associated with the "Golden Age," let's begin by finding out when you feel the "Golden Age" started, what made it "Golden," how long it lasted, and what caused its demise.

MINER: It started the minute CBS began to challenge the prior dominance of NBC. Did you realize that NBC went on the air with a regular schedule as early as 1939? It could have been '37. It was a full decade later that CBS launched its first rebuttal, Toast of the Town. You probably think of it as

The Ed Sullivan Show. It was CBS's answer to The Texaco Star Theater with Milton Berle. The fateful date was June 20, 1948. That same year CBS presented Studio One as an answer to the Philco Television Playhouse, November 7, 1948.

What made it "Golden" was the fact that it began in New York, that its standards were theatre standards, and its maximum audience was roughly ten to fifteen percent of the potential television public -- a relatively affluent, well-educated and preponderantly mature audience, twenty-five to fifty years of age. What is of equal importance is to recognize all the things that the Golden Age was not. Its idolaters would have us believe that its productions were not only literate and provocative, but just as slick and technically sophisticated as anything we see on the air today. This nonsense has given our detractors all the ammunition they have needed to defame and belittle the true contribution that was made during those primitive years.

Technically, the Golden Age was still in short pants. It was, as you well know, a far-from-dependable black-and-white medium. Its camerawork was washed out; its lighting shabby; its methods of reproduction deplorable. Despite these shortcomings, television in the early fifties had the excitement of a reckless, pioneering adventure; its people were young and its source material covered the entire range of classic literature. This was on the dramatic side. In variety and comedy it would be hard to find a more talented group than those assembled by Max Liebman for Your Show of Shows -- apart from Sid Caesar and Imogene Coca, there were Neil Simon, Carl Reiner, Mel Brooks, etcetera, etcetera, etcetera. Nor has television ever produced a better comedy series than I Love Lucy or The Honeymooners.

In a nutshell the Golden Age was crude, inept and desperately poor. Studio One, an hour-long dramatic series, was sold to Westinghouse in 1949 for $8,100. At the same time the era was young, undaunted and, in its aspirations, rich. Anything that joyous is rich as Croesus.

SCHAFFFNER: But where did it end? And why?

MINER: It ended the day I Love Lucy went on the air. While accurate, that is perhaps misleading. Actually, the Golden Age suffered a slow demise -- it lasted another seven to eight years. But I Love Lucy made the move to the West Coast inevitable; it also meant a swift surrender to Hollywood standards. Theatre standards would inevitably be abandoned, which we well knew would sound the death-knell to that brief era. Roughly it lasted a decade; by 1955-56 it had breathed its last. Those whom the gods love die young!

SCHAFFFNER: That's accurate, but misleading. The Golden Age suffered a slower demise. Playhouse 90 was Studio One extended to an hour and a half. You ought to know. You were trying to sell the idea to CBS before you left in '52.

MINER: And I almost did -- with one big difference. I never said the stories had to be originals. I only asked that they pack a wallop that could last for ninety minutes. A lot of shows on Playhouse 90 were simply dragged out; they could better have been told in an hour. This was one of the weaknesses of the series. We didn't as yet have enough good writers to build the kind of schedule the Playhouse needed.

SCHAFFFNER: Was that the real flaw in the idea?

MINER: No -- only a part. The Play of the Week proved that an audience could be held for four full hours, if the writing were taut enough and passionate enough and unrelenting.

SCHAFFNER: The Iceman Cometh.

MINER: Yes. But that's a specious answer. It isn't the true reason for the failure of Playhouse 90 and the demise of the Golden Age. What killed them both was commercialism, crass, crude, and shortsighted.

SCHAFFNER: The cost was too high.

MINER: Since no one could afford the whole show, more than one sponsor would have to be found. And where could you find the idiot to foot so staggering a bill without sole and exclusive identification? Westinghouse had had Studio One for its very own; they were inseparable. Who could ask General Electric to pay more for Act II of Playhouse 90?

SCHAFFNER: They pay more today.

MINER: That's why I said "shortsighted." Do you know what Play of the Week cost for two hours? Somewhere around $45,000. You tell me what two hours of prime time would cost today, not that Play of the Week was sold at network scale. But as it ran out of rights to buy, and your sponsors ran out of money to spend, the Golden Age staggered to a sad requiem. Its life span was a fraction over one decade, twelve years at most.

SCHAFFNER: But it was fun while it lasted.

MINER: The most fun I ever had in my life. Pioneering is, for me, a kind of tonic. I thrive on it. Add the sweet breath of success, and it is an intoxicating brew. For a few short years everything I touched turned to gold. Not literally; I wasn't growing rich, my salary was a pittance, but for a time applause was a lovely substitute for the harder currency.

SCHAFFNER: How much recognition were you given in those early years? Formal recognition, that is. Inside the industry you got plenty, I know, but from the public?

MINER: Are you talking about awards?

SCHAFFNER: Exactly.

MINER: Oh dear God, they were pretty sleazy at that time. They didn't mean very much, I'm afraid. But whatever there were, I got. From Look, Sylvania . . . I even got an Emmy so early they won't honor it today. Most of them I'd never heard of. All that mattered, to me at least, was the job I'd taken on. I became an addict, twenty hours a day, seven days a week. I didn't even have time to get tired. I'd had enough heartbreaks in my time, disappointments, failures and humiliations; this was my lucky day, and I was loving every moment of it. Fortune smiled.

> I can enjoy her when she's kind,
> But when she flutters in the wind,
> And spreads her wings and will not stay,
> I puff that prostitute away.

You should know, you were part of it. It was a loverly interlude, wasn't it?

SCHAFFNER: It was that.

MINER: We could forgive a lot of beatings for one eve-ning like Smoke with Leueen MacGrath and and Chuck Heston, or your Waterfront Boss. They carried their own reward.

SCHAFFNER: But it's only in retrospect that we appreciate how reckless we were.

MINER: Practically everything we did in those days was reckless. Bob Saudek mentioned the other day, speaking of the Museum of Broadcasting, that the greatest demand for any show from the early years, and greatest by a sizable margin, was The Battleship Bismarck. That stunned me. It was close to the last show I would have guessed the young people of today would have wanted to see.

SCHAFFNER: And I.

MINER: For many years I have thought of The Bismarck
as a quasi-failure. Even in 1950 it seemed a near disaster. But
one thing I can't deny, we were taking one hell of a risk. To
think we could sink a full-scale battleship in a studio sixty-five
feet long by forty feet wide. No producer in his right mind
would try it today. He'd get an honest-to-God battleship and
sink it in the Pacific; or he'd say it couldn't be done. We were
more foolhardy.

SCHAFFNER: Perhaps you did it a little better than you
seem to remember.

MINER: I'm not so sure. But one of the reasons I've
always dismissed The Bismarck as an attempt that failed is
that a year later we did a show about two submarines in an
Arctic storm.

SCHAFFNER: The Last Cruise.

MINER: Right. And the production we gave it was so
much better than The Bismarck, it's always held a special
place in my heart. The Cruise wasn't just foolhardy, it was
crazy!

SCHAFFNER: (a smile) That was the general reaction
around the store, as I remember.

MINER: I'm sure. It began with Fran's* announcing, as
we were having breakfast, that she had just read a fascinating
review of a new book called The Last Cruise. She was almost
afraid to mention it to me, I might try to do it on Studio One.
That was all I needed. I got the book and read it that morning;
by early afternoon the rights to The Last Cruise were ours.

*Frances Fuller, actress, educator, Doctor of Humane Letters,
and Mr. Miner's wife, who died in 1980.

The big problem was that fifty percent of the crew of that disabled submarine were going to have to go out on deck to survive for thirty-five minutes in a raging Arctic storm. To top it off, the entire crew had to be evacuated to a sister submarine across a single wobbly plank, one foot wide by two inches thick. Risky? So what? If they'd actually done it at sea, we should be able to do it in the relative calm of a television studio.

SCHAFFNER: Could anyone believe you could put two submarines into Studio 42?

MINER: Well, the second sub wasn't much more than a fragment, as you remember. That's all we needed, and its being foreshortened allowed us to rock it fore and aft. The big baby was rocked from port to starboard.

SCHAFFNER: I get it. Sort of a corkscrew motion.

MINER: Exactly. Some of the cast were actually seasick. But it was one basic piece of camerawork that made the whole production possible. The forward deck of the actual submarine measured something like 165 feet. The most we could squeeze into Studio 42 was fifty-five to sixty feet. No one could be expected to accept such a toyland substitute. But by using a twenty-five millimeter lens and shooting through the oval frame of the sub's escape hatch, the deck seemed to stretch from here to the afterlife. Forgive me, I tend to exaggerate a trifle at times.

But the madness I'm about to describe really happened. You can't reproduce the roar and pounding of a true Arctic storm without some danger. For the quieter moments we used four heavy fire hoses with a foreground haze from a rack of sprinklers. It was when the huge waves pounded the deck that the actual danger began. For this we used a whole array of bathtubs mounted on the grid above the stage; I'm afraid to say how many; I think in actuality we used thirty. Off the coast of Iceland it may have seemed no more than a puddle, but inside the four walls of a television studio it made one hell of a splash.

Those bathtubs presented a logistical problem that none of us had anticipated. The time allowed on Studio One between Dress and Air was just two hours, but to rig and fill those tubs took three and a half hours. That meant we had to run our Dress without trying out our most critical effect. We knew those tubs were going to cause some havoc, but how much none of us knew. We had no choice but to take the chance. Remember, we were still "live" in those days; no retakes, no second tries. It was one of the few times my hands were damp before we hit the air.

SCHAFFNER: (a smile) You were in your element.

MINER: Well, perhaps. (a smile) And for fifteen minutes it was almost a milkrun. It was a hell of a show, even if Jack Gould found it less absorbing than Henry James. One episode told the whole story. As the crew was climbing out on deck for the first time, one man had been rehearsed to slip overboard, only saving himself by grabbing hold of a thin rail along the edge of the deck, until a comrade could come to his rescue. But the scene had never been done with all the effects. And so, just as the man stretched out his hand to his struggling comrade, the first bathtub of water landed on his back. It was such a gargantuan shock, he lost his grip on the other seaman's wrist. According to the script, that was the moment when we should have cut to another part of the action, but this was too tense a moment to miss. I saw the director was wavering, still uncertain; there was no time to debate. "Stay with it," I shouted. And so he did until the rescue was completed.

SCHAFFNER: For how long?

MINER: An hour? Two minutes? It might have been less. Actually, in terms of strict network timing, two minutes is a lifetime, and with the evacuation still to come, it was clear we were not going to make it up. Which we didn't.

SCHAFFNER: What did you do? Run over?

MINER: No. We had a cushion. I had corralled the real Captain of the lost submarine to round out the evening and given him a sizable cut in case we were in trouble. At least I'd been that forehanded. Seeing the last crewmen making their escape, I started out into the Studio to tell Captain Ramirez (I think that was his name) to put in the cut I had given him. I was aglow with success, which only made my imminent moment of truth all the more shattering.

As I stepped into the Studio, I stepped into four and a half inches of water. It was over my shoe tops. One glance at the cameras, and I realized the water was all but up to the cable connectors. Can you imagine the holocaust if just one drop of water had short-circuited those cameras? It's a paralyzing thought. And the weight! Dear God! We were located directly above the Main Lobby of the Grand Central Terminal. It had a ceiling mural valued at $450,000, not to mention the human lives at stake.

The ending was bathos. No camera was short-circuited, no operator was broiled, no one was killed; and the pumps had the Studio dry by 4:30 a.m. without a crack or blister in the ceiling below. But how close, how close!

SCHAFFNER: I'm still back with those men on that plank. Didn't even one of them fall off?

MINER: Oh, yes, eleven. No, that's wrong. Only nine fell off. Two got pneumonia. But we did have two broken arms, a broken ankle, and a dislocated thumb. The rest were assorted bruises and abrasions.

SCHAFFNER: I hope you suffered some pangs of guilt?

MINER: Not a one! I loved every minute of it. In retrospect I recognize it was scarcely a sample of responsible behavior, but at the time it was an enthralling stunt. Nor was I alone. Perhaps just because we skirted disaster so closely, our laughter was tinged with relief. No, that's today talking. In 1951 I was delighted with the job we'd done. It was a point of pride. So it was for most of those around me. I felt younger than I had in a very long time.

SCHAFFNER: Now I'll have to look up that kinescope.

MINER: There's the pity! Perhaps a stronger word is justified -- tragedy! All that remains of all we sweated to produce are a few scraps of bloody awful film.

SCHAFFNER: Kinescopes were our crown of thorns.

MINER: I looked at what was left of The Last Cruise about ten years ago. It was to weep! The picture quality was so degraded, I could scarcely recognize what we had put on the air with such immense pride in 1951.

No one will ever again see the Golden Age as it was. Technically we left much to be desired, but had we been as bad as those washed out, often fuzzy kinescopes would have us believe, not just the Golden Age, all of television, would long since have been interred and forgotten. But damn it to hell, we were better than that, a lot better (a laugh). I can't imagine why I'm getting so worked up, especially with you. We shared the same unhappiness in recognizing that nothing we did would survive as we had done it. Our salvation lay in the fact that each day was so full, we were given no chance to bemoan the future of our handiwork.

SCHAFFNER: True. One thing has been bothering me ever since I began to look into your career. As we've been talking, Studio One has been the all-but-exclusive focus of our discussion. What I find hard to credit is that at the same time you were also producing The Toast of the Town with Ed Sullivan, The Goldbergs and Mr. I. Magination. How did you do it? How did you find the time?

MINER: I don't know. That's not being coy, I honestly don't know. I've thought about it often in the last few years, and I remain as mystified as you. After all, I not ony produced Studio One, I wrote about eighty-five percent of the scripts for three and a half years, something over a hundred hour-long dramatic shows in all. With the other series, I had very competent assistants, but I still kept pretty close track of them. I even directed the first eleven weeks of The Goldbergs. The one nearly acceptable answer I can give is twenty to twenty-two hours a day seven days a week. I seldom slept more than four hours a night for close to five years. To which you may also ask: "How did you stand it?" To which I can only reply: "I don't know." It must have offered me some immense reward, some massive gratification, that was adrenalin to the spirit.

And, of course, I paid a price. I smoked too much and drank too much. I was a wretched father, an even worse provider. My top salary for all those years at CBS was $500 a week, and no residuals. That's some measure of my financial slovenliness. Money seldom entered my mind until NBC offered me, well, let's just say it was a colossal amount more than CBS ever granted me, with lavish residuals to boot. And so when CBS refused to meet my modest demand for a raise to $750 a week, I walked. Yet -- and here's the bitter irony -- I was convinced, almost from the start, that I had done the wrong thing. I never had one rewarding, truly happy day at NBC. The shadow of the General was crass and joyless; the shadow of Bill Paley was sprinkled with sparks.

SCHAFFNER: So you moved.

MINER: It wasn't until I bought off my contract and took over Play of the Week that the excitement and the zest returned. Play of the Week was the last major series to be produced in New York. It was the last series to accept the primacy of theatre standards and theatre quality. After three years on the Coast it was a shot in the arm to find literacy and excellence once again in good repute.

SCHAFFNER: (a laugh) Now, something I find somewhat more mystifiying. According to my notes, you were born in

1900. That means you were pressing fifty before television began to take root. Isn't that a little late to start pioneering?

MINER: I suppose it was, but frankly the idea never occurred to me at the time. And now at eighty I can look back over this stretch of years and realize that my life has been made up of three quite separate careers. Each of them covered some fifteen to twenty years; 1924 to 1939, the theatre; 1930 to 1959, television; 1964 to now, the American Academy of Dramatic Arts. Each has demanded its quota of that particular brand of energy and dedication usually associated with youth.

SCHAFFNER: Your years in the theatre were so full, I find it hard to understand how you could have deserted it for the nothing that was television in 1939.

MINER: Security! I was scared. That might seem improbable in light of the success I had had throughout most of the thirties. But early in 1939 I had suffered a devastating failure in Jeremiah. It was a bust to remember. I was underwhelmed with offers for a period of six months. It was the first time I'd ever been out of work since I went into the business in October of 1924. I was growing restless. I was . . . Oh, let's be honest. I was close to panic. A regular salary check, even a relatively modest one, seemed infinitely more attractive than the risks and gambles of a free-lance director.

But to give the devil his due -- that's me! -- the various pragmatic reasons for my decision were buttressed by an equally persuasive and far more profound philosophy. The same stubborn conviction that had driven me into the theatre in the first place was now driving me out. Ever since my days at Yale I had held the belief that the theatre was a laggard art, that it flourished only in the aftermath of war and only for the victorious. They were, as a rule, the irrepressibly young.

SCHAFFNER: Can you give a for instance?

MINER: A few, not many! Have you ever stopped to count how many periods of explosive theatre there have been in the last 2,500 years? There've been pitifully few, so few it makes each one of them both evanescent and precious. The twenties was one of those periods. For that I am belatedly grateful, belated because most of us who lived through that decade had no adequate awareness of the awesome scope of our good fortune. To have once been so blessed should have been privilege enough for any one mortal to ask. But with the birth of television I was about to be granted a second glorious opportunity. The golden decade in television was less important and less lasting than the theatre of the twenties and thirties but its excitement was just as infectious and its ultimate impact just as prodigious (a laugh) . . . I've lost the thread. Forgive me, where were we?

SCHAFFNER: No apologies needed. I was asking you to give me an example of a period in the past when the theatre had burst ito life.

MINER: Right, right, right you are! So, let's see. The first example on which most of us in the Western World agree is Greece. Aeschylus, Sophocles, Euripedes, all were contemporaries of Pericles. They flourished at the peak of Athenian dominance. As the Spartan Wars dragged on, that magnificent theatre began to wane. Before the Pelopennesian Wars were ended, tragedy had been replaced by satire, exaltation by bitterness. By Aristophanes' time, the robes of nobility had been replaced by the sackcloth of the common man.

And how short a time it lasted! Fifty years? Not much more than that. From the pinnacle to the depths could be encompassed by a single lifetime. Then what an arid waste! The Romans had dramatists, but no single explosive era of native theatre. The doldrums held sway for a good thousand years more.

The next proudest age was in France; their theatre was ushered in by Louis XIV and his final domination of Europe. Corneille, Racine, Molière, all flourished during these boisterous years. But once again tragedy was transmuted into satire, and, as those towering figures faded from the scene, they left no heritage of lofty creativity, only a memory of prouder times. Once more these vibrant days were crowded into a scant fifty years.

The Shakespearian era came as a swift response to the Armada, to England's subjugation of Spain, its rulers and its people. Victory breathes a permeating elation that brings the impossible and the incomparable well within the reach of man. I have long believed that without the Armada there might never have been an Elizabethan theatre.

SCHAFFNER: You're serious, aren't you?

MINER: Oh yes, very! (laughs) Does that make me sound like some Apocalyptic monster advocating war and pestilence?

SCHAFFNER: To tell the truth, it does.

MINER: It's an illogic that I cannot rationalize, but I've recognized it for a very long time. It's not a question of asking: "Is war good?" It's a question of asking: "How much good has ever come out of war?" We created a haven in this country for the oppressed, the religiously persecuted and the enslaved. Were we the children of good or evil? While creating a magnificent sanctuary, we massacred, and all but annihilated, the natives of this land. That evil will haunt us for generations to come. Would that the good and the evil could be separated, but no one has ever devised a way. For every victor, there must be someone to suffer the "agony of defeat."

So let's get back to the Armada. That mighty assemblage of firepower was in 1588 bent on destroying England. Every Englishman's life, his home and his family were threatened. How might he be expected to respond when the word reached him that those ships with their guns and armor and fighting men were finally buried beneath the waters of the sea? He exulted. What else? He danced in the streets; he walked taller than he had walked since Beowulf! But what about the Spanish mother of that seventeen-year-old drummer boy who had gone to sea for Spain, for glory and for God? What else can we expect but tears and pain? Perhaps that's not as it should be, but who is to say it's not as it was, and always has been?

SCHAFFNER: How old were you when you began to think like this?

MINER: I was in my teens. Oh, its application to the theatre came later. I was at Yale studying with Johnny Berdan. He was one of the few stimulating teachers I'd met at New Haven. The beginning for me came early. You see, I was a part of the World War I generation. I'd spent nineteen months overseas -- I was at the front from Belleau Wood to the Armistice, 16th Field Artillery, 4th Division, Regular Army! (a laugh) Elite stuff, what?

SCHAFFNER: How old were you?

MINER: Seventeen. I tried to enlist at fifteen, but I got caught. Oh, I was a very patriotic young man, Mr. Schaffner. I was also shot with luck. Five days after I enlisted, I was on the Atlantic.

SCHAFFNER: Five days? Didn't you have any basic training at all?

MINER: Oh, yes! Three months in the ROTC at Yale. We even worked with a battery of French 75's. And who do you think was our Commanding Officer? Ray Massey! And God in Heaven, was he ever an alluring hunk of martial manhood! For me, he was the British Empire's No. 10. I'll always remember him that way.

SCHAFFNER: What sort of child were you then?

MINER: I was a brat. I was a shameless fake. On the outside I appeared, I suspect, pretty solid. Beneath, I was a tremulous twerp. I was scared, not of any actual danger or hurt, I was afraid of being afraid. The idea of cowardice was never far from my mind. It was, more than anything else, what drove me into uniform. I professed to a lot of noble principles, national honor, all the regular hogwash, but in my heart I was still in wet pants. It's strange, looking back. I was a cocky little bastard in so many ways, but the very thought of a bullet in the head, or a hunk of shrapnel in the gut, or above all a bayonet . . . ugh!

SCHAFFNER: And that changed? I should have thought that being in action, seeing so much blood, so much mutilation, would only have made the nightmare more harrowing.

MINER: And so it might, if I'd been through Cambrai! You may find this hard to credit, but in all my six months at the front, I never saw a single person killed. I saw the after-stages. I saw the face of a one-man-tank driver with his skull burned white; I saw death in every obscene shape and condition. I had four cars blown out from under me -- I was a Reconnaissance Driver for the Regiment. I survived interminable bombardments by shell and mortar fire, but I never saw anyone in the act of dying.

Luck pursued me. I never suffered so much as a bump or a bruise to my pretty little body. A Chocolate Soldier Warrior, I! One thing only mattered to me; I hadn't run away, I hadn't tried to hide. It had been close often enough; it must have been that nothing had had my number on it. I believed that with a kind of fervor. I believed I wasn't meant to die -- yet! At seventeen years of age I felt older than God and considerably more competent.

SCHAFFNER: Was this feeling widespread?

MINER: Yes, I believe it was. Not always in the same form as mine, but in essence, yes. What had taken over was an individual and national arrogance, an intoxicating and youthful arrogance that permeated our lives for a decade. Six years later, as I entered the theatre, this indomitable assurance was still with me.

And so, stronger than ever, was my belief that in the postwar years we were going to build one hell of a theatre. It never occurred to me to equate what we were about to achieve with the glory and stature of Elizabethan England, but there was an electricity in the air, an excitement; perhaps it was naive, even sophomoric, but it got us out of bed in the morning without benefit of a cattleprod. I believed that, before we were through, our American theatre was going to matter. It was going to be recognized. And I was not alone.

SCHAFFNER: Where are we now? 1923? 1924?

MINER: 1924. What a year that was! Incredible! It is only lately that I've begun to realize how much we took for granted. The rare and remarkable were mundane, even usual. Do you know how many shows were produced on Broadway that year? I don't know either, but I'll hazard a guess that it was around 200. Maybe 250? Who knows? And how many in 1979? 45? 50? The twenties, with their momentum carrying over into the thirties, were the greatest years the American theatre has ever known. The emergence of Eugene O'Neill would have been enough to justify the boast. Look at this one man's contribution during this ten-year span: The Emperor Jones, All God's Chillun Got Wings, Beyond the Horizon, Desire Under the Elms, The Great God Brown. There were more, I'm sure, but my mind has gone blank.

SCHAFFNER: The Hairy Ape, In the Zone, Strange Interlude.

MINER: Yes, oh yes. How could I have forgotten Strange Interlude? It was a turning point in my life, and a disastrous one at that.

SCHAFFNER: I didn't know you were with the Theatre Guild that early. They were the producers, weren't they?

MINER: That's right, but this was a long time before my association with them. I was still working as Guthrie McClintic's assistant. I had been ever since The Green Hat. I don't know how many people know that O'Neill wrote Strange Interlude for Kit Cornell. He not only wrote it for her, for four months he refused to take "no" for an answer.

SCHAFFNER: You mean to say Kit Cornell turned down Strange Interlude?

MINER: No, Guthrie did. As his assistant, I had been a part of their household for a good many years. I was expected to read any scripts that came in. When I got through with Strange Interlude, I was mesmerized. I thought it was something Kit couldn't afford not to do. All spring and early summer I suffered through long evenings while Gene pleaded with Kit to change her mind. It was fruitless. Guthrie was still her Svengali; she could not make a move without him, and the alternatives he kept offering her were cheap and dismal. I all but took a walk off the Queensborough Bridge.

In the end, Gene gave up. Strange Interlude went over to Lawrence Langner at the Guild. I was so stunned, so outraged, so damn sick to my stomach, I was driven to let Guthrie know how deeply I felt. Finally, I asked for a moment to speak with him. He looked at me somewhat quizzically.

"Is something troubling you, Tony?
"Yes. There is . . . "
"Let's have it."
"Well, Guthrie, I don't think you ought to direct Kit any longer. And I don't think you ought to choose the plays for her to do."

I have never been by temperament politic! My tenure as Mr. McClintic's assistant terminated somewhat abruptly. I didn't see either of them again for a long time.

As a matter of mature judgment I am far from certain my fervent responses were justified. Kit was a great human being as well as a great figure in our theatre. She was not a great actress. Possibly she did need a person who knew her limitations, who could protect her from overreaching her capacity. Also, in sober judgment, Strange Interlude was not the play I had thought it was at the time. And yet, as a general principle, I still believe that Guthrie was not the best judge of properties for Kit Cornell. Certainly her career took on added stature and dignity once Stanton Griffis and Conger Goodyear undertook to finance Katharine Cornell, Inc. On their insistence she, not Guthrie, was to be allowed to select her own properties.

Her first such venture was The Barretts of Wimpole Street. While it did everything for Kit it was supposed to do, she never knew how sad a blow it turned out to be for me. My bid for the rights had already been accepted; I was to sign the contract within a couple of days. It was at that moment that Kit made her bid to produce the play. Alice Kaiser, the agent, promptly accepted her offer; mine went into the trashbin. Who could blame her? Certainly not I. But I cannot deny that it hurt. It hurt a lot. At that point in my career I could well have used a Barretts of Wimpole Street. But The Barretts needed Miss Cornell. It was her finest performance.

SCHAFFNER: You were fond of O'Neill, weren't you?

MINER: I was overboard. I still believe he was the best we have known. He re-established, and singlehandedly, our respect for tragedy.

SCHAFFNER: But surely O'Neill was not the only one who made the twenties so exhilarating.

MINER: Dear God, no! That would be like saying that Dryden made an era. It was an exuberant time, spring kept busting out all over. I have no notes in front of me, but a host of examples come to mind without much prodding: George

Kelly, Elmer Rice, George S. Kaufman and Moss Hart, Marc Connelly, John Howard Lawson, Bob Sherwood and Sidney Howard, Max Anderson, not to mention the cupboardful of foreign playwrights, largely fostered by the Theatre Guild, who became familiar to American audiences in that lively decade: G.B. Shaw, Luigi Pirandello, Ferenc Molnar, O'Casey, and Paul Vincent Carroll.

And let's not forget that we were, at the same moment, unleashing a galaxy of glorious and indigenous musical talents. Irving Berlin had been discovered some time before, but it was the twenties that gave us Jerome Kern, Rodgers and Hart, Arthur Schwartz and Vincent Youmans, Cole Porter, Oscar Hammerstein and the Gershwins, Ira and George. It's a formidable list. In this department the British had little to offer. Ivor Novello? (a laugh) Noel Coward was the exception.

No, I never felt that O'Neill was the solitary symbol of the twenties. What swept us along was an irrepressible wave of self-assurance, of lighthearted generosity and reckless exuberance. It was most youthful. This assumption of invincibility all our own was inherited from 1918. Its music was the barrage.

SCHAFFNER: Barrage? What does that mean?

MINER: Just that, barrage! Miles and miles of French 75's, G.P.F.'s six-inch howitzers, 14-inch rail-mounted naval guns -- all letting loose a massive bombardment of spiralling metal in haphazard, but intoxicating rhythm. Ask anyone who was there. If he denies its allure, he's either a liar or . . .

SCHAFFNER: . . . or on the other end of that avalanche of steel.

MINER: Ah, yes! That might not be quite so intoxicating. And yet, it had its appeal, too. Once you have survived eight, or eighty, hours of that kind of pounding, there comes a kind of glow, knowing you have joined a rather exclusive club.

That's one of the most terrifying things about war. It's a despicable, loathsome, unnatural Circe, but a Circe nonetheless. Decent young farmboys become quite as much its slaves as George S. Patton. And, untinged by the bitterness of defeat or surrender, the intoxication of victory can last a long time, a generation can inherit its fascination. That's unpopular philosophy, and thoroughly illogical. But then, is there any illogic to compare with the will of God?

The appeal I'm talking about has nothing to do with the monstrous insanity of Hiroshima or Vietnam. They represented such an orgy of inhumanity, no victory could allay the horror. It is scarcely the atmosphere in which a rambunctious creativity might flower.

SCHAFFNER: Does that mean you totally dismiss Tennessee Williams and Bill Inge, Arthur Miller, Lorraine Hansberry and Bob Anderson? They turned out some pretty exciting stuff in my book.

MINER: Of course they did. The laws were still operating, but the conditions had changed, utterly, devastatingly. From Pearl Harbor on we did nothing but win. After the first fiasco in Africa, we did nothing but win. In all of Europe, aside from the Bulge, we did nothing but win. We were victorious so long before Hitler or Tojo were ready to concede defeat, that surrender, when it came at last, had lost the tang of surprise. Miracles are made of rarer stuff, and without a touch of the miraculous, there could have been no Thermopylae, there could have been no Armada, there could have been no Belleau Wood. Dunkirk comes closer to qualifying than Waterloo.

SCHAFFNER: What went wrong in 1945?

MINER: Tennessee Williams, Bill Inge, all the others you mentioned began to write after the war was ended. But notice one thing; they were not exultant. All were writing in evident

sadness about a day and a time that was past. Nostalgia is a
dead-end street; it is only a race for tomorrow that travels a
joyous highway.

SCHAFFNER: And so you remain convinced that World
War I was the big gun, that it gave birth to the twenties and
thirties in theatre, in literature, in music, in industry, in
essence, in everything, is that it?

MINER: Exactly! I've always felt that the first play to
speak directly to our postwar frame of mind was What Price
Glory? Its candor and its earthiness, its gusto and its passion,
were all peculiarly American. It epitomized the irresistible
surge of our national optimism. How ironic that this play
should have been written by a man who only a bare six years
before had spent a term in jail as a passionate pacifist! Max
Anderson had never even been in the Army, much less overseas. Obviously it was his collaborator Laurence Stallings who
gave the dialogue its authenticity, its spice and its salty mas-
culinity. Compare this classic of its day with Journey's End,
which remains the most poignant and accurate reflection of
the British state of mind after their four exhausting years of
struggle. It is not to belittle R.C. Sheriff to recognize that
behind the acrid wistfulness, the quiet courage and the
nostalgia, the mood was one of wan and waning futility. Its
music was somewhere between a madrigal and "Johnny Comes
Marching Home." This is not to impugn its validity, only to
note the vast gulf that separated our mood and that of our
theatre from the mood of any other theatre of its day.

To close out the twenties, I know of no play that
better displays the boisterous vitality of the latter half of the
decade than The Front Page. Under the mantle of satiric and
often outrageous melodrama, Hecht and MacArthur created a
mood of irresistible irreverence, of youth without malice.
Different as it might appear in character from What Price
Glory?, it was, I feel, the culmination of a single decade's
statement. It was male chauvinism at its unapologetic best. It
was at once sentimental and hard-nosed. Yet beneath its
boyishness there was often a wisdom considerably more mature
than we are wont to encounter among the playwrights of
recent years.

Just look at how Hecht and MacArthur handled the deplorable conduct of the Mayor and the Sheriff of Cook County. Their stupidity so far outweighed their venality, they soon became the objects of hilarious laughter. Compare this with the mirthless and soggy righteousness with which we treat corruption in this post-Watergate era. Were a playwright of the seventies to portray the blatant skullduggery of the political machine in Hecht and MacArthur's Chicago, the breast-beatings and mea culpas would rival the Wailing Wall. I prefer the sense of proportion and the humor that were prevalent in those less solemn years.

I've grown weary of the kneejerk morality that has grown so prevalent of late. Ben and Charlie weren't insensitive, nor were they bereft of moral outrage. They were, however, objective enough to recognize that the price we pay for a democratic society is petty thievery and greed, and, on occasion, considerably more than petty. Political machines feed on nepotism and privilege. America was a country so huge, its destiny so commanding, it could absorb the frailties of a few tinhorn politicians and sleazy crooks without deflecting its purpose nor diminishing its stature. That is why Hecht and MacArthur were able to laugh, and know that we would laugh with them.

SCHAFFNER: How much did those writers of the twenties owe to the other legendary figures of the day, the actors, directors, scene designers who helped to bring their plays to life?

MINER: Plenty. Actors particularly. It was a lush time.

SCHAFFNER: I suppose the Barrymores were the bellwethers.

MINER: I'd have to agree with that, although I unfortunately missed many of their finest performances. I never saw Jack Barrymore's Hamlet, for instance. I did see enough, however, to know that the Barrymores' fame was well deserved. I was present at a very special performance of Peter Ibbetson with Jack and Lionel. Lionel's son had died that day, and that tragedy had lent an unforgettable poignancy to the evening's performance. I never saw The Jest. I never saw Ethel at her youthful peak, but I did see The Constant Wife and The Corn Is Green, enough to respect her claim to being part of our theatre's royal family. Emerging from the world of musical comedy, they had set a standard that became the hallmark of American acting. They had style. But Hollywood had no use for the kind of breeding and dignity, the aristocracy if you will, they had to offer. Ethel took flight; Jack and Lionel surrendered. It's sad. They might have contributed so much more.

SCHAFFNER: These were the years before the crash of '29, right?

MINER: Right. Though I would just as soon you hadn't mentioned that unhappy event. Over the years I've been blessed with my share of good fortune, but October 29, 1929 wasn't one of the shining days. It marked my first directorial credit on Broadway, a play called Week-end by Austin Parker. It wasn't a bad play, and I got good enough notices to satisfy any beginner. Unhappily no one ever read them. Some of my best friends called me weeks after the show had folded to ask, "By the way, Tony, what ever happened to Week-end?"

SCHAFFNER: (a chuckle) Humpty Dumpty had a great fall!

MINER: Well, it was my start. Every job I got over the next couple of years I owed to Week-end. And the Market Crash did not destroy the theatre at one blow; its momentum carried over into the thirties. It was a single progression from 1919 to 1939.

SCHAFFNER: There was, of course, no off-Broadway then.

MINER: Very little -- the Provincetown Playhouse, what else? And no off-off-Broadway whatever. It was still an opulent time. What gave that theatre its unique flavor was the stockpile of talent that was available to every producer and writer with a play to cast. Look at the number of magnificent actors we had! Laurette Taylor, Holbrook Blinn, The Lunts, Louis Wolheim, Pauline Lord, Richard Bennett, Grace George, Ina Claire, Arthur Byron. How many have I forgotten?

SCHAFFNER: Alice Brady? Jane Cowl?

MINER: (a laugh) Wow! I should be ashamed. Jane Cowl was an alumna of the Academy.* But it was not the established performers alone that mattered; it was the stockpile of young people who gave these years their excitement: Spencer Tracy, Eva Le Gallienne, Edward G. Robinson, Osgood Perkins, Tallulah Bankhead, Walter Huston, Helen Hayes, Melvyn Douglas, Shirley Booth, George Abbott. How many remember that, before turning director, George Abbott played the lead in John Lawson's Processional opposite June Walker? And good he was, very good indeed.

SCHAFFNER: And what about Ruth Gordon in Saturday's Children? And Lee Tracy in Broadway?

MINER: And Lee again in The Front Page, with Os Perkins and Dorothy Stickney. And, not incidentally, Frances Fuller.

SCHAFFNER: Now, an uninspired, but obligatory, question. What has been for you, the most unforgettable performance you have ever seen?

MINER: If you'll accept an answer in three parts, I'm ready.

---

*American Academy of Dramatic Arts, of which Mr. Miner was Chairman of the Board.

SCHAFFNER: I accept.

MINER: Male: Larry Olivier in Oedipus Rex. Female: Pauline Lord in Anna Christie. Male and female: the Pitoeffs in Six Characters in Search of an Author, Paris, 1922 -- it might have been 1923.

SCHAFFNER: The first answer doesn't surprise me. Only a great actor could hit the heights he did. The other two I find mystifying. What was so special about Pauline Lord in Anna Christie?

MINER: Magic. I know of no other word to describe it. When Pauline Lord appeared for the first time in that waterfront saloon, there was a long moment of silence in which we were given a chance to size up this forlorn and pitiable creature. Her helplessness was heartrending, it came close to being ludicrous. But when she spoke, it was with the voice of desolation, of complete and abject defeat. As the scene progressed, we began to glimpse a lonely farm child, utterly convinced of her total inadequacy. Even when she had been forced to give herself to the boys on the farm, she had been a failure. She didn't even have the makings of a first-rate tart. Every word she spoke was torn from her with such pain, we ourselves began to suffer even as she. It was an anguish so compelling, it remains unforgettable and unforgotten.

Some twenty years went by before I read the script of Anna Christie for the first time. My memory had been too indelible, I thought, to need refreshment. What confronted me on the printed page was a body blow. The coarse vulgarity of line after line built up a picture of nothing so much as a case-hardened broad who'd seen it all. Not a glimmer of the Anna Christie for whom I'd once felt such searing pity.

What had Pauline Lord done? Could she actually have spoken those words? It was a stupid question; of course she had. The only answer was that Lord so completely understood the devastating despair of that child, it mattered not one whit what vulgarity, what profanity, she was asked to speak. Somehow she managed to make us understand that the words she uttered were nothing but the habitual patter of her surroundings. They had nothing to do with the feelings she wanted so desperately to express. Indeed, the words meant so little to her that we scarcely heard them. That's acting!

A few days ago Walter Kerr was writing about her performance in They Knew What They Wanted. He recalled the same baffling mystery about Miss Lord.

SCHAFFNER: That leaves the Pitoeffs. They have never been anything but names to me. What was so special about their Six Characters?

MINER: Oh, Lord, let me think. How can I hope to explain it? Did you happen to see Tyrone Guthrie's production at the Phoenix?

SCHAFFNER: I did indeed.

MINER: Then you probably remember that the critics gave it their full stamp of approval. Guthrie was a colorful character; he did Gilbert and Sullivan better than anyone alive. As a Savoyard he was a master, probably the best to be found either side of the Atlantic.

SCHAFFNER: But -- ! (a laugh) I gather you have some misgivings about his understanding of Pirandello.

MINER: I do, indeed. It was as though he'd never bothered to read the script. What the Pitoeffs did was so daring, none but the greatest of artists would have had the gall to attempt it. To build to the climax of the play the two actors in the rehearsal scene attempted to reconstruct an actual incident in the lives of the father and mother. You remember?

SCHAFFNER: Moderately well so far.

28

MINER: Good. Now what Guthrie did was to make the two actors ham up the scene so badly the audience began to titter. When at last the true father and mother took over to play the scene with some sense of feeling and dignity, the audience's response was respectful, if less than tempestuous. It was a safe and pedestrian way of attacking the play.

The Pitoeffs scorned such a lack-lustre approach. They let the two rehearsal actors play the scene with all the spirit and passion they were able to summon. The audience's response was full-blooded and spontaneous. Only as the applause had begun to fade did the Pitoeffs step in. The "No! Stop it!" was an agonizing cry. An abrupt and tingling silence fell over the theatre. The next ten to fifteen minutes were among the most thrilling and exalting I've ever experienced, certainly unmatched until Jason Robards' confrontation with his brother, Edmond, in Long Day's Journey Into Night. When transcendent daring is matched by transcendent passion, the risks are stupendous. But, dear Lord, the rewards!

SCHAFFNER: It's the kind of thing we've been led to expect from Orson Welles, but somehow never get. Which reminds me, how did he get lost in the shuffle?

MINER: Monstrous! Perhaps it was because we were accenting the twenties, and Orson was so peculiarly a part of the thirties. But surely he cannot be bypassed, he was too massive a figure. (a laugh) And is!

SCHAFFNER: How do you rate him?

MINER: Waste! Among the most tragic cases of waste our theatre has suffered in this century. The senseless financial trap that has kept him idle for all these years should never have been allowed to happen. He should be acting and directing today. It's sickening to see so gifted a figure dribbling away a stupendous talent in card tricks for Johnny Carson and commercials for Paul Masson.

He had the equipment and the passion to reach the heights. As an actor in the theatre, he had magnificent presence, a God-given voice and superb dramatic instincts. His record as a director in the theatre was in and out. He was blessed from the start with a glittering visual inventiveness. That's what lent such excitement to his Julius Caesar. His The Shoemaker's Holiday was joyous, gutsy and amateurish. His Henry IV, Part I was unforgivably bad. So much for his record in the theatre.

Citizen Kane was something else. All that explosive energy, that carefree recklesness, that incomparable visual imagery, was given professional polish and precision by magnificent craftsmen. The result was a masterpiece. It remains his supreme work. But that was in 1939. How pitifully little has been built upon that dazzling foundation. As I said at the start, a waste, a deeply saddening waste.

SCHAFFNER: Did you ever have any association with him?

MINER: Only once, and a somewhat ludicrous episode it was. I had just done Bury the Dead with a group of actors who had clustered around me, calling themselves the Actors Repertory Company. One of them, I rather think it was Will Geer, had struck up an acquaintance with a young, virtually unknown composer named Marc Blitzstein. Marc had just completed a bitter, little musical, The Cradle Will Rock. It reeked of social significance; I presume that is why Marc was eager for me to have it. Perhaps you never knew that throughout the thirties I was known in Hollywood as "The Red Director of New York." I was all but blacklisted.

SCHAFFNER: (a laugh) You're kidding.

MINER: Oh, no, I'm not. And for a time I was in fact an emotional rebel -- I believed the sun was about to rise out of the Kremlin's walls. I hadn't read Das Kapital then, nor Lenin nor Engels nor The Communist Manifesto. While my awakening occurred well before the Moscow Trials, I was still guilt-ridden. So there we have it. Marc liked my politics and was ecstatic about my work on Bury the Dead. We met in a restaurant over a couple of drinks; almost before the second sip Marc let it be known he thought I could do no wrong; if I wanted to do his script, it was mine for the asking.

Over the next two months we held auditions and completed a large share of the casting. I even began working out the kind of production I thought the show should have. I was blithely undisturbed by the fact that some silly legality had held up our signing a contract; it was too apparent that Marc had no intention of letting anyone but me do the job. Thus, the chronology of ensuing events is a little hazy. Suffice it to say that somewhere along the line Orson had got hold of the script of The Cradle Will Rock and Marc had seen Orson's production of Doctor Faustus. Orson was at the time working with W.P.A. money. He had never had to give much thought to the dollars and cents, and never did.

With Marc it was instant infatuation. He was totally mesmerized by the lavishness of Doctor Faustus, not to mention Orson's ebullient charm. He was like a girl after her first embrace; for him the Actors Repertory and Tony Miner held no further charms. I did all in my power to persuade him that The Cradle didn't need so opulent a setting as Orson had proposed. It would, I argued, overpower the play. Even at the time I had begun to doubt that Marc was hearing one word I said, and, without a a signed agreement, there was no weapon for me to use to force his hand. The inevitable soon followed. Marc gave his script to Orson.

As rehearsals progressed, reports began trickling in -- we had loads of scouts in Orson's camp -- reports concerning the sweep and the grandeur of Mr. Welles's production. We also knew that Marc's state of mind was still euphoric. This continued up to Dress, when for the first time, some observers felt the production tended to diminish the show's impact, that it had, in fact, been more effective on a bare stage. The issue will never be fully resolved, since the show, as Orson conceived it, was never seen.

SCHAFFNER: Why not? What happened?

MINER: A scowling or a smiling fate -- take your pick. You were probably too young to remember, but there was in Washington at that time a pale precursor of Joe McCarthy.

SCHAFFNER: Martin Dies?

MINER: Martin Dies it was. He and his Sub-Committee were against everything but motherhood. Second only to his distrust of Stalin was his paranoid obsession with Hallie Flanagan and the W.P.A. The perfect target for his outrage was the pinko production "that fellow Welles" was planning to put on with W.P.A. dollars. His ignorant, even vicious misinterpretation of anti-Americanism achieved an ephemeral triumph at the exact moment when The Cradle was scheduled to open in New York. Under a Martin Dies edict, the first night audience -- I was among them -- found itself facing a darkened theatre.

Who eventually arranged the makeshift solution I've never known -- probably Jack Houseman -- but after an angry wait of roughly an hour, we found ourselves parading uptown to the Century Theatre at 59th Street and Seventh Avenue where the show would go on under "limited" conditions.

SCHAFFNER: How did they manage it? Were there even any lights?

MINER: I can't remember. I think there was something more than a work-light, but I'm not sure. This much: Marc was at a piano center stage; the actors were seated on stools set in a semicircle around him. Now wait a minute! I seem to remember some of the early voices coming from the first tier boxes. It was starkly simple and unadorned. Indeed there were moments, any number of them, when the staging was almost exactly as we had planned it for the Actors Repertory Company some six to eight weeks earlier.

And that's where the absurdity begins. The morning critics not only gave The Cradle Will Rock a royal send-off, they reserved for Orson Welles their special accolades.

"Who but Mr. Welles would have had the inspired sensitivity to give this play so simple and unadorned a production?"

This is not a direct quote, but it sums up the aisle-sitters' response.

SCHAFFNER: (a laugh) Did accidents like this happen often?

MINER: I've heard of quite a number. But for my own part one in particular stands out.

SCHAFFNER: Give.

MINER: It was on the opening night of The Front Page in New York. I've already covered my abrupt departure from McClintic's employ. What salved the bruise for me was the fact that I'd written a play about Rasputin with Marya Mannes, who was then Jo Mielziner's wife. A day or so after I left the McClintic home on Beekman Place I got word that Jed Harris was interested in Rasputin. Jed was already, in Noel Coward's words, "Destiny's Tot." He'd already produced in sequence Coquette, Broadway, and The Royal Family. Selling a script to him in that Year of Grace, 1928, was little less than Sutter's Gold. As it happened, Jed and I had been in the same class at Yale, but due to my being overseas for two years and his dropping out well before I returned, we'd never met.

Ostensibly the play had been bought for Holbrook Blinn. Jed insisted that Blinn was crazy about the script, he only wanted a couple of weeks to rest, and he'd be ready to meet with Ma Mie (that was Marya's nickname) and me. In truth, I've always suspected that Jed's true reason for buying the play was rather more devious. Before Jed began skyrocketing into prominence, Guthrie had been the fair-haired boy along the Big Stem. For years Jed's envy of Guthrie had been obsessive. What better way to show his disdain than lavishly to praise Guthrie's protégé, to "discover him," to nurture this exciting new playwright whom Guthrie had been too insensitive to recognize? I'm not exaggerating; Jed was that devious. Sadly enough for Ma Mie and me, not to mention the American theatre, Holbrook Blinn was killed a few weeks later in a fall from his horse. Rasputin is still collecting dust in a rusting file.

In the interim, Jed had me put on the payroll as his personal assistant. The Front Page was due to go into rehearsal in a few days with George S. Kaufman as director. The night before the first reading, Jed had brought me in to ask a favor. Kaufman, he said, was starting off as the director of the show, but Jed had no assurance he was up to the job. Would I pose as the Stage Manager and report back to him if I found that George was seriously hurting the play? I should never have agreed, but with Rasputin still pending, my baser instincts won the day. I was afraid to brush Jed's request aside. The whole thing was a swift fiasco. In barely forty-eight hours George had spotted the hoax and confronted me with it. I confessed. Eduardo Ciannelli soon took over as Stage Manager.

As opening night drew near Jed became paranoid about the end of the First Act. It was a madhouse, with a jail-break setting off alarms, phones ringing, lights going on and off every few seconds, and in the middle of this bedlam the curtain coming down at a precise moment and at a precise speed. Absolute precision was obligatory, or the entire First Act might be ruined. It was something I'd learned to do well and calmly; as a result I was called on to step into the breach.

This much for explanation. Outside the window to the Press Room there was a large open trap into which Dorothy Stickney would plunge to her death in Act II. In the basement below were eight "Cops" with rifles whom I controlled with hand signals. Above my head was the signal light for the curtain, but the Curtain Man was on the other side of the stage.

The moment the jail-break occurred, an alarm sounded, the Reporters broke loose in all directions, phones rang, lights went on and off, all precisely on cue, at which point Lee Tracy dashed on stage and grabbed his phone to the Examiner. That was the cue for the first shot to be fired. I gave the signal. Lee was screaming, "Duffy!" into the phone, when I caught sight of the curtain coming down slowly, just as it should, except for the fact that we still had a page and a half of script to go. I signalled for more shots, and lo, up went the curtain. Lee kept on shouting. More shots. Down came the curtain. Lee, in a towering rage by this time, kept shouting, more at me, I suspect, than at Duffy. More shots. Up went the curtain. Four times! Finally, with pandemonium at its crest, Lee spoke his final words, the curtain fell, and stayed down. The boys in the basement had run out of shells.

The chewing out I took from Jed a moment later was horrendous. I couldn't blame him, I'd wrecked the show. My personal misery was not allayed until the following day when the morning papers arrived. Along with the general raves, a large share of the critical community picked out that "magnificent handling of the First Act curtain" as evidence of Jed's unassailable genius.

SCHAFFNER: What did really happen? Did you ever find out?

MINER: A bulb with a loose connection. Pretty absurd, what? The guns from the cellar, being aimed upward, had inadvertently peppered the curtain light, which, by some freak of chance, had been loose in its socket. Every time a shot went off, out went the light. When the guns were still, on came the light again. The Curtain Man on the other side of the stage thought Tony Miner had gone bananas. Still the good soldier, he had dutifully done what the light commanded. The unmatchable timing had been the handiwork of the gods.

SCHAFFNER: We've covered the playwrights and the actors; what about those who found a suitable habitat for the rich of Holiday, the robots of R.U.R., and the dream-world of Liliom?

MINER: (a smile) Gordon Craig's little changelings?

SCHAFFNER: (a laugh) All right, scene designers!

MINER: That's where the twenties were in luck. When the playwrights and producers needed them most, they were there, eager and able.

SCHAFFNER: How many of them did you know personally?

MINER: Most of them; all the best ones. The one who set the pace for the decade was Robert Edmond (Bobby) Jones -- no relation to the golfer, though they were about the same age. Bobby had a sense of unadorned dimension that was hauntingly beautiful. One job of his remains indelible. It was his set for The Green Bay Tree. It came late, but it was still one of his finest.

The designer who transcended and outlasted Bobby was his one-time assistant Jo Mielziner. He, too, had a spectacular sense of scale. The vastness of his bridge scene from Winterset (Act I and III) only accented the stinginess of the basement apartment for Act II. Those massive steampipes seemed to press down on, and all but smother, the actors. But the great thing about Jo was his flexibility, his capacity to supply the most effective background that the script demanded, whether it were a lush and luxurious setting for Anatol or a tasteless, drab and airless apartment on the upper West Side for Lucky Sam McCarver.

While these two dominated the scene for many years, there were ever so many others with genuine imagination and daring. Some will argue that Norman Bel Geddes was the greatest talent of them all; certainly many of his designs were breathtaking. His weakness lay in a tendency to overpower the actors, to reduce them to a pygmy scale. Witness Phil Barry's John. Guthrie McClintic was captivated by the colossal size of the courtroom Norman had designed for Herod and Herodia. I confess I, too, fell victim to its spell in modular form. Once I saw it in the shop, however, my heart fell. Painted a glorious Chinese red, those twenty-four foot walls were massive enough to thoroughly dominate the scene. Norman had just begun, however. Even the Contractor had become apprehensive, apprehensive enough to give me a ring. He thought I'd better come down and see what the Master had wrought. What I encountered was not these massive walls alone, but a series of gilded frescoes sixteen feet high, depicting Azur-bani-pal cum chariot in the act of spearing an enraged lion. Beautiful? Yes, oh yes! But once set up in a theatre, even Ben Ami and Constance Collier were reduced to toy-shop scale. The lovely but fragile Anna Duncan was totally obliterated. Perhaps Norman did not single-handedly kill the play, but surely he contributed his quota to its demise.

Freddie Jones's untimely death robbed us of a soaring talent. While he rivalled Norman in his use of mass, he never diminished, but rather enhanced, the impact of the play. Witness The Criminal Code where his monstrous front curtain, a huge granite wall eight feet thick, nearly turned a run-of-the-mill prison drama into a minor classic. It lent to the claustrophobia of prison life a vivid and inexorable terror.

SCHAFFNER: Others?

MINER: Don Oenslager's gigantic pine branch framing a bleak Alaskan landscape for 200 Were Chosen was both awesome and supremely simple. Mordecai Gorelik was signally inventive in a constructivist style. Lee Simonson was enormously gifted, supplying affectionate and effective backgrounds for a host of Theatre Guild productions during the twenties and thirties. I worked with all of them, and none ever let me down. They were the playwrights' collaborators. Their work had vigor and size and a glorious range of imagination. Few, aside from Oliver Smith and Ruben Ter Arutunian, have matched them. Take that for what it is, a personal and highly prejudiced opinion.

SCHAFFNER: Should I expect anything else?

MINER: No.

SCHAFFNER: (a laugh) And now, where are we? What about the directors?

MINER: Directors were another matter. There were four or five great designers at least; there were no great directors. That, I hasten to repeat, is a personal appraisal. Guthrie McClintic was relatively prolific, but ninety percent of his successes were with Katharine Cornell. My memory is far from the best, but I feel reasonably confident that his only successes away from Kit were The Dover Road, Mrs. Partridge Presents, Saturday's Children with Ruth Gordon, the Medea with Judith Anderson, and Winterset. All but the last two were in the twenties.

Then there was Philip Moeller, but he worked exclusively for the Theatre Guild. Ernest Milton did a magnificent job with He Who Gets Slapped, but I can't remember another show of his. There was also Peggy Webster, especially Peggy Webster. She deserved all the acclaim she got, possibly more. But there again, she worked in almost nothing but Shakespeare, and with Maurice Evans. Her range was limited.

Finally, and some will contend he should have headed the list, George Abbott. His reputation is so prodigious, it's somewhat surprising to find that his start in the twenties was far from spectacular. To begin with, he was for nearly a decade an actor. As a director the first hit of his that I recall was Coquette with Helen Hayes. This was followed by Broadway with Lee Tracy. A good start, no argument. But not many remember the lean period that followed. From Broadway to Three Men on a Horse was a long eight years, 1927 to 1935. Eight years, twenty-two failures. Moreover, aside from Coquette, I can't remember a single serious play to add to his credits. It was the four farces, Three Men on a Horse, Room Service, Boy Meets Girl and Brother Rat that won him acceptance as one of our finest directors. Yet the George Abbott we acclaim today won his major accolades, not as a stage director, but as a director-producer-co-author of a veritable parade of musical comedy successes throughout the forties, fifties, and sixties. There have been many durable directors in pictures, Cecil B. De Mille, John Ford, Willie Wyler, George Cukor, etc., but in our theatre Abbott's longevity stands alone. Truly he has well earned the title "The Grand Old Man of Broadway."

Jed Harris had a sunburst of hits in the twenties -- Coquette, Broadway, The Royal Family, The Front Page -- but in all of these he acted as producer. His directorial phase only came along in the thirties. My life was intertwined with Jed's all through the next decade, culminating in Uncle Vanya, which remains, for me, the crest of my career in the theatre.

Now here's something truly to confound a legend of our craft. We of the theatre, of all the arts in fact, are supposed to be, by nature, egotists supreme. In common parlance that's a euphemism for voracious scoundrels. Well, I've lived in this business for upward of fifty years and, discounting one thoroughly vicious episode with Jed Harris, I've never met an underhanded or unscrupulous manager or producer. I've heard of them in pictures, I've seen a few in television, but in the theatre I've never had any reason to blame my failures or disappointments on the malice of another. Even the one time I was fired -- that was from On Your Toes -- I could never ask for more generous treatment than I was accorded by Dwight Deere Wiman.

SCHAFFNER: That's a long way from the common belief.

MINER: I know. That's why I thought it was important enough to mention. If there's been anything I've said that sounded like a personal apologia, and so many memoirs are little else, it was inadvertent. For my successes I've often had others to thank, frequently Lady Luck. But for my boo-boos I've seldom had anyone but myself to blame.

SCHAFFNER: As you've been talking I've thought: Can anyone be that objective, that devoid of spite? It would be easy to conclude it was all an act, but I know damn well, you being you, that it wasn't. Tell me, have you always been this impartial?

MINER: God, no. I've had my spells of envy and greed, but they came along somewhat later. You see, for the first eleven years of my life I was an invalid. I never saw spring except through a windowpane. All my dreams, all my longings, were physical. I was too frail ever to consider being tops in anything; being able to compete was all I asked. You see what that meant? I had no goal except to be physically adequate. I didn't want to paint or play the piano or draw or write, or even be President. I just wanted to be accepted. One thing more: I had no father -- he died when I was two -- nor even a brother. I had two sisters, but they were four or five years older than I. They were never objects of envy; I was, in fact, rather fond of them. It wasn't a very stimulating, much less competitive, environment.

SCHAFFNER: Where did all that energy of yours come from?

MINER: I have no good answer. I only know the sick put up a mighty struggle to be strong. Is that an answer?

SCHAFFNER: Possibly. But there's something missing. At least you must have been abnormally ambitious. Doesn't that imply some ogre to be overcome?

MINER: Oh, I had my share of ogres to overcome, yes. But they were mostly creatures I'd observed outside my immediate "family" -- the stinking rich, especially the nouveau riche; the well-dressed; the loud and the popular. These were the ogres of childhood. Ambition only began to flourish with the advent of manhood. Yet even then, and again and again, those seizures of acquisitive hunger and secret greed were tempered by some trick of fate, some twist of fortune, that dispelled the darkening clouds of spite. I have held grudges, but seldom for long.

SCHAFFNER: But at least you have held them. Good. And what was the moment of utmost misery?

MINER: Well, let's see -- The hours of misery I remember best were my years at Yale. Coming out of the Army, I returned to New Haven through inertia. The only future I could see was as a teacher, and for that I needed a degree. And so I simply drifted. I landed back in those ivied halls, aimless and without joy. God in heaven, how I hated Yale! Its mean and puerile principles, its narrow-minded values, its smug superiority. I hated Yale, which Yale returned in full and abundant measure. I was ignored. (laugh) I started to say "disdained," an inadvertent admission that some random traces of a youthful unhappiness still rankled. But -- and here's the critical point -- before this misogyny had destroyed me quite, I had enrolled in Magdalene College, Cambridge.   From the moment I set foot in that wondrous town, it was, for me, as though the sun had risen. I had found wonder once again, and not, this time, through a windowpane.

SCHAFFNER: What was so different?

MINER: All the things that mattered. At Yale all that mattered for the vast majority of the student body was the extra-curricular activities, the Sophomore and Senior Societies, sports and the Yale News. A person's academic standing was a matter of signal unimportance. When I won my Phi Beta Kappa, it was of so little value to me, I hid the key under a pile of socks. It opened no doors for me; it merely strengthened my classmates' conviction that I didn't quite belong, like all those little Jew-boys from New Haven High. At Cambridge the difference was at once apparent and startling. The only "big men," aside from the Captain of the Crew, the Captain of the Rugger team and the Speaker of the Union, were the Double Firsts.

A high scholastic standing was the "open sesame" to most of the worthwhile doors in Cambridge. How word of my Phi Beta Kappa managed to precede me I never discovered. I only know the word was out, and the tangible rewards were swift. In less than a week I learned that the tutor assigned to me was the best the College had to offer; I.A. Richards was already well recognized throughout the British academic world. The one other American working with Richards was J. Hall Paxton, an equal "nobody" in the Debrett of New Haven. Some years later Hall was to lead a fantastic and heroic hegira of some thousands of souls from China to Azerbaijan. It brought on his death, but it was a colossal accomplishment.

The essence of Cambridge lay in its mixture of the ages. It began with one vital and permeating distinction. It is routine for a young man to enter Yale at eighteen; four years later he graduates, and is accepted as an educated man. No one ever graduates from Cambridge. Distinguished scholars of eighty and youngsters in their teens are all part of a single undergraduate community. They live next door to each other, they eat together, they have tea together, they argue and laugh together. At Yale you enter as a class and leave as a class; when you enter a college at Cambridge, you join an adult community, you are treated as an adult and are expected to behave as an adult. It was a heady tonic for one who'd spent three years in the intellectual playpen of New Haven.

Soon I found myself on an intimate footing with Frank Birch, a highly regarded historian from King's College who had been a close friend of Rupert Brooke; with Sir Arthur Quiller-Couch, Shakespearian scholar and critic extraordinary; with C.K. Ogden, renowned publisher and close friend of I.A. Richards; with Maynard Keynes and his entrancing lady, Lydia Lopokova. Can you imagine a young undergraduate at Yale being allowed to befriend a group of mature figures of equal

42

stature to those I've listed? I was accepted, and I was having the time of my life. There was no room for bitterness. If there's a better solvent for spite than a generous jigger of approval, I've never found it. It's a hell of a lot better than a slug of Jim Beam -- though Jim Beam does pretty well by itself at times.

SCHAFFNER: You speak as one who knows, but we've been at this for some time now, and I haven't yet seen you take a drop of anything.

MINER: Penance for the sins of my immoderate youth! My grandfather kept warning me from the age of ten: "Moderation, young man, moderation in everything -- especially in moderation!" Unhappily, I only gave heed to the last three words. The truth is, I worked so hard and lived so hard, drank so hard and smoked so hard (five packs a day for fifty years), the gods decided at seventy-six that I'd had enough of the good things of this world. They began to reclaim some of the gifts they had bestowed, a couple of legs below the knee, the major sight in my left eye and a good percentage of the feeling in my right hand. (laugh) That will teach you! And assuredly, it has! I haven't had a drink or a puff of a cigarette in many a year. But you want to know the cockeyed irony of it all? I feel younger, I feel better and I'm getting a hell of a lot more out of life than I had for some three to four years before. What kind of punitive justice is that?

SCHAFFNER: You almost make me look forward to eighty.

MINER: You'll love it.

SCHAFFNER: You make it too easy for me to get distracted. Where were we?

MINER: Somewhere between 1925 and '35. I was still in the theatre.

SCHAFFNER: And so were some other able and gifted
figures.   How able? How gifted? How, in fact, do you rate
your contemporaries and their achievements, specifically directors? You've mentioned so few. There must have been others.

MINER: Perhaps the most widely ignored fact about
directors in the theatre is the brevity of their prominence.
With a very few exceptions the creative dominance of even
the finest directors lasts a bare fifteen years. Those who
peaked in the twenties had mostly begun to slip by 1935-36;
those of the thirties seldom outlasted World War II; and those
who won wide acclaim in the postwar years -- Elia Kazan,
Josh Logan, Bobby Lewis, etc. -- were in meager demand by
the close of the Vietnam era. A director's years of triumph are
few.

SCHAFFNER: That I accept. But a couple of names
intrigue me. George S. Kaufman.

MINER: As a director, George was never in the same
class with Abbott, or McClintic, or Welles. In the twenties he
was largely known as a playwright. His first directorial assignment was The Front Page; that was 1928. While he received
critical bouquets for his performance, I can attest to the fact
that, having sat through the rehearsals from the start, it was
Jed Harris who deserved the directorial accolades, not George
Kaufman.

SCHAFFNER: (a smile) All but the First Act curtain.

MINER: (a laugh) All but that wayward curtain! . . . One
other director warrants inclusion, though he is associated with
an earlier generation.

SCHAFFNER: Who?

MINER: Arthur Hopkins. The name evokes an instant smile. Arthur was so sensitive and self-effacing, it's hard to visualize him as an active part of a generation in revolt. Unhappily for me I missed most of his greatest productions; I was either in the Army, or abroad. As I said before, I missed Jack Barrymore's Hamlet; I missed The Jest. They were, I suspect, the high points of Arthur's early years. But of those productions I did see, I'd have to go with Holiday.

SCHAFFNER: Holiday? I expected you to say The Petrified Forest.

MINER: No, I don't think so. Aside from the magnificent performance by Bogie, Petrified Forest was far from a distinguished play. I stay with Holiday. I confess his discovery of Hope Williams -- actually he'd found her in Paris Bound -- may have colored my judgment, but I still think it was his most sensitive and daring performance. Why "daring"? Well, I'm just remembering that, in addition to Hope, he picked Donald Ogden Stewart out of left field. Two unknown amateurs as leads in one show? That takes the kind of daring most people call foolhardy, and I loved him for it.

SCHAFFNER: Were you close friends?

MINER: Warm, yes; close, no. Actually, the most revealing picture I can give you of Arthur came to me second-hand from Os Perkins.

SCHAFFNER: Tony's father.

MINER: Tony's father. Arthur, he said, was like no other director he'd ever met. For hours and hours he'd sit in silence in the dark of the house until you'd want to scream. But then quite suddenly, and at the most unpredictable moment, he'd stand up and call you down to the footlights. When you got there full of apprehension, he'd look up and whisper: "Son, don't you think you might find another way of doing that scene?" Or reading that line, or closing that door? Never a "Do this" or "Don't do that." Just a whisper, a suggestion, and a smile. But his taste and sensitivity were flawless. And when he asked an established actor to do something in a different way, he was actually breaking the mold of tradition, he was making the actor create something fresh and untried, and often, for that very reason, arresting and true. His unique ability lay in making the great greater. He had little aptitude for, nor interest in, making the novice good enough.

This still does not fully explain the mysterious capacity of this remarkable man. It is true that, as Hollywood began to entice the talent he had found and fostered to desert the theatre for films, he suffered, but he did not surrender. Past the mid-term of his life he began foraging for new talent. Little enthusiasm as he might have felt for this task, he was the unchallenged master of its usage. Witness: Hope Williams in Paris Bound, Clark Gable in Machinal, Humphrey Bogart in Petrified Forest. He shunned the spotlight, but he was a figure of immense consequence in the shape of a pint-sized Santa Claus.

SCHAFFNER: I like that. Ask anyone to name the major theatrical figures of the twenties and how many will include Arthur Hopkins?

MINER: Almost none. He was too gentle and too quiet. I dare say he would have found applause outside the theatre hideously embarrassing. And a little noisy.

SCHAFFNER: Yes. Yet I still sense a gap. Maybe I haven't asked the right questions. Were there no giants in the twenties and thirties?

MINER: Yes, one: Lawrence Langner. I should perhaps have said the Theatre Guild, but Lawrence stood so high above the other members of that Board, he stood alone. I can't pretend that this is entirely impartial; my relations with

Lawrence were too close and lasted too long. To be fair, Terry (Theresa) Helburn was a powerhouse, almost on a par with Lawrence. She was full of zest and imagination. The two of them were a formidable pair. But had there never been a Terry Helburn, there still would have been a Theatre Guild; had there never been a Lawrence Langner, there would have been no Guild at all. Let me give you some facts, reminders, if you will, of what the Guild meant to our American Theatre for thirty years.

SCHAFFNER: How many members of the Guild Board were there?

MINER: Substantially, six. I was, as I have said before, still in the Army of Occupation when it started, 1919. They called themselves The Washington Square Players then, and, aside from the fact that they launched Katharine Cornell, I know little about them. Very soon, however, they became the Theatre Guild, consisting of Terry Helburn, President; Lawrence Langner -- I've no idea what Lawrence's title was; Helen Westley, actress; Phil Moeller, director; Lee Simonson, scene designer; and Maurice Wertheim, financial advisor. So it remained until 1937, when, due to a long bout of intramural wrangling, Alfred Lunt and I were elected to the Board. We would, it was hoped, re-invigorate the Guild with new ideas and fresh vitality. On both counts, we failed. In 1939 I adapted and produced one prodigious flop, Jeremiah, after which I moved into television. Thereafter, my contributions became so minimal, I resigned. That was 1941. I don't know how long Alfred lasted. His contributions, however, were about as minimal as mine.

But a few simple facts will confirm the magnitude and extent of the Guild's effect on our theatre. With a subscription season of five productions a year, they undertook, not only to discover and encourage a group of young American playwrights, but simultaneously to introduce American audiences to the best British and European dramatists of the 19th and 20th Centuries. Lawrence had been peculiarly aware that, while we had emerged from World War I as a mature industrial power, within the arts, and particularly within the theatre, our record was dreary and uninspired. Among the major nations of the Western World, we were all but ignored. What the Guild undertook to do was to transmute this humiliation into a position of commanding respect. I doubt that any of them thought this could be achieved in less than twenty-five to fifty years -- certainly not within a single decade.

SCHAFFNER: How close did they come?

MINER: Well, let's see. I'm no statistician, but these facts are substantially accurate. Within five years they had completely changed the face of the American theatre and the tastes of the New York audience. Between 1925 and 1929 they had fourteen successes in a row. By 1926 they had assembled the most formidable acting company this country has ever seen. Certainly there has been none since to compare with it.

SCHAFFNER: How many of that company did you know?

MINER: I was only starting out then. Besides, I've never had an encyclopedic mind, but most of them I knew -- Alfred Lunt and Lynn Fontanne, Helen Westley, Henry Travers, Dudley Digges, Claire Eames, Tom Powers, Edward G. Robinson, Richard Bennett. In addition, of course, they were able to call on practically any major star along Broadway -- some I knew, some I didn't -- Ina Claire, Roland Young, Freddie March and Florence Eldridge, Helen Hayes, Helen Mencken. Enough? When your batting average is fourteen hits in fifteen tries, you're bound to command a certain amount of attention.

SCHAFFNER: How do you account for that record?

MINER: (a laugh) Lawrence had a pretty good answer to that. The members of the Guild Board disliked each other so heartily, they could never willingly agree on anything, least of all a script. Ergo, when they did, it had to be a dilly. And, of course, the subscription season had a lot to do with it, too.

But what made Lawrence so impressive a figure was the fact that the theatre was, for him, no more than an avocation. His primary concern was patent law. Langner, Parry, Card and Langner, which he set up when little more than a boy, became the largest international patent law firm in the world. Name any Goliath in American business or industry, and the odds are ninety to one they were among Lawrence's clients -- DuPont, General Motors, General Electric, Westinghouse, take your pick. When we opened <u>Both Your Houses</u> in Pittsburgh during FDR's inaugural week -- this was not precisely a good time for business, you remember -- Lawrence picked up some three million dollars' worth of legal accounts in two days. When in the forties the Guild's subscription campaign fell on hard times, Lawrence got Warren Caro to organize the Theatre Guild-American Theatre Society, a booking operation. It could well be that, without them there would be few or no road companies in this country today. Finally, he gave his life to the founding of the American Shakespeare Festival in Stratford, Connecticut. It has never lived up to his dreams -- far from it -- but I tend to believe that is because he didn't live to see it through. He didn't die too young, just too soon. But for thirty years there was no one in our theatre to challenge his stature.

SCHAFFNER: It's so diametrically opposed to the picture I've had of the man.

MINER: (laugh) Devoid of humor? Politically inept? Penny-pinching?

SCHAFFNER: That's right.

MINER: All of them true -- to a degree! Yet, in essence, false. Lawrence was not without humor, but his humor was a touch old-fashioned and highly intellectual. His "lack of humor," which became a legend, applied in fact to the Board as a whole. Their conduct was monstrously crass and uncivil. Have you ever heard Alfred Lunt's famous remark? After playing a whole Dress Rehearsal of a Sam Behrman comedy to the accompaniment of whispers, the shuffling of papers, the stomping of feet up and down the aisle, and all without one trace of a chuckle, Alfred strode down to the footlights and announced: "I'd as soon feed caviar to a horse as try to play comedy to this assemblage."

SCHAFFNER: Beautiful!

MINER: Politically inept? Right on! And no one quicker to admit it than Lawrence. In fact, he delighted in telling stories on himself. One that has always enchanted me: The Guild was doing a multi-scene play about Richard Wagner with Wilfrid Lawson as star. The opening night out of town was a chilling affair. While Lawson played every scene brilliantly, he played no two of them alike. Each was a different Richard Wagner. This was a common British failing of the thirties; it was even true of John Gielgud's otherwise enthralling performance as Hamlet. But it was killing Wagner.

For what reason it's still difficult for me to fathom, the Guild selected Lawrence to meet with Lawson to try to get from him a more coherent attack on the part. In the Dressing Room Lawrence was for a time graciousness itself, but eventually he was forced to confess that the Board had at moments found it difficult to understand what Lawson was trying to say regarding the character of Wagner. It had seemed to them -- here Lawrence was struggling to choose his words particularly carefully -- let us say, contradictory.

"Maybe you can explain to me how you saw the man, Wagner."

"Gladly, old boy. Gladly," Lawson said jauntily. "You see, I've been studying Wagner ever since you sent me the script last spring. I've read everything I could, I've talked to dozens of people. I've, if you like, 'burned the midnight oil.'" This was spoken with a tolerant smile. "Finally, just about a month ago, to be exact, the whole thing became clear to me. Wagner was an actor! In every situation, in every confrontation, he quickly grasped what the other person expected of him, and there and then he became that person."

"Excellent!" said Lawrence. "Excellent! Now I see just what you've been after. I quite understand your belief that Wagner was, in essence, an actor. But why did you feel you had to make him such a very bad actor?"

SCHAFFNER: (a laugh) No! No! I don't believe it!

MINER: True! True!

SCHAFFNER: What happened?

MINER: "Wagner" lasted a very short time! -- Lawrence the cheapskate! This was a common canard about the Guild as a whole. I never found it true. But with Lawrence the reverse was glaringly apparent. Example: in 1936 I was negotiating a contract with the Guild. I felt I deserved a raise, a rather sizable raise, in fact. The pivotal issue was a sliding scale of royalties from .01% to .04% of the gross. A meeting was set for Friday afternoon; those present were myself, Lawrence, Terry Helburn, and Warren Munsell, the Guild's Business Manager. As I was outlining my proposal, I saw Lawrence turn to Terry and surreptitiously shake his head. At the mention of royalties, Warren lowered his eyes and began nervously tapping the desk with a pencil. Assured though I was that I was not going to make the sale, I kept on doggedly to the end.

Terry was the first to break the ice. "Tony, dear, we love you, and we'd love you to do this show, but honestly, four percent of the gross? It's unheard of."

Come Monday afternoon we met again. Lawrence at once took the floor to say he'd given my proposal a lot of thought over the weekend and felt he had a fair solution to offer. He hadn't gone very far, however, when I began to realize that he was offering me considerably better terms than I had dared to propose. A glance revealed that Terry and Warren were equally confused and dismayed. A moment later Terry felt compelled to cut in, calling Lawrence's attention to the fact that his figures were far better for me than any I had suggested. A moment of thought, and a twinkle came into Lawrence's eye.

"I must have been thinking a little too much about Tony and a little too little about us. A weakness of mine. You'd better take over, Terry. You're better at this sort of thing than I am."

SCHAFFNER: How did you make out?

MINER: Out of sheer embarrassment they gave me just about what I'd asked for in the first place. No, I don't think anyone can justly accuse Lawrence of penny-pinching.

SCHAFFNER: I'm stunned! It's so far from anything I've ever heard about Lawrence Langner. How can any one man evoke so much unwarranted venom and rancor?

MINER: Big winners have few friends, and the bigger, the fewer. Envy plants a poisonous seed. I'm grateful to you for giving me a chance to set the record straight.

SCHAFFNER: Close as you were to the Guild, how come you've scarcely mentioned Phil Moeller as a director?

MINER: For a very good reason. Over all the years I barely spoke to Phil above a dozen times. I had no intimate association with him whatsoever. You see, my tenure with the Guild was in large measure due to an intramural consensus that Phil had run his course as a creative director. There is seldom much love lost between the deposed and his successor. Understandably the chilliness and embarrassment were almost entirely one-sided; I held no ill will toward Phil, but he chose to maintain toward me a polite, yet distant, posture.

This in no way affected my appraisal of his work. Much of it was, by me, journeyman and predictable. He displayed, however, recurrent flashes of imagination and emotional intensity that could not be dismissed. His concept of suspended animation to frame the thought processes in Strange Interlude was, not alone magnificent, but magnificently simple. His handling of Shaw and Molnar was exemplary, often better than that. And yet, for some reason I cannot justify, his work was seldom, for me, exciting. He was -- .

Damn it, I've no right to pass judgment on Phil Moeller. He was of another generation, another school, against which I was in revolt. Competition that active is seldom fair. The best I can do is to repeat a story told me by a young spear-bearer from Elizabeth and Essex. It gives a far more vivid and revealing picture of Phil Moeller than anything I can supply.

From the start there'd been trouble with the curtain of Act II. Alfred and Lynn were superb, but the climax of their big scene remained a dud. By the end of the third week this had become far more than an irritant; it threatened calamity. Gloom pervaded the stage of the Guild Theatre. As the door closed behind Alfred's exit, the Stage Manager announced in a weary and listless voice: "Curtain." There was a dark pause, a preamble to doom. Suddenly Phil erupted from deep in the darkened fastnesses of the house.

"No!" he bellowed. "Stop! I've got it! I've got it!"

In a burst of excitement he leapt onto the stage and descended on Lynn. No one but she could hear what he said, but, as she nodded, he grabbed a rehearsal chair and swung it into place in the footlights, his arms folded across the back. Turning to the Stage Manager, he announced: "No curtain this time! Not till I give the word. Is that clear?"

"Yes, sir."

A moment later Alfred made his entrance and the scene began, building, as it had so often before, and ending on an impassioned note. Turning, Alfred started for the door. The door opened; the door closed, only this time the curtain did not fall. Once alone, Lynn began in mime to express the rage, the frustration, the agonizing admixture of passion and hatred

that consumed her. As her anguish reached its terrifying cre-
scendo, Phil leapt to his feet, his right arm thrust upward, his
fingers splayed.

"Now!" he roared. "Now, after that exquisite arabesque
of agony -- COITIN!"

That was Phil Moeller, the intellectual and the street
kid. One never altogether obliterated the other. They were
father to his genius and also to his ever-threatening insecurity.
Nothing has ever so persuasively explained, for me, Phil
Moeller's coming so close to being an inspired director -- and
missing.

SCHAFFNER: (a laugh) That's beautiful!

II

MINER: Why have I been carrying on about a bunch of dead dodos, whom no one knows, nor gives a damn about? I've been boring the hell out of you, haven't I?

SCHAFFNER: If I'd been bored, I'd have let you know well before this. No -- I'm still with you. I feel that behind all you've been saying there was a purpose, but I haven't been able to give it shape.

MINER: (a smile) Let me give it a try. My concern is for the young. They are threatened day after day by the illusion that those who have found success were born to success, that once you strike it big, you have it made permanently, you will be big forever. I hold the hope that by exposing the fact that my successes were merely interludes between long stretches of uncertainty, apprehension and failure, this would act as a cold bucket of candor to shock them out of their inertia. Some fragment from my past may evoke in some youngster some-where a flash of recognition, a recognition of himself, of times when he had suffered too much or too little, had got drunk on hope or withered in despair, and believed this was due to some shortcoming in himself, some doleful weakness he was unable to surmount. As he is wont to believe this is unique, I am say-ing it is both diurnal and ubiquitous. Triumph is never everlast-ing; it is absurdly finite. Is that any sort of answer to your question?

SCHAFFNER: Yes, but I still have a lot to learn about the work of Worthington Miner.

MINER: (deadpan) I thought you knew me well enough to know that I always save the best till last.

SCHAFFNER: All right! I don't pretend to be an authority on your career in the theatre. But quantitatively alone, I recognize you must have ranked reasonably high in your day. How many shows did you do in your fifteen years?

MINER: All told? God knows. On Broadway? Roughly thirty. But it wasn't really fifteen years, more like ten. I'd had five years before I picked up my first directorial credit.

SCHAFFNER: Thirty productions between Week-end, October, 1929, and your departure for television, August, 1939. If my notes are accurate, that averages out to three shows a year. What's more, I spot here a number of years when you had three shows playing at the same time; one year you had four. Where did you find the time?

MINER: I was young. I was under thirty when Week-end was done. That's no record, of course. Jed Harris had five productions and four smash hits by that age. But no, it wasn't youth, and it wasn't energy, alone. I was, I suspect, acutely sensitive to the temper, the passions, and the humor of the postwar years.

SCHAFFNER: How did you get started?

MINER: Luck.

SCHAFFNER: You must have had a lot more going for you than luck alone.

MINER: (a laugh) So call it destiny! My stepfather was in the importing business, high-grade worsteds from Verviers in

Belgium. You couldn't get much further from the theatre than that, could you? Yet it just so happened that his Sales Manager, a delightful old cuss named Harold Gould, was an active and ardent member of the Comedy Club. He also happened to be a lifelong friend of Walter Hampden. And so, when I got back from Cambridge with spotlights in my eyes, having fallen in love with the theatre, Harold Gould undertook to give me a note to Hampden, who was just setting out on a fourteen-week road tour with Cyrano de Bergerac. It was exactly ten days after I'd stepped off the gangplank of the Majestic. (a smile) Luck? Or Destiny?

SCHAFFNER: O.K., O.K.!

MINER: When I arrived at the rehearsal hall, I discovered that just that morning one of the extras had fallen ill, and so Walter was able to offer me a job. There and then I was hired.

I was so unprepared that, in my delight at being taken on so suddenly, I forgot to ask the price. It was thirty-five dollars a week. Even in 1924 that was scarcely a lavish sum for living on the Road. Thanks to Heaven and the United States Regular Army, I'd been taught to play poker by professionals, many of them pretty good with the second card. I'd learned to spot the fast dealers before I lost my shirt. In fourteen weeks I more than doubled that thirty-five dollars a week playing poker with the stagehands, the extras and the horse wranglers during Act Three.

But the real stroke of "destiny" came when I got back to New York. It was all due to my being born in Buffalo, New York, in a house on North Street. The house happened to be across the way from the one in which Kit Cornell had been born two years before. . . . I got back to New York in January. At dinner a few nights later, my mother came up with an item she'd clipped out of the paper that day. Katharine Cornell's name, it seems, had been stricken from the pages of the Social Register.

SCHAFFNER: In 1925? Why?

MINER: She was an actress. My mother was highly amused. "Which reminds me," she said. "Did you know, Worthington" -- she always called me by my first name -- "did you know that Kit was born in Buffalo?"

Indeed I had not. "Why didn't you tell me?" I asked.

"I didn't think of it. She's just opened in Candida and they say she's quite good. Why don't you go and see her?"

That was impossible for some weeks -- our matinees were on the same days as theirs. But the moment Cyrano closed, I slipped into a mid-week matinee and sat enthralled. I thought Miss Cornell was both glowing and exquisite to look upon. When the final curtain fell, I raced back to her dressing room, handing in a note from my mother. Although I was warmly greeted at once, I failed pathetically to find the words to express my feelings. I merely sat like a mute dimwit. Fortunately Kit was, as always, gracious beyond measure. It ended with her asking me to have tea with her and Guthrie the following day. I did. Guthrie never arrived; some crisis with the casting of The Green Hat had prevented him from coming, but he called to make a date with me in his office the following Monday.

SCHAFFNER: How many get a break like that?

MINER: Not many. But -- and this is not easy to accept -- I was too young and too naive to appreciate the break it was.

I arived at Guthrie's office on Monday, 11:00 a.m. sharp. A coolly polite secretary informed me that Mr. McClintic was tied up; it might be some time before he would be free. I was offered a plush sofa to lessen the discomfort of waiting.

My idea of a tolerable wait was little more than twenty minutes. As the hands of the wall-clock approached

12:45, my patience wore thin. I rose, put on my hat and started toward the door. The secretary looked at me in some dismay.

"Mr. Miner," she said, "you're not leaving? I know Mr. McClintic intended to see you. Miss Cornell suggested it."

"I realize that, but I've been here an hour and a half now. Besides, I have a lunch date at one o'clock."

The lunch date was true; I did not mention the fact that it was with my roommate and quite easily cancellable.

"Can I say you'll be back this afternoon?" she asked. "I know he'll be very upset at missing you."

"Oh, certainly," I replied. "I think I can make it by -- let's say four o'clock."

"I'll tell him," she said. What she thought was: Oh, little boy, you've got just as much chance of seeing Guthrie McClintic at four o'clock as I have of being twenty-one again.

I wasn't listening for nuances. And so, at 3:55 I walked into the office to announce I was back. What greeted me was such a reversal of form, I was caught completely off guard.

"Oh, Mr. Miner. Good! Mr. McClintic's been waiting for you. Just let me tell him you're here."

Her manner was both effusive and deferential. McClintic must have suffered more pangs of guilt than I had expected. Before I could fully collect myself, the door opened and Guthrie appeared. He was scarcely an imposing figure. I've never been certain whether he'd had polio as a child, or was merely double-jointed. In either case, his wrists were oddly bent and, when he moved, it was slightly crab-wise. He never moved directly forward; one shoulder invariably led the rest. This helped to relieve my imminent panic, but still failed to explain his excessive cordiality.

"Come in, Mr. Miner, come in! I couldn't be more distressed at our missing each other this morning. I do hope you'll forgive me."

"Oh, that's perfectly all right," I said. "It's just that I had another date."

"So I've been told. But now you're here, let's get right down to business. You want to learn as much as you can about the theatre, and as fast as you can, am I right?"

"That's it exactly," I smiled. "I realize it's a bad time of year, but your wife was so gracious, I thought I should have a talk with you as soon as possible."

"That's where fortune is on your side. I happen to have an opening at this very moment. Wasn't it Napoleon who asked the vital question: 'Is he lucky?' You obviously are. That's a mark in your favor."

"Well, I've had my good days and bad days," I said.

"This must be one of the good ones. Kit goes into rehearsal next Monday with The Green Hat, and I haven't yet signed a Stage Manager. It's as good a place as I know to learn the business."

"How right," I said. "Miss Cornell mentioned The Green Hat but it never occurred to me there'd be anything going into rehearsal this late in the season."

"It's a tryout," he said. Then with a smile: "She was quite taken with you. I can't think of any other way to explain it."

"When did you say you were starting?"

"Monday. Elgin Theatre. 10:30 a.m. The producer is Al Woods. He owns the Elgin." He smiled. "I promise to be punctual this time."

And so I had my first Class A job. I'd had enough experience in England so that nothing too dire occurred during the first three weeks. It was, in fact, no more than a day or so before we were to leave for Detroit that Guthrie arrived at rehearsal with a portly companion some fifty years of age. They soon entered into a whispered conversation at the far end of the stage. After no more than two or three minutes, Guthrie signalled me to join them.

A chill of apprehension went through me as I crossed the stage and sat down opposite him. What dire thing had I done, however inadvertently, to bring on this disaster? His first words did nothing to assuage the foreboding.

"How much experience have you had up to now?"

This was it. I was going to be fired. I told him all there was to tell -- my theatrical work at Cambridge and fourteen weeks carrying a spear for Walter Hampden.

"How old are you?"

"Twenty-five but I've been bald since I was seventeen," I said. "The steel hats we wore overseas did it." And then I added: "Is there something dreadfully wrong that I've done?"

"Oh, no," he said. "Not at all. But opening nights are rather terrifying, the first time out at least. That's why I've asked Ed" -- his last name eludes me -- "to come with us to Detroit. He's an old hand and can be a big help if anything goes wrong, which it often does."

"I think I can handle it," I said, a little hesitantly.

Guthrie smiled. "I'm sure you can. This is just, oh, you know, call it insurance."

"Well," I said, "whatever you say."

And so we moved on to Detroit. I handled the set-up and the show itself. In spite of Murphy's Law, there were no catastrophes. The portly Mr. Ed most thoughtfully stayed in the background. When the show was over, Guthrie came backstage, and the whisperings began again. After what seemed an unconscionable length of time, he came up to me.

"Well," he said, "Ed tells me you handled yourself like a veteran. Besides," he added, "the stagehands seem to like you. That's often the biggest hurdle for a beginner. I guess it pays to be bald."

The next day, Mr. Ed went back to New York, and I was on my own, all of which I owed to a hairless skull.

SCHAFFNER: What did your being bald have to do with your getting the job?

MINER: Guthrie had hired the wrong man. When I had gone back to his office that Monday afternoon at four, Guthrie was expecting another person entirely. He was a forty-two year-old stock broker who had made a fortune at an early age and had decided that he wanted to try his hand at the theatre. Guthrie was to give him that opportunity in exchange, God willing, for some sizable financial support for one of Mr. McClintic's future ventures. The moment Guthrie saw my bald head, he apparently concluded I was that forty-two year-old man; the boy from Cambridge had been the furthest thing from his mind. I'd been so late, I'd arrived at someone else's appointed hour.

SCHAFFNER: When did you find out?

MINER: Not right away -- almost a year later, in fact.

SCHAFFNER: And our balding millionaire? What ever became of him?

MINER: I've never known. I think he changed his mind and went back to building a fortune on margin.

SCHAFFNER: And went bust in the Crash.

MINER: Probably. Howsomever, five weeks later we were settled in for a run in Chicago. After Detroit Guthrie had gone back to New York for a few days, returning with Al Woods for a Saturday matinee. After the show Guthrie took me aside to ask in a thoroughly casual tone: "By the way, Tony, how would you feel about taking over as my assistant in the fall?"

The price he proposed was $25 a week. I raised no objections.

SCHAFFNER: And how much from Al Woods? $35?

MINER: That's right, but he'd boosted my salary to $45 before we reached Chicago. I said awhile back that managers had always been generous with me. Well, hear this! Guthrie had hired me originally for $25. Inside two weeks Al had boosted it to $45. When we opened at the Broadhurst Theatre in New York, Al hiked it again to $75. At Christmas he made it $125. When we went on the road the following fall, he boosted it to $200, and all of this without a word of prodding from me. Thus, at the end of a little over a year I was earning, with Guthrie's $25, $225 a week. You know how much that would mean today?

SCHAFFNER: A thousand dollars?

MINER: More like $1,500. And for a Stage Manager! It was another age. It meant a lot to know that, when you did a good job, it was recognized and rewarded. That's how the old-timers thought. Young talent was rare, and the competition was fierce. It was a cheap way to buy a young person's allegiance.

SCHAFFNER: Great for you, but how many others were that fortunate?

MINER: More than you might imagine. It was common practice then. Raises weren't yet computerized.

SCHAFFNER: I had expected to find you'd struggled for years before the first break came along. Now you tell me it was Easy Street for Tony Miner from the start.

MINER: That's right. Only I wasn't Tony Miner yet. The christening didn't take place till after the opening in Detroit.

SCHAFFNER: How come?

MINER: Coincidence. You see, the opening of The Green Hat happened also to be Kit's birthday. There was, of course, a party after the show. I'd gone back early to help out with drinks and other chores, when Kit turned to me and said: "What in the world are we going to call you? I've spent a month saying 'You!' or 'Look!' or 'Hey!' I cannot, and will not, call you Worthington. Haven't you ever had a nickname?"

"No." I had answered a little too quickly. "That isn't true. Truth is, I've had too many, all of them repulsive; things like 'Dit' and 'Cupid' and 'Minner Ditricals.'"

"No, no, none of those will do."

"Well, my nephew has had trouble with Worthington, too. He calls me Worthingtony."

"Perfect! You shall be 'Tony' from now on."

And so it was. No one but my mother has ever called me anything else since that evening in the spring of '25.

III

SCHAFFNER: Do you consider the thirties your decade?

MINER: Yes. But it was not the creative bombshell the twenties had been.

SCHAFFNER: Why not? What was missing?

MINER: The momentum was still there at the start, but by '36 to '37 the steam was spent. What isn't generally appreciated about the twenties is the fact that it wasn't only a great era in the theatre, it was a great era for the country as a whole.   While Alfred Sloan was creating General Motors, David Sarnoff was creating RCA, William S. Paley was founding CBS, Juan Trippe was founding PanAm, Harry Luce was founding Time, Inc., and Harold Ross was creating The New Yorker.   And music! Toscanini, Stokowski, Casals, Paul Robeson. The impact of the decade was stupendous.

SCHAFFNER: Including quite a number of prominent writers.

MINER: Hemingway, Faulkner, Willa Cather --

SCHAFFNER: -- Scott Fitzgerald, Sherwood Anderson, Steinbeck.

MINER: Not to mention the veritable avalanche of poets
-- Robert Frost, T.S. Eliot, Steve Benét --

SCHAFFNER: -- Edna St. Vincent Millay, Carl Sandburg,
Edwin Arlington Robinson --

MINER: -- Robinson Jeffers. Was there ever such a
gusher of lyric talent in so short a space of time?

SCHAFFNER: If there were, I can't name it.

MINER: And who, who could have predicted that this
vast wellspring of talent could all but dry up?

SCHAFFNER: Surely Sandburg went on writing. And
Frost. And Edna St. Vincent Millay.

MINER: Ah, yes, indeed. Most of them did, but they
were nonetheless children of the twenties. And it's the surge
of new talent that I'm talking about. That was the difference
between the twenties and thirties. The twenties were
aggressively secure; the thirties were still proud, stubbornly
proud, but secretly uncertain. The twenties attracted and
encouraged new talent; the thirties bred desertion and flight.
Even a writer of outstanding promise, like Clifford Odets, had
emerged, flowered and fled to the West, all before 1940. There
were no vestiges left of the momentum of the twenties to
carry over into the war years. There were but two prewar
plays of genuine distinction: The Philadelphia Story, and There
Shall Be No Night, but in both cases their authors, Phil Barry
and Bob Sherwood, were initially discovered during the
twenties. The biggest war-time success was Angel Street, and
even that was written many years before. I know. Against
Fran's advice, I had turned it down. (a laugh) I could be wrong,
you see. It was called Gaslight as a movie, and it made Shep
Traube, who was, himself, a child of an earlier time.

The forties' main distinction lay in a wholly new approach to musical comedy. The revolution that raised this native art to a new literate plateau began with adaptations of Theatre Guild productions from the twenties and thirties: Green Grow the Lilacs and Liliom. We know those productions today by other names: Oklahoma! and Carousel. Ony as the decade was drawing to a close did a new crop of playwrights and directors begin to emerge: Arthur Miller, Elia Kazan, Joshua Logan, Bob Anderson, Bill Inge. It was but another instance of the theatre's decline during a time of tumult, only to emerge again into a fresh, vibrant and creative art after the bombs were still. This was not as great an era as the twenties but it was cut from the same patten.

And so, though I was spurred into going into the theatre in the twenties, and was acutely in tune with that postwar decade, all my working years were in the thirties, years of gradual sterility and disaffection, reaching a climax of disillusionment after the Moscow trials of 1937-38. I was of the twenties in my tempo, my willingness to take a chance on new ideas and new people; I was of the thirties in my shame at being relatively comfortable and solvent while too many of my contemporaries were struggling through bankruptcy and destitution. It bred all around me an ill-read and poorly informed radicalism, a sympathy with the extreme left that was sixty percent sentimentality, thirty percent guilt and only a marginal amount of informed conviction. My accomplishments and failures can only be appraised against an understanding of this atmosphere of misery, the smothered misery of being among the chosen few. Why me?

SCHAFFNER: Which gives us a better appreciation of the kind of theatre to which you contributed so many productions, including, I must assume, a certain number of failures.

MINER: Ah, yes, a plentiful lot! It helped me to develop a very tough hide at a very early age.

SCHAFFNER: But you must have had a large number of hits as well, or you wouldn't have been in such continuing demand. Have you any idea how many successes there were?

MINER: That's hard to say without knowing what you
mean by the word "success." Nowadays a show has to run a
year or more to qualify. In the twenties and thirties -- and
before air-conditioning -- precious few survived the sweatshop
days of August. There have always been freaks like Choo-Chin
Chow and Abie's Irish Rose, but for the most part thirty weeks
was, in my fledgling years, a respectable season. Actually, it
was part of our whole economy. Would you believe that ninety
percent of the shows I did in those ten years, musicals
excluded, came in under $20,000? The average weekly nut ran
between $10,000 and $12,500. That meant that, if a show
lasted roughly twelve weeks, it was on an average in the
black. Thus, a twelve-week run was generally accepted as the
break-even point between success and failure.

SCHAFFNER: On that basis, how many did you have?

MINER: Well, starting at the beginning, there was Up
Pops the Devil, by Al Hackett and Frances Goodrich, August
1930. When I first read the script it had a rather nice title:
Let's Get Married, but the Shuberts wouldn't allow the word
"marriage" to appear in the title of any show they backed.
Seldom, however, did they saddle a production with as unhappy
a title as Up Pops the Devil. Even with this handicap, the
show lasted a full season.

By mid-year I was again in rehearsal with a far bigger
success, Five Star Final. How I got an assignment that expensive and that important at that stage of the game is one of
those twists of fate that would be considered the hallmark of
a third-rate writer in search of a plot.

You will recall that after suggesting he should never
again try to direct Miss Cornell, my association with Guthrie
McClintic had come to an abrupt end. In the summer of 1928
Guthrie took a translation from the French called Jealousy to
Al Woods with the idea tha Al should produce the play with
Fay Bainter and Guthrie in the two, and only two, leads. In
spite of his misgivings regarding Guthrie as an actor, Al
bought the idea on the assumption that Guthrie would, of
course, direct. By the time the contract was signed, Guthrie

had begun to panic about playing so exacting a role without some objective and professional guidance. This turned out for several reasons to be more of a hurdle than he had anticipated.

1. Al Woods was sold on Guthrie as a director and wanted no one else.

2. Guthrie had already signed a contract at a sizable fee.

3. There were only two directors in the business whom Guthrie would even consider, and each of them demanded full credit and authority. This Guthrie could not afford to offer without seriously antagonizing Al Woods.

Up to that point, Al had been Guthrie's only Mr. Moneybags. Here was his dilemma. The one person he trusted was me; but how could he endure the humiliation of giving that assignment to a young twerp he had kicked out of this house less than two years before?

You may well imagine my incredulity when Guthrie called a day or so later to offer me the job of directing him in a new play for Al Woods. He explained why he could not offer me any official credit for the job, but he was ready to hand over half his fee, $500 per week, plus one-half of one percent of the gross. This was far too intriguing and financially rewarding for me to refuse.

Although I was fully ready to accept the deal before putting down the phone, I insisted, for reasons of politics, on reading the script before making any final commitment. Within an hour the script arrived by special messenger. I dearly hoped it was a zinger, and it was. At least it read a whale of a lot better than I had dared to expect. And, if Guthrie were ever to play any part in the world, this was it. All his physical handicaps and disabilities were, in this case, ready-made assets. In addition, less than a year before I had played Fay Bainter's husband in Fallen Angels; we had got along well enough to make me anticipate no serious obstacle to her accepting me as director. My heart was, shall we say, at ease as I called Guthrie back to accept his proposal.

I said: "Yes." Guthrie said: "Good." By noon the following day I had signed a letter agreement. The die was cast.

The modus operandi was simple. I was to sit in the back of the darkened theatre and make notes to be given out later. When, and if, Al Woods came in, I was to pretend that Guthrie had invited me to take a look at his performance. Far from arousing his suspicions, the arrangement seemed to delight Mr. Woods. How better could he check on whether Guthrie was lousing up his play or not?

On his very first visit I was able fully to reassure him. "Forget it, Al. Guthrie's so damn right for this part, the whole thing's beginning to sing." He never quite believed me, of that I'm convinced, but it brought him a moment of solace.

The opening was in Stamford, Connecticut. For the whole First Act Guthrie was like a girl at her first prom. I've seldom seen anyone in the theatre so beset by nerves, and for good reason. Guthrie, as I've said, was eccentric, so eccentric that the audience could not for an agonizingly long time accept him as Fay's incomparable lover. By Act II he'd begun to win them over -- he was quite a hell of an actor, you know -- and to make them forget his physical shortcomings. When the curtain finally came down, the applause, if not thunderous, was at least respectful. That, by itself, was gratifying. Given two more weeks before coming into town, success seemed quite a possibility.

There was but one flaw in an otherwise cheerful evening. Jed Harris -- I was working for him by then, you remember -- had unpredictably driven out to Stamford, probably to gloat over Guthrie's ignominy. Once his eye spotted me, he guessed that I had had some secret part in directing the show. He seemed at the start to take this surreptitious moonlighting of mine with gracious good nature. But this was out of character for Jed. He knew very well that I was going to be needed in Hartford and New Haven. And so, predictably, he gave me the needle where it hurt the most. As a parting shot he invented a chore for me that made it impossible for me to travel with the show.

I've mentioned the fact that at the final curtain there was a decent amount of applause. There was one, however, who did not applaud. That was Al Woods. He felt that Guthrie was not only mannered, but physically unacceptable in the part, and he didn't hesitate to speak his mind. To buttress his conviction, "Guthrie McClintic" was a name no one in Hartford had ever heard of; as a result, business was dreadful. The upright citizenry of central Connecticut was not ready to accept Guthrie as a great Latin lover, no matter how well he played the part.

On its way back to New York, Jealousy was scheduled for a split week in Mount Vernon. It was the only Broadway production I ever heard of that ever did play that pot-hole. On that same morning Guthrie, and half of New York, myself included, read in the New York Times that Al Woods was replacing Guthrie McClintic in the lead role of Jealousy with Jack Halliday.

It was so crass, so cruel a way of doing things, I could scarcely believe it. Before the day was out I knew that Guthrie was both stunned and outraged by Al's betrayal. Thus I was far from surprised to learn a day or so later that Guthrie was about to sue Al for the lion's share of Fort Knox. It was an untidy affair that left deep scars and bitter hurts on both sides.

Fay was in a panic about changing over to Jack Halliday with only two weeks' rehearsal and without either Guthrie or me on hand. Obviously Guthrie was out of the picture; quite as obviously, so was I; I could never again be discovered in the darkness of the Elgin Theatre. Since, however, Guthrie had already paid me $2,000, I felt an obligation to do what I could to ease Fay's mind. Thus it was agreed that, as often as possible, I would come to her apartment and work with her and Jack. This was not as wild as it may sound, since Jealousy was a two character play; it could have been rehearsed in a public restroom.

I deliberately did not attend the opening; the last person I wanted to bump into at that juncture was Al Woods. The notices were over-generous, and Jealousy settled down to a successful run. And yet, and this is truly sardonic, I have always believed that, with Guthrie, the play might have been a far greater success, and certainly a more interesting play, than it ever was with Jack Halliday.

There remains the major madness in this entangled incident. The following year Al Woods got hold of a play called Five Star Final by Louis Weitzenkorn. In the course of normal events Al would have given the script to Guthrie to direct. It was a big show, presenting major technical problems, multiple scenes and a cast of thirty. In addition, it was known to have a most difficult and irascible playwright. Louis Weitzenkorn was a tough little newspaper man once trained by Bayard Swope, the famous Managing Editor of the old World. Al needed an experienced powerhouse to tackle the job, but after signing Arthur Byron to the lead, he still had no director. Things were geting pretty ominous as the weeks passed. The final and decisive event was relayed to me by Sam Hoffenstein, poet and legendary Press Agent for Al Woods. After weeks of frustration, Al arrived in the office one morning in high spirits to announce he had found just the director for Five Star Final.

When Sam asked: "Who?", Al responded, "Tony Miner."

Sam exploded. "Tony Miner! He's ony a kid. What makes you think he's up to a job like this?

A twinkle came into Al's eye. "I don't know, Sam. But this is for sure -- it's going to make Guthrie yowl like a stuck pig."

That's how I got the assignment that made my career possible.

SCHAFFNER: Incredible! And it gave you two hits in one season. Don't tell me you took on another?

MINER: Yes indeed, I did, I did. And a most memorable show it was, too.

SCHAFFNER: Memorable? I've just looked it up, and it only lasted about ten weeks.

MINER: Ah, but it got one of the most unforgettable reviews ever written. "The House Beautiful is the play lousy."

SCHAFFNER: That was it?

MINER: That was it. It was Dottie Parker at her best. She was critic for the New Yorker at the time. And she was right. It was a louse of a play. But it also happened to give my professional standing an incomparable boost. And it did quite as well, if not better, by Jo Mielziner. It was reprehensible; we should have blushed, both of us, but it worked like a charm.

SCHAFFNER: Why reprehensible?

MINER: Because we both knew the play was a stinker at the time we agreed to do it. We should have turned it down. But we also knew it was the spring of the year and jobs were far from plentiful. Moreover, Channing Pollock had had other dreadful shows that, bad as they were, had yet made Crosby Gage a tidy fortune. Who were we to argue with the erratic whims of the New York box office?

But the decisive factor for Jo and me was the script's reliance on our finding a solution to a prodigious technical challenge. We were well aware that, if we licked that problem, the aisle-sitters would laud our efforts, regardless of the success or failure of the play.

SCHAFFNER: Go on.

MINER: The stunt was to transform, before an audience's eyes, a sweep of New Jersey countryside into the living room of a comfortable suburban cottage without a break in the action. We found the answer, and it worked. The applause was spontaneous, and the critics were enchanted, so enchanted that even the play itself was treated gently and with tolerance by all, barring of course, Dottie Parker. Jo and I were riding high. Three sets of good notices in one season were enough to give me a royal send-off in my chosen profession. I felt only the smallest twinge of shame at not having let Crosby know from the start my true opinion of the play. Ironically enough, if I had, it would have made no difference whatever. He'd have replied: "I know, my boy, I know. And so was The Enemy, but it made a lordly sum."

In addition to his undeniable charm, Crosby was an intellectual and a scholar. He spoke Latin with relative fluency. He was equally at home in the twelfth and thirteenth centuries. He knew Channing Pollock as well as I did. That's why he never blamed me for the failure of the show, why at the first opportunity he asked me to do another show for him, I Loved You Wednesday. Taken all in all, it was a most happy windfall for me and, in the end, no one was seriously hurt, not even Crosby himself. Some months later he confessed that he had put $50,000 into escrow to cover the losses he anticipated on the show. It was worth it to keep a money-making play-wright in his camp. "You know what it actually set me back, Tony? $18,568.23." This figure is only roughly accurate.

I'd like to round this off by stating that House Beautiful had been responsible for my being asked to do Reunion in Vienna. Unhappily, I can't; it was Five Star Final. Lawrence Langner and his wife, Armina Marshall, had come backstage one night during the first two weeks of the run and had asked me to drop by the Guild the following day. I did, and was given the script for Reunion. It became my first assignment for the fall season of 1931.

SCHAFFNER: This is all pretty early, isn't it?

MINER: Very.

SCHAFFNER: How was it working with the Lunts? And
at that age? Were they willing to listen?

MINER: Oh, they'd listen! God in Heaven, how they'd
listen! Provided, that is, provided what you said made sense. If
not, beware!

     I don't really know why I said that. It sounds as though
they had been monsters. Nothing could be further from the
truth. But what I found hard to adjust to was their way of
working. They taught me to think a long time before saying
yes or no.

SCHAFFNER: It wasn't easy then?

MINER: No. As a director, you can understand why I was
apprehensive from the start. First of all, I was far from wild
about the script. Bob Sherwood had written the second act
three years earlier; the next year he had written Act Three;
then, after an interval of two years, he'd finally tackled Act
One and dashed it off in eleven days, or some equally hurried
length of time. And it showed. Bob knew everything about the
character he had written for Alfred; every gesture and syllable
was true and believable. But he never made up his mind who
Lynn was from one scene to another. She was one woman in
Act One, another in Act Two, and a hopeless hodgepodge in
Act Three. Proof? This much: Reunion was never again a
success with any other actress, Ina Claire, Diana Wynyard, God
knows who else. No one lacking Lynn's stubborn, peasant mind
could ever hope to carve out a single credible character from
the contradictory dialogue she was given to speak. That she
could also make the creature alluring was merely miraculous. I
have always felt the play's success was due more to Lynn than
to anyone else.

     But you asked: "Did they listen?" I'll give you a sam-
ple. I'd never worked with a team like the Lunts. I felt it was
important to test their acceptance of my authority before we
started rehearsal, and so I asked to meet with them to which
they readily agreed. It was late afternoon a few days later.

Almost at the start I confessed that I was disturbed by two things: first, Lynn's part. With that they were in full accord. Second, and this applied to both of them: mannerisms. I was shaking inside as I spoke the word.

SCHAFFNER: (a laugh) You should have said "stylized."

MINER: "Mannerisms?" said Alfred with frightening intensity. "When? Where?"

"Now don't get excited, Alfred dear." Lynn tried to quiet him down. "It may have happened without our knowing it. Let's hear what Tony has to say."

Fortunately I'd done my homework; I'd listed more examples than I ever intended to use.

"I've admired you both so much, I can't bear to see you become -- " I hesitated some time before speaking the word "-- usual. No, that's not the way I want to put it. Let's just say, doing what the audience expects you to do instead of surprising them, doing something they've never seen you do before, or never have seen you do in just that way. And so, delighting them."

"Go on," Alfred said. "Be specific."

I was. By the time I had given them two or three examples, I stopped.

"You obviously know what I'm talking about," I said.

"Go on. I want to hear more."

"No," I laughed, "I've talked quite enough. I just didn't want a scene, anything that could be avoided, in front of the cast."

"Good," said Alfred. "It will do us good."

"Oh, Alfred dear, you'd go out of your mind. You forget how vain you are." She began to laugh. He turned to me.

"She's a dreadful woman," he said. "She's the one who needs the reminding." He suddenly broke into his most radiant, most irresistible smile. "But just watch out, young man. She notices things, too! Don't let her catch you in a mannerism! Oh-ho!"

"He's such a liar," Lynn said. "It's not true, any of it."

It ended on that note. And if my contribution to Reunion did nothing more, it presented Alfred and Lynn more nearly devoid of mannerisms than they had been in years. It lent a freshness to their performance that allowed the magic of their uncanny charm to shine through.

The adjustments I had to make, amusing as they may seem today, were anything but amusing to me at the time. I had been in the habit, borrowed from McClintic, of sitting around a table for the first week or ten days of rehearsal, examining the mood and purpose of the play, the individual quality of each character and the tempo and thrust of each scene as it fitted into the overall structure of the play. It had worked well for me up to then, allowing the actors to make notes without interrupting the flow of the scene, and permitting the mechanism of putting the actors on their feet to go forward without stopping for character analyses and line readings.

But Alfred and Lynn had had the script for three months. They had substantially learned their lines before the first rehearsal and knew, to a very large degree, what they wanted to do with those lines. For them every hour spent around a table was spendthrift of time, and they were far too impatient to tolerate a waste of that irreplaceable commodity. Fortunately I was flexible and able to work faster than most in this aspect of the craft, but it still cost me a number of long and sleepless nights.

My second adjustment was to the Guild. I was forced into a nasty situation before the end of the first week. I was in the middle of working on a scene with Alfred and Lynn when I looked up and spotted Lawrence Langner sitting along the sidelines. I still disliked him intensely and disrespected him even more. He was sitting over at one side of the room, whispering quite audibly to some member of the cast. It had been his habit to drop in on rehearsals at will. Indeed, it had been the habit of any member of the Board who so desired. I, on the other hand, had never let anyone into a rehearsal of mine except by invitation. Not certain what I should do, I took Alfred and Lynn aside and asked: "Do you like having people sit in at rehearsals?"

"God, no!" Alfred said. "But it's an old Guild custom."

"Then would you object if I tried to break that custom?"

His answer was a grin of delight. If I had the stomach for it, they'd be overjoyed.

With that much encouragement I decided to risk an ugly confrontation. Lawrence was smiling as I approached.

"Well, Tony, how are things going?"

"Rather well, so far," I answered. "Only one thing. I'm not used to having people come into my rehearsals without being invited."

Lawrence laughed. "But we've always come to rehearsals, old boy. We come and go whenever we like. No one has ever objected before."

"I know," I said. "But it would disturb me very much. I also know that Alfred and Lynn would prefer it if you left."

He stared at me for some time with a puzzled expression. Then, and without a word, he patted my shoulder and left.

When I turned around Alfred and Lynn were utterly incredulous. Slowly they began to grin. I had made Guild history. Nothing could have given me a better send-off. They'd resented these intrusions too long.

But a part of my reason for revising my opinion of Lawrence was the fact that never, ever, did he show the slightest resentment toward my highhanded behavior. If anything, he seemed more gracious and friendly toward me afterward than before. And never again did he try to come into a rehearsal of mine. Neither did any other member of the Board. Lawrence, I felt sure, had taken care of that. My respect for him developed slowly, but it had begun.

The most difficult adjustment came later in rehearsals. Around the second week Alfred came up to me before the rest of the cast had arrived.

"Tony, Lynn and I did some work last night in that sticky spot in Act Three. Do you mind if we show you what we've done?"

I agreed, naturally. Without further ado he and Lynn went through an eight- to ten-minute scene so slickly rehearsed and polished that my first instinct was to applaud. But I didn't; I hesitated. Something whispered to me that all was not quite right. While I was still pondering, Alfred came to the footlights.

"You don't like it," he said, "so, forget it, forget it! It was just an idea." And then he laughed. "Don't look so mouldy, lad. We'll find it the next time."

That was not an isolated incident; it happened again and again. My problem was to realize that nothing could satisfy those two but a spontaneous "Hurray!" Anything less, and they would throw it out. No hard feelings, no recriminations. But sometimes, in throwing out a scene, they'd throw out some moments that were delicious, beautiful. It was a tough, but exciting, way of working. I adjusted to it with repetitive jitters, but an inner delight. What a pity that never again would I encounter any other actors who were willing to put in that much time and effort without showing a trace of resentment if it were tossed in the trashcan. They were two very great human beings. I've never met their equal since.

Objectively, I always felt I did a skillful, but, best of all, an inconspicuous job with the play. And with the Lunts.

Certainly it was a "loverly" evening of theatre, for which I felt no shame.

An incident occurred when we were on the road, however, that dealt an all but mortal blow to my future in the theatre. When Reunion opened in Pittsburgh it was a flop. By the time we reached Cleveland two weeks later, it was still shaky and unwell. The pitfall lay somewhere in Act Three, but it was a "somewhere" not one of us had been able to spot. It was on Wednesday that we got word that the Guild, meaning Terry Helburn and Lawrence, were coming to the Saturday matinee to take a look at the show. Bob Sherwood and Harold Freedman, his agent, were arriving with them. All of us knew this foreshadowed a swift interment of the venture.

Alfred and I went into a most apprehensive conference. We still believed in the show, but we couldn't deny that the patient was a poor and shaky thing. After a melancholy hour a spark suddenly appeared in Alfred's eye. He grabbed the script from me and began to read in feverish intensity.

"This is it!" he declared. "Tony, it's here! This is where we lose them every night, right here!"

A glance told me he was right, but I couldn't yet see why.

"It's happening too soon," he went on. "That's what's wrong. The audience isn't ready yet."

It was the clue we both had needed. Reading ahead another ten to fifteen pages, I saw what we all had missed for so long; those ten to fifteen pages cried out for transposition. They belonged to a later part of the story.

"It's staring at us!" I said. "All we have to do is lift this whole damn scene and put it in here. All it needs are two simple joins to get us in and get us out."

Alfred hesitated. "Bob will kill us," he said.

"So let's ask him."

We got on the phone, only to find that Bob was out of town, and no one knew where he could be reached. We were still up against a fateful deadline. In the end our decision was to try it out. Next evening would be Friday. If it worked, it might salvage the show. If it didn't, what had we lost? We'd go back to what we had before the harpies arrived on Saturday.

The effect of that transposition was startling, even to us. For the first time the audience gave the last act a loud ovation. When I got back to Alfred's dressing room, he greeted me with that marvelous, mischievous grin of his. "I'd like to see those executioners use their meat-axes on us now."

We both laughed in a happy glow of confidence. We could not at that moment imagine that our handiwork would be greeted with anything but gratitude and the warmest of thanks.

What in fact transpired at the matinee on Saturday was so stunning, it was many hours before I could accept it. When Bob heard those few makeshift lines I'd written to make that all-important transposition possible, he flew into an ungovernable rage. I was accused of an effrontery unheard of and unforgiveable. Why, Bob wanted to know, hadn't I even had the courtesy to ask his approval? Our efforts to convince him that we had tried were fruitless. Our assurances that the few lines I'd written were only temporary patchwork were brushed aside. Bob and Harold continued to insist that I'd committed an unthinkable act. They also, and for no reason I could ever fathom, refused to accept the fact that Alfred had had any part in it. Harold's words were: "It'll be a long time, Tony Miner, before you get another script from one of my clients." This was a formidable jolt. Throughout the thirties Harold controlled seventy-five percent of the best playwrights in the business.

Despite this outcry, our transposition remained in the script for the evening performance. For this I felt sure we had Lawrence Langner to thank. Before the opening in Baltimore, Bob had rewritten those few phrases. Notwithstanding his unbridled fury, Bob had finally accepted my "effrontery." This became the script with which we opened in New York.

Time eventually healed the wound. Bob and I remained friends until his untimely and tragic death. Harold's thaw was somewhat swifter. Within a month I was getting other scripts from him; one of them I did the following season; it won the Pulitzer for 1933. Within the theatre world, however, the more vicious aspects of the story took a far longer time to die. As late as 1939 Phil Barry flew into a rage when the Guild suggested that I direct The Philadelphia Story.

"Let that bastard massacre one of my scripts? Over my dead body!"

It scarcely smoothed the way for me in the years ahead.

SCHAFFNER: Brandt & Brandt was Freedman's agent, right?

MINER: Correct. And because of Harold, it became in the theatre an institution. It wasn't a good idea to incur Harold's ire during the Depression years.

SCHAFFNER: So, what next?

MINER: Oh Lord, let's see. It wasn't next, but it comes to mind: Her Master's Voice. Author: Clare Kummer. Stars: Roland Young and Laura Hope Crews. Featured: Elizabeth Patterson and Frances Fuller. That was not, as you might suspect, a case of nepotism; Max Gordon had signed Fran for the part months before I even came into the picture.

Her Master's Voice was a sizable hit, but it wasn't, for me, a happy experience. There was constant friction during rehearsals and, when it was all done, I felt little, or no, pride in my workmanship. By my own estimate, it was a professional, but undistinguished job, superficially slick, but with little freshness and less imagination.

SCHAFFNER: Why?

MINER: Politics. Even worse, family and maternal politics. And let's not forget Laura Hope Crews, her dear self. It
wasn't that she was a bitch, which she was, but that she was
the kind of actress I couldn't abide. She was skin-deep and
greedy. She represented the cult of acting I'd spent my professional years trying to discredit and replace. What made things
even more insufferable was the fact that Clare Kummer had
written the play for Laura, and Roland was Clare's son-in-law.
I thought the play was his; Laura thought it was hers, and
would stop at nothing to see that it remained so. The first
time I caught her deliberately trying to kill one of Roland's
laughs, I called her on it. To my bewildered fury, Roland came
to her defense, not as an actor, but as a dutiful son-in-law.

        After all, Laura was Clare's bosom friend, and Clare
was Marjorie's mother, and Marjorie was Roland's wife, and so
on and so on . . .

        If there was one thing that drove me berserk it was a
set that put the fireplace along one wall with a chair or sofa
illogically placed with its back to it. Clare's script called for a
large wing chair to be set center stage, its back to the
stairwell, the fireplace, and even the sofa with which it was
designed to serve as a group. With rehearsal chairs it was not
particularly disturbing, but for me, it was a constant sore. Day
after day I would place it in its logical position; I wanted to
be able to live in that room. Nothing could have mattered less
to Laura. One day I happened to catch her twisting that chair
into its unnatural position. I blew my top.

        "Miss Crews -- " Before I could go on, Roland stepped
in.

        "Oh, come now, Tony. What are you getting so worked
up about?"

        "Why is that goddamned chair sitting there in the mid-
dle of the stage?"

        "To play scenes in, old boy."

The cast's laughter was at my expense. Roland was a love of a human being; he was also an enchanting actor, and, having spent his youth in Laura's kind of theatre, he was easily able to adjust to its artificialities, which I so intensely deplored. I should have been able to smile, to have taken it all more lightheartedly. I couldn't. Worst of all, that chair proved to be a very simple and effective place to play scenes. While I could do nothing to smother my discomfort, I secretly fumed. No one else seemed to care that those scenes might have played at least as well, perhaps better, had that damn piece of furniture been placed in a more rational position. But what Clare wanted, Laura got.

My mood became increasingly sullen, so sullen, in fact, that when at one point on the road Max Gordon suggested he see what he could do to ease the troubled waters, I offered no objection. This led to the one joyous moment I can recall from the whole adventure. After an hour of coping with Laura's acquisitive tactics, Max burst out: "Oh, come on, Laura, what in hell do you want?"

Fast as a cat she replied: "I want all the lines!"

To be fair, there was a twinkle in her eye as she spoke. She was capable of undeniable charm; she never could have become a star of that magnitude without it. And when she wasn't lying, her frankness was often disarming. But these were oases in a dreary desert of bad temper, stubbornness and egotism. Well, as I say, we got a hit. But frankly by that time I, with apologies to Rhett Butler, didn't give a damn.

SCHAFFNER: (a laugh) But where were all those "socially conscious" jobs that won you the title of "The Red Director of New York"?

MINER: There weren't all that many, three, maybe four, and one of them wasn't left-wing at all, it was about farmers from Minnesota trying to cope with an Alaskan winter. My first really "Red" production was Let Freedom Ring by Albert Bein. With a cast of fifty-five I soon found that handling crowds was instinct with me. I shone at it. Quite objectively, I don't know anyone who did it better up to Agnes De Mille and Jerry Robbins. Nowadays, Bill Ball is good with crowds, and Franco Zeffirelli is a master. In the thirties, however, there was no one in the same league.

Let Freedom Ring was a marginal success. I did, I thought, one of my better jobs with it, but the reviews were lukewarm, all but one glowing notice from Brooks Atkinson. It was enough to allow us to survive for a respectable number of weeks at the Broadhurst Theatre. After that Freedom moved down to the Theatre Union, Eva Le Gallienne's old stomping ground on 14th Street, where it kept running into the following summer. It wasn't one of the greatest plays of the decade, but it had some lovely lyric writing, and a number of stunningly poignant moments.

The cast, all unknowns, became the nucleus of the Actors Repertory Company. It was an odd assemblage; no great stars emerged from its ranks. The only ones you might have heard of were Tony Ross and Will Geer. Still, for some reason, when they worked with me they attracted attention. More than once they were given the kind of notices you keep to brighten the waning years. Away from me, they couldn't seem to cut it. I have no idea why. It was a group with perennial promise and, as unendowed promises are wont to do, they had their day in the sun, a scant three years, after which nothing but an unrecorded dark. They represented no revolutionary principle to secure them a niche in memory.

SCHAFFNER: What were some of the other shows you did with the Repertory Company?

MINER: It began while they were still down at the Theatre Union. Almost completely on their own, the kids put on an evening of one-act plays. I only came in for the last few days. Again, as a group, their notices were close to raves; the best of the lot was Paul Green's Glory Road. It was one of the best things Green ever wrote, and we gave it a taut and moving production. It was something to remember.

Then there was Bury the Dead by Irwin Shaw. It was famous in part for the fact that its first production cost $660.

I designed the set; it was built on the stage by the stage crew. It was done as a benefit for a left-wing magazine out to raise money for Loyalist Spain. When, however, it was brought up-town to the Fulton Theatre, now the Helen Hayes, the nut was $13,500. For what?

SCHAFFNER: Featherbedding for Local 802, what else?

MINER: Precisely. The play was, of course, a plea for peace. In that day and age that was for the critics like motherhood. Our reviews were overboard.

SCHAFFNER: But an exciting evening -- that seems clear. I also see here by my notes that you had other labor problems along the way, one of them formidable.

MINER: That it was. And the answer we found was so foolhardy, we should never, by rights, have got away with it.

SCHAFFNER: Tell me more.

MINER: It began with the fact that Bury the Dead only ran an hour and five minutes. That was not a full evening of theatre. The curtain-raiser we'd come up with was another play by Paul Green which looked like a zinger. All was aglow up to five days before opening when the Writers Guild, with no substantial warning, pulled a strike. Paul Green's opus had to be scratched. Why Irwin Shaw wasn't affected I can't recall, but he wasn't. Bury the Dead remained in the clear. Perhaps because it was written for radio originally. I don't know. But how in hell were we going to fill thirty-five to forty minutes to start the evening?

Cancellation seemed the one rational response, but I got stubborn. I insisted there had to be another out, and the company agreed. Only one flaw: none of us had the foggiest notion what that "out" might be.

SCHAFFNER: So what did you do?

MINER: We decided to ad lib.

SCHAFFNER: Ad lib? For thirty-five minutes?

MINER: I kid you not. We decided to have two wounded veterans review the historical scene from 1914 up to that point in the mid-thirties when "the war that was to start tomorrow" could pick up. Of course, we depended heavily on music to carry along the mood.

SCHAFFNER: What music?

MINER: That was the problem. To evoke nostalgia we had to use any number of standards, but the moment we touched a standard we ran into Grand Rights. The one way out was to use less than four bars of any one number.

SCHAFFNER: Which was no "out" at all.

MINER: On the contrary, it was our salvation. The score was prepared by a young actor named Fred Stewart, and it worked. It worked so well that Dick Rodgers claimed it was the best evening of theatre he'd seen in years.

SCHAFFNER: And what did you use for a script?

MINER: Ad libs! The two wounded veterans began reminiscing on the porch of a hospital. Other actors interrupted, bringing in word of the assassination at Sarajevo. Two secretaries took down every word. Each evening we'd keep what was good, throw out the rest, insert actual speeches by Petain,

Lloyd George, Wilson, and a whole array of every-day Joes on the streets of London, Paris, Berlin and Chicago. We went through the War of 1914 to '18, the League of Nations, the Market Crash, and Prohibition. We still had Stalin and Hitler for toppers.

SCHAFFNER: In five days?

MINER: In five days. And here's the kicker. It got more than a few professional responses that were better than those for Bury the Dead! Is that to be believed?

SCHAFFNER: No.

MINER: It happened. (a laugh) I was there. And a long way it went toward softening the blow of being fired from On Your Toes.

SCHAFFNER: That wasn't your last?

MINER: No. The last, and best, was 200 Were Chosen by E.P. ("Worth") Conkle. Scratch that from the list of successes. It was, sadly enough, a flop-aroo, backed, unpredictably enough, by Harry Luce and Jock Whitney. What should we call it? A posh stinker? We'd be wrong. It was no stinker, far from it. In my book it was one of the best plays I ever did; it had the best set Don Oenslager ever devised; and it was the best example of group acting I ever saw up to West Side Story. Yet it was unmercifully panned by every critic in New York. Its dialogue, built around colloquialisms that sang to a rhythm of their own, was casually ignored. Its dismissal left, I confess, a hurt that lasted a long time.

Which makes the aftermath all the more sardonic. Some four years later Worth Conkle told me that, since the day we closed in New York, not a week had gone by without 200 Were Chosen being played somewhere in the United States.

And this for a clincher -- in all those productions, good and bad, there had never been a half-hearted review for the play. Most had proclaimed it a tribute to our 20th Century American Theatre.

On the other side of the ledger, there was I Loved You Wednesday. It wasn't much of a play, but the cast list carried a certain fascination: I Loved You Wednesday, starring Frances Fuller; featuring Humphrey Bogart and Rose Hobart. Not to mention a bit player, suffering through an unhappy divorce from Maggie Sullavan. Are you ahead of me? Hank Fonda.

SCHAFFNER: Beautiful. How well had you known Bogie before this?

MINER: Oh, we'd been close friends for a long time. It was Bogie's lowest ebb. He had just blown a career in Hollywood; he was still on the books as a white-tie-and-tails juvenile. In the year before I gave him the job in I Loved You Wednesday, he made a total of $165 -- at least that's what he told me. He could, of course, have been exaggerating, but not by much. He had been married to Mary Philips for about three years. Mary was one of the best actresses I ever worked with, very like Eileen Heckart today. No star, but she had everything else. Her $500 a week kept them going. For Bogie, this was a constant humiliation; he didn't submit to being "kept" with ready nonchalance. Day after day he'd come around to borrow a quarter from me, or four bits or a buck, to buy his way into one of the Chess Parlors along Sixth Avenue. By evening he'd drop by to pay me back. Far more important, he'd have a dollar or two in his pocket to pay for his lunch the following day. It tore at his guts to ask Mary for the price of a hot dog. I Loved You Wednesday put a few dollars in his pocket, but it didn't make him an actor.

SCHAFFNER: What did?

MINER: Mary Philips. She alone saw how great Bogie could be. And, in the end, a small group of his friends, of which Fran and I were a part, began to see him as she did. You see, Bogie had begun in Cradle Snatchers as a gigolo type. During his marriage to Helen Mencken she was the serious actress, the star; Bogie was rated a puff-paste playboy. From the moment he married Mary Philips she recognized the passionate intensity that Bogie had managed, all too successfully, to hide. It was a year or so after I Loved You Wednesday that she persuaded the stock company in Falmouth, Massachusetts, to take on Bogie as well as herself for the summer. She also got them to agree to put on Seventh Heaven as the final bill of the season with Bogie in the part of Chico. They must have been hungry indeed to get Mary, to accede to such terms. Up to that time Bogie had never indicated the slightest capacity to play this Parisian gutter rat.

Happily for all of us Mary's instinct was right. The production and Bogie's performance were immediate sensations. From the moment he emerged from the sewers of Paris, Bogie captured the audience and held it spellbound until the final curtain.

Word of his performance travelled fast; it reached New York before he did. The transformation was extraordinary. He had become, almost overnight, a different human being. No longer the lines of apprehension and bitterness around the mouth. He had proven what he could do, and no one was ever again going to take that away from him.

The next sequence of events was, and remains, almost too improbable to record. Fran had gone to see Arthur Hopkins about a part in a play he was doing in the fall with Leslie Howard. A few seasons before she had played opposite Leslie in The Animal Kingdom. She had been so glowing, it was not surprising that he should want her with him again. She came home with a script which she was just finishing when I got in from rehearsal.

"How is it?" I asked.

"Marvelous!" she said. "I don't know whether Arthur is going to want me for the part, but he should. But, oh, Tony," she went on, "there's such a part for Humphrey! It's as though it were written for him."

I read the script that night and agreed. It was for Mr. Bogart the chance of a lifetime.

An evening or so later we were at Humphrey and Mary's apartment with Jeffrey Kerr and Miriam Howell, a well-known agent at the time. The subject of the play came up. The script was, of course, The Petrified Forest by Robert E. Sherwood; the part was that of Duke Mantee. The problem was to get Arthur and Bob to give Humphrey a chance to read. Neither of them had seen him in Seventh Heaven. Thus, for them he was still a one-night stand for Alice Brady. They were not easily to be persuaded that he had either the depth or the authority to give convincing stature to so commanding a figure.

It was, as I remember, Jeffrey Kerr who first suggested the scenario for our little caper. Within moments all of us were contributing bits and pieces to its improbable development. Fran was to supply the script. She still had the copy Arthur had given her; she agreed to get it to Humphrey the following morning. He would need a day or so to study the part. Jeffrey undertook to get Bob to come over for an evening of bridge. There would, of course, be no hint that Duke Mantee would be one of the foursome.

With a critical assist from Mary, Humphrey's initial hesitancy was transformed into wholehearted compliance. The game became, for him, a living reality. Soon he was treating it like opening night. First he gave his hair a crewcut that looked for all the world like a San Quentin crop. With his naturally thick hair he had no trouble producing a five o'clock shadow within a matter of days. Black shirt, black tie, shoulder holster -- God knows where he had picked it up -- he was to the manner born a complete Mantee.

When Bob arrived Humphrey slipped into the bedroom. Jeffrey was magnificent; with disarming skill he led Bob into a discussion of the play. How was casting going? When were rehearsals going to start? Bob was still without suspicion. Everthing seemed to be going well with The Forest, he said, the one exception being the part of Duke Mantee. God knows how many actors they had seen, but no one so far had come even close. At this moment the door to the bedroom opened and Humphrey appeared, quite as though he had nothing on his mind other than a hand of bridge. I won't try to describe the expression on Bob's face. There was a moment when I actually thought he hadn't recognized Humphrey, and it might be that he hadn't. It might be that all he saw at that moment was the ghost of Duke Mantee.

The ice was partially broken as Jeffrey tried to smother a laugh, but Bob was still too shaken to recognize the note of reality. Only as he began to appreciate that this was a rag, something we had cooked up for his benefit, could he begin to share our mood, to recognize the basic seriousness of our purpose, to accept the possibility that Humphrey Bogart might indeed be the actor they had been looking for. A couple of drinks and a couple of laughs later, he and Humphrey were off to the bedroom for that momentous reading.

When they emerged some half an hour later we all knew at a glance that we were halfway home. Bob was clearly persuaded; all that remained was for him to persuade Arthur. His excitement was so genuine, we were convinced that his chances of failure were joyously slim. And so the long search for a Duke Mantee was ended. I don't think any of us got around to playing bridge that night. As for the rest, or so they say --

SCHAFFNER: -- it's history. God, that's a story. How many others know it?

MINER: Well, now, let's think. Of that original cabal, Fran and I are the only ones still alive. Now you! As you may imagine, there were many reasons for keeping it secret. There was but one sour note to the whole escapade: Fran lost the part to Peggy Conklin. Leslie always insisted that Peggy was signed before Fran ever got to see Arthur. I wouldn't know.

SCHAFFNER: Why would he ever do a thing like that?

MINER: Embarrassment? He liked Fran, and he was a very shy man.

SCHAFFNER: One thing. The moment you began telling that story, you began calling Bogie, Humphrey. And you kept calling him Humphrey right through to the end. How come?

MINER: We were back in the thirties. He was known to us as Humphrey then. Bogie came along a couple of years later. It's a way of spotting whether someone really knew Bogie as well as he pretends. It will expose a lot of fakers.

SCHAFFNER: That's not an easy act to follow.

MINER: It shouldn't have worked. It was too barefaced. Or was it just that the timing just happened to be right?

SCHAFFNER: How important do you think that is, timing, I mean? Can bad timing actually kill a good play? And vice versa, can good timing turn a bad play into a smash?

MINER: It's happened to me both ways. Week-end opened the night of the Market Crash. It wasn't, as I've said, a great play, but it was good enough to have eked out a respectable run.

SCHAFFNER: But nights like that don't happen often, say once a century. How often is it valid? How much more often is it merely an excuse for deserved failure?

MINER: More often the latter. Yet bad timing can still be calamitous. Look at Blind Alley. It got close to rave reviews. It was recognized within months as a semi-classic in its genre, and so it remains. But it had the misfortune to open the night of the Louis-Schmeling fight. I'd guess that that piece of bad timing cut short its run by at least six months, maybe a year. An even better example, Dame Nature. It was the most captivating comedy I ever did.

SCHAFFNER: I don't know it at all.

MINER: Why should you? It didn't last long enough. It was a Pat Collinge adaptation from the French, and a job she did! It was about two kids in Paris who have a child at less than the legally acceptable age. The father was fourteen, the mother a year younger. The two lovers were played by Lois Hall and Montgomery Clift. I had done the show in late summer in Westport and Mount Kisco as a try-out for the Guild. In each case the notices had been glowing with ovations after every performance. It seemed as sure a success as I had ever had; sensitive, delicate, and loaded with warm and rippling laughter. It possessed the kind of childlike purity we struggle so often to capture and too often fail. Not Dame Nature! It sparkled.

        We opened at the Booth Theatre on the night Hitler invaded Czechoslovakia. The stomp of Storm Troopers' boots drowned out the fragile voices of two teenage children in love. As I watched the audience, especially the critics, solemnly entering the theatre that night, I knew. I didn't even wait for the curtain to go up. I walked over to Sardi's and got drunk. Dame Nature lasted a bare four weeks; without Guild subscription, it might have folded in as many days.

SCHAFFNER: But didn't you ever get a boost?

MINER: Oh, yes, oh, yes. Max Anderson's Both Your Houses for one. It opened the night after FDR's First Inaugural. It was not Max's best effort by a long shot, but it came along at a most opportune moment to expose the venality of Congress. The opening night audience gave it a tumultuous reception, while the critics next morning showered it with extravagant acclaim. To top it off, a few weeks later Max was awarded the Pulitzer Prize. Perhaps he had earned such recognition in other years, but not with Both Your Houses. Read it, and you'll see what I mean. But history turned it into a prestigious success and a sizable money-maker.

        Though I viewed the play with scant approval, two things about its production were peculiarly rewarding. One was learning why Mary Philips could handle a bitter and acerbic line better than anyone else in our theatre. Two was confirming my belief that many members of the Group were topnotch actors, not because of anything they derived from Stanislavsky, but because of the exacting disciplines they had acquired many years before the Group came into being.

SCHAFFNER: Great! First Mary Philips.

MINER: It was spring of the year. Otherwise, I'd never have been able to persuade Mary to play so small a part as that of the secretary. About ten days into rehearsal I'd set up a partial run-through so that the Guild might pass on two wildly unorthodox pieces of casting. They involved the two leading parts. The first was Walter Kelly, George Kelly's brother. Walter was an old-time vaudevillian with an act he'd made famous for some twenty-five years, "The Virginia Judge," but he hadn't acted in a legitimate play since he was a boy. The other was a complete unknown who'd wandered into my office some year and a half earlier. I'd never seen him on a stage, but something about him had lodged in my memory. His name was Shepperd Strudwick. The part he was playing was that of an idealistic young Lincoln, a sort of precursor to Jimmy Stewart. His was, of course, the leading part, with the whole production resting on his shoulders. It was to be his first appearance on Broadway.

The run-through, as far as these two "outrageous" bits of casting were concerned, was a succès fou. Not one member of the Board had a word of complaint. In fact, I got nothing but effusive congratulations for my perception and daring in coming up with two such remarkable unknowns.

"But that Mary Philips! What in the world did she think she was doing? Playing Pollyanna? She's dreadful! What we need is a case-hardened bitch, not a sob-sister!"

To tell the truth, I myself had been shaken. Mary's performance was so sentimental, it was just about as bad as they said it was. On the other hand, I'd seen Mary too often; I knew what she was capable of doing. And so I was able to persuade the Guild to give me a few more days to work with her, to find, if I could, what lay behind the bland and saccharine performance she had given.

The next morning she and I went into a huddle. The moment I asked her why she had played the part as she had, she broke into that rich, Irish laugh of hers.

"Oh, Tony, Tony, Tony! That's just me. If I were to play a bitch as a bitch from the start, I could get some laughs, sure, but the audience wouldn't give one good damn about me as a person. But a woman who has once been young and vulnerable and full of ideals, and then been mortally hurt, that's the kind of person the whole world takes to its heart. She can be as sharp and cutting as she pleases, and those out front will love her still. They may even be in tears. I'll feed in the bitchery before those scavengers come back another time. Trust me." And she did.

It's a lesson I've never forgotten. On top of which Mary gave an incomparable performance. No more complaints were ever heard from the Guild.

SCHAFFNER: That's good. Now how many did you have from the Group in that cast?

MINER: (a laugh) Oh, Lord help us, half the Ways and Means Committee! Morris Carnovsky, Joe Bromberg, Russell Collins, Roman Bohnen. There were at least two more I can't remember. I didn't use any Moscow Art Theatre vocabulary with them, nothing but straightforward shop-talk. The older members of the Group were, as I've said, disciplined professionals. It was only the younger ones who made incivility a by-word.

SCHAFFNER: Those who mumbled and interrupted rehearsals and behaved like children. It was a common type well into the fifties. How much of that was due to Lee Strasberg?

MINER: Ah, now you're asking me to tread on treacherous soil, Mr. Schaffner. I've nothing against Lee; I've seldom even met him. But he is the Studio and I'm Chairman of the Board of the American Academy of Dramatic Arts. I cannot pretend to be totally impartial.

This may come as a surprise to you, however. As early as 1908 Charles Jehlinger was teaching emotional recall at the Academy; that was nearly twenty years before Stanislavsky's An Actor Prepares reached these shores. By the time the Group was becoming idolatrous of the Moscow Art Theatre, Charles Jehlinger had long since recognized that emotional recall was not a panacea, but merely a tool, one of many tools the actor should be asked to master.

SCHAFFNER: I hadn't known that. But with that vaunted objectivity of yours, surely you can offer an appraisal of Lee as a director. What were his credits? Men in White --

MINER: Which won the Pulitzer.

SCHAFFNER: And The Three Sisters, which didn't. Come to think of it, that Pulitzer was awarded to Sidney Kingsley, not to Mr. Strasberg.

MINER: As Both Your Houses was awarded to Max Anderson, not to me. Lee was a person of the theatre and a damn fine actor. You can't take that away from him. He directed two important plays; one I liked, one I didn't.

SCHAFFNER: He was also a teacher.

MINER: Ah, that's where our principles and our values begin to diverge.

SCHAFFNER: Have his theories been repudiated?

MINER: Professionally, probably yes. Academically, no. The Method is still sacrosanct in the Drama Departments of most colleges and universities throughout the land. We at the Academy know. We spend too much of our time asking young people to unlearn the popular notions they've been taught.

SCHAFFNER: You question everything that Lee Strasberg
advocates.

MINER: No. That implies a first-hand knowledge I totally
lack. I've never sat in on one of Lee's classes, I've never seen
him conduct a rehearsal. How can I judge him? What I do
deplore is the conduct of the many young people who have
served their novitiate under "the Method." I deplore their den-
igration of so many disciplines I feel an actor is obliged to
respect. They lack skill and they lack illusion.

There is wide-spread confusion regarding the Group,
the Studio, the Method and Lee Strasberg.

The Group was fostered by the Theatre Guild as a sort
of Junior Theatre Guild Acting Company. They were able, well
trained, and well disciplined. They were, moreover, deeply
affected by the kind of group acting for which the Moscow Art
Theatre was famous. Inevitably this brought them into contact
with Stanislavsky. But, since they had already acquired the
disciplines and skills Stanislavsky took for granted, they were
accorded the highest critical acclaim. Unhappily their productions were somewhat less financially rewarding.

It was a good many years later that Cheryl Crawford,
Gadge Kazan and a handful of others launched the Studio; Lee
Strasberg wasn't even among the original team. The Studio was
not a way of teaching actors; it was a place for seasoned
actors to meet, to argue, to brush up on neglected skills and,
at its best, to offer those actors a chance to widen their range
as performers. So far, so good.

Soon, however, young actors began clamoring to join
the Studio, but, since many of them were totally untrained,
Lee Strasberg was the obvious choice to set up a school for
them.   The Method was merely the name the old Group had
given to the version of Stanislavsky it endorsed.

Inevitably one of those students turned out to have
remarkable ability and fire. His work attracted the attention
of Elia Kazan, as a result of which he was assigned to the lead
in A Streetcar Named Desire. This was, of course, Marlon

Brando. That was all that was needed to make the Studio, the Method, and the name, Lee Strasberg, household words across the land. Brando was a great personality. Irrational as it may seem, this was disastrous because it carried the implication that his shortcomings and amateurish ineptitudes were also worthy of active emulation. "If Marlon can mumble, why shouldn't I?"

Such was the thirty-year malaise from which we are just now beginning to emerge.

SCHAFFNER: I see by my notes here that you did a couple of musicals: On Your Toes for one. Why haven't you discussed them?

MINER: (a smile) Vanity. I've never been particularly proud of my record in that department. I'm not a musician. Nonetheless I was called in to try to salvage a musical, a big one by Arthur Schwartz and Howard Dietz, with Charles (Show Boat) Winninger and Libby Holman in the leads. That little beauty was called Revenge With Music, and by all the laws it should have been a smash. It wasn't. It was a dog.

SCHAFFNER: How did you make out?

MINER: Not well enough. I came close, but a miss is as good as a you-know-what. The other, On Your Toes, I did and got fired one week before the opening in New York. I was fired, and I deserved to be.

SCHAFFNER: How come?

MINER: I had the poor judgment to believe that Larry Hart could rewrite the book in the style of Noel Coward. Instead, he got drunk. He got drunk, and I neglected the show for a week too long. So, I got the boot, and George Abbott took over. My contributions, particularly two offbeat pieces of casting, had been so important to the show's success that Dwight Wiman not only insisted on leaving my name on the program as director, but continued to pay me my full royalty as long as the show ran. Remember, I said I'd been fairly and justly treated by producers, and often beyond the call of contractual duty. This was such a case.

SCHAFFNER: What were the daring pieces of casting? Not Ray Bolger?

MINER: No, Ray was set before I came into the picture. The first was Tamara Geva. But the stroke of near genius was Monty Woolley as Diaghilev. Monty had directed a production of Rhesus by Euripides while I was still at Yale; I had appeared in it as a Messenger. But Monty had never set foot on a Broadway stage. Dwight had also known Monty; thus he was able to understand my "cracked-brain madness" as another producer might not. Fortunately it turned out to be a piece of inspired madness. It made Monty a star, or perhaps "prima donna" would be a better word, but it also made On Your Toes. Dwight did not forget.

Less than a week after the opening of On Your Toes in New York, Bury the Dead opened at the Fulton. The reason I was able to handle both assignments was that we had already, as I've said, done Bury the Dead as a benefit. And thereby hangs a tale. We rehearsed On Your Toes at the 46th Street Theatre. With Dwight's permission, I was also permitted to rehearse Bury the Dead in the foyer. Whenever Fran came to the Stage Door to pick me up, for dinner or whatever, the doorman would announce: " On Your Toes on stage, lady. Bury Your Dead in the lobby."

SCHAFFNER: I like it! How many shows is that? I got lost a long way back.

MINER: Some of the successes meant far less to me than some of the near-misses. There's one which doesn't fit any category. It came near to being a smash, but wasn't. It sold out the first Saturday matinee, and was sold to pictures within one week for $150,000. In those days, that was quite a hell of a price for an established writer; for a newcomer like Victor Wolfson it was all but unheard of.

SCHAFFNER: What was the play?

MINER: Excursion. It got such good notices it seemed certain to last a couple of seasons. My recollection is that it folded in less than twenty weeks. I was off base almost from the start. I couldn't fathom why. I was usually good at structure; with Excursion I made one blunder after another. I never did find a solution.

SCHAFFNER: Solution or no, there must have been a reason.

MINER: There was. The author hated his people, not all of them, just the two leads. He killed his own show because of a personal venom.

SCHAFFNER: When did you find out?

MINER: In Philadelphia. It was a little too late; we were due to open inside a week. We'd met for a story conference after the show. Everyone's nerves were frazzled by then; I offered one tentative suggestion with cautious diffidence. I thought it might make the guy and girl a little more appealing. Victor exploded.

"No!" he shouted. "I'm not going to do those two little stinkers any more favors! Let them sweat!"

"Why?" I asked.

He'd had one too many whiskeys, I suspect. It invoked a candor I hadn't encountered before. "I hate those little bastards!" he said. "I've always hated them!"

We were at a stand-off. It was insane, but he remained adamant. He invented some weird symbolism to cover his stubbornness, a paraphrase of the Spanish Civil War. No one believed him, but no one could budge him, either.

I had hoped to make Excursion into a hit. My work with the actors had been good, nearly good enough to salvage an ailing script, but my structural suggestions only messed up what they were designed to cure. Jack Wilson, the producer, got so frustrated, he insisted we discard all the rewrites that had been done, some of them good, and go back to the original script. The end result was a beautiful first act, an adequate second, and a bummer for a last act.

Early in the game Arthur Byron had taught me to ask one pivotal question about a script: "Who are you rooting for? If you don't care about anyone, watch out." Here with an author despising the very ones he, and we, should have cared about most, I knew we were lost. There was much that was charmingly written, much that was brilliantly played, enough to make an opening night audience cheer. It took a while for the public to discern that the play, itself, was a cold fish.

SCHAFFNER: Was that the show where a Coney Island ferryboat took off to sea?

MINER: That's the one! That was the finale of the first act, which inspired a telltale incident. I don't often get angry, uncontrollably angry, that is, but this time it was explosive. The moment when the passengers on the ferry realized they were putting out to sea was a moment of genuine terror. Three weeks into rehearsal I decided to have a run-through of Act I. It was on that same day that Victor elected to sneak into the theatre. Not long after we'd started I thought I detected whispering somewhere in the house; turning, I saw that he was talking to Jack Wilson. It was evident that he did not approve of something he was seeing. When, however, we came to that final moment of panic, he could no longer contain himself.

"Stop!" he yelled. "Stop! This is not my play! This is not my play!" He descended on me in a fury. "I've never seen such desecration. It's criminal what you've done, Tony Miner!"

I had the reserve control to give the cast a ten-minute break before turning back to Victor. "Now," I said, "say what you have to say."

I found a large part of Victor's rage inarticulate, but there was nothing inarticulate about his fury at the way I had handled the finale of the act.

"They're loud," he shouted.

"I know. I've taught them to be."

"But that's not the way people behave at a moment of terror."

"Of course not -- so long as it's only a 'moment.' But sustained terror needs an entirely different dimension and outlook. How long do you expect this terror to last? An hour?"

"This is ridiculous! You're just trying to irritate me. The curtain will be coming down in two minutes. That's how long!"

"That's where you're wrong, Victor. My guess is six minutes. That's a lot more than two minutes. Now, Jack, if you'll take Mr. Wolfson out of here for half an hour, I'll play the end of Act I for you as I see it."

Jack managed to steer Victor out of the theatre without further incident. When they'd left, I called the cast back and asked them to play the scene for me. It was loud. There was a lot of shrill shouting; there was some violent, but pointless, rushing about, and one final scream. Again I called them together and congratulated them. "Now," I said, "I want you to make two small changes for me. First: wherever you've been shouting or screaming, don't! Whisper." I too was whispering. "Some lines may be lost, but that can be fixed. Second: wherever you've been rushing about, don't. Try, but find your feet too heavy. If you do move, don't ever end up where you started to go. Stop, think, and then go somewhere else."

Three weeks of shouting had set up a vocal and physical pattern that was desperately hard for them to break. It was torture to turn an uproar into a whisper. But a sense of genuine terror started to infect the entire cast. We spent some twenty minutes ironing out the rough edges, adding some new and truer business and, at the end, we inserted one climactic moment. Then I called Jack and Victor back into the theatre.

At the first whisper a tremor went through the crowd. There was quiet, but it was the quiet of genuine fear. Haltingly, jerkily, by fits and starts, the word went around the deck, causing others to come up to the rail. What movement there was, was aimless. A child started to cry, and the mother put a hand over her mouth: "Shh!"

And then, when the tension was drawn close to the breaking point, a young street-urchin broke through to the rail and stopped, stunned. After a moment of utter stillness, of suspended animation, he mouthed, without sound, the simple word: "Christ!" As an echo the ship's foghorn sounded, and I hand-signalled the fall of the curtain.

There's a reason for not allowing authors into rehearsals without the director's permission. Writers write; they seldom know how the actor, even less the director, goes about bringing life to those inanimate words. The shortest distance between a printed page and a final performance is seldom a direct line. It pays to be devious at times.

SCHAFFNER: What other trickery did you use?

MINER: Anything that came to hand. Sometimes a prop will do. Did you ever see <u>Father Malachy's Miracle</u>?

SCHAFFNER: No. But what if I had?

MINER: You might have wondered why, with all the marvelous Irish actors in this world, we chose Al Shean, the Marx Brothers' uncle, to play Father Malachy.

SCHAFFNER: He must have had something very rare to offer.

MINER: That he had. But there were moments of apprehension along the way. I can still feel an icy shiver remembering the scene where he tackled the Cardinal, the Delegate from Rome. The Cardinal scored several times during the early part of the scene. On these occasions and with each setback, Al would slap his temple with an open palm, and almost exclaim, "Oy, oy!" No objection of mine did the slightest good. In a split second he would go Lower East Side.

At the close of the run-through I took the Stage Manager aside and asked him to bring a Missal to rehearsal the following day. This he did. Before rehearsal I took it to Al, explaining what I wanted.

"Here's a book, Al, a very holy book. I want you to carry it with you from now on. Never let go of it, no matter what."

"Like this?" he asked, holding it up in one hand.

"No," I said. "Both hands! And never let go of it on pain of Judeo-Christian excommunication!"

I'd no reason to believe he had the foggiest idea what I was talking about, but he agreed without argument. Shortly afterward I said I wanted to pick up with the Cardinal scene. We'd barely started when I had to remind him.

"Book, Al! Both hands!"

It became a threnody accompanying the whole scene.

"Book, Al! Both hands! Book, Al! Both hands!"

The frenzy with which he eventually clutched that Missal began to seep through his entire performance. The intensity was like Jack Klugman's. Al was, to begin with, a fine actor; but, as his knuckles went white, his anguish and his belief took on an heroic stature. He was convincing, endearing and hilari ous, all at once. His performance was both moving and joyous. It was acting at a very high level. He may once have been Gallagher and Shean, but in Father Malachy's Miracle he was the most fervent little Catholic priest in all of Ireland.

SCHAFFNER: Father Malachy was written by a Canadian, wasn't it?

MINER: That's right. It was an adaptation by Brian Doherty. He died a few years ago. He founded the Shaw Festival in Niagara-on-the-Lake and did a whale of a job with it. But he never wrote another play. Too bad. He was a fine talent.

SCHAFFNER: Cancer?

MINER: No, even sadder and more senseless -- fat. With an assist from the juice, of course. I understand he gave up the juice toward the end, but the fat was still with him. In his later years it was hard to remember that in 1937 he had still been quite a hell of a tennis player. Brian was a man of humor, a fine mind and a salty companion. The fat and the drink were a saddening sickness.

One fascinating sidelight on Father Malachy. It was boycotted by the Jewish community of New York. I don't mean to imply that it was organized, but night after night you could seldom spot more than a half-dozen Jews in the house. Why? God knows. With Al Shean in the lead, what reason could they have had to assume we were anti-Semitic? But it hurt at the box office, and a grievous and costly hurt it was.

SCHAFFNER: So, where are we?

MINER: Later than you think. 1938.

IV

SCHAFFNER: You spent some time in Hollywood. Before, or after, <u>Father Malachy</u>?

MINER: Before. Two summers, 1933 and 1934. It was a sad and expensive experience. In the end I had the poor sense to break my contract. If I had waited another twenty-four hours, I would have been given the gate with pay. That stupidity cost me more than I could afford. It was a sophomoric outburst of pride and disgust.

SCHAFFNER: Creative differences, as the saying goes?

MINER: No, not even that. At the time I felt abused. I blamed studio politics. There was some of that, too, but the true fault was my inexplicable failure to master even the simplest principles of the motion picture camera. Considering how quickly I learned to use a television camera, even to creating a distinctive style of visual storytelling, it remains inexplicable to me why I was so pedestrian and inept as a film director in 1933 and '34.

SCHAFFNER: How many pictures did you make?

MINER: Three, I think -- maybe four. One was a remake with Connie Bennett, Joel McCrea and a fine old Hollywood title, <u>Bed of Roses</u>. It was a ludicrous show. Nonetheless, and

106

Miner, age about three, in Greenwich, Connecticut

A

Miner, seated center, with the members of his class at Kent School, c.1917

Somewhere in France, World War I. Miner at left.

C

Miner on hockey team at Cambridge University, England, about 1922.

Lee Tracy and Frances Fuller (later Mrs. Worthington Miner)
in The Front Page, New York, 1928.

E

Frances and Tony Miner in California shortly after their marriage, 1929.

F

"The Red Director of New York." Irwin Shaw's Bury the Dead, 1935.

Courtesy of the Billy Rose Theatre Collection, The New York Public Library at Lincoln Center, Astor, Lennox and Tilden Foundations.

G

Miner, center, in control room at CBS directing "Studio One," c. 1949

H

Miner, right, with Kaiser Aluminum Hour directors. Clockwise: Franklin J. Schaffner, Fielder Cook, George Roy Hill.

I

Miner directs Grace Kelly for a "Studio One" production of
The Rockingham Tea Set, 1950.

J

Miner acts in a "Studio One" as an emergency fill-in for Yul Brynner.

K

Seated from left: Mary Elizabeth, Tony and Fran; standing center: Margaret Miner, with cast members from Frontier, 1954.

L

Robert Redford, Tony and Frances Miner at student seminar: American Academy of Dramatic Arts, about 1966.

M

Frances and Tony Miner in They Might be Giants, a feature film directed by Anthony Harvey, 1972.

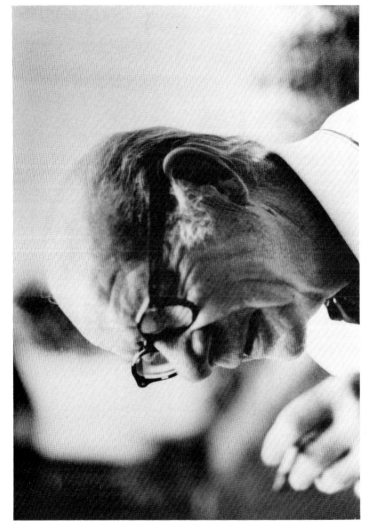

Tony Miner, age about 74, in Brooklyn, NY.

O

Miner with Lillian Gish at graduation, American Academy of Dramatic Arts, 1978.

P

despite my having no idea what I was doing, it ended up earning some $350,000 -- a modest but most acceptable sum for 1933. I could never see that I'd done that much, but at least it didn't blacken my name. For that I had to wait until the following year.

Out of the whole two summers, only two incidents stand out, neither having anything whatever to do with my creative ability, or lack of it.

SCHAFFNER: What were they?

MINER: The first was of no particular moment, aside from a possible giggle or two. When I arrived in Hollywood in February, I was at once rushed into the breach in a crisis situation. A spy picture I urged RKO not to do the year before was already ten days into shooting with Connie Bennett and Gilbert Roland. At that moment they were in the midst of a most passionate affair.

The story was cheesy enough by itself, but the dialogue was unspeakable. Bob Benchley and I were assigned to rewrite the script, keeping, if possible, twelve hours ahead of the camera. One swift look, and Bob and I knew there was nothing to do but make the words intelligible. What was ungrammatically inane we tried to make grammatically inane. It was not an assignment we could take seriously.

To make it at least tolerable, we invented a novel modus operandi. Bob would tackle the first half of a scene up to a designated spot; I'd pick up from that point and continue on. The first time his five pages arrived in my office they read beautifully up to the final payoff. To throw it over to me he had inserted something so filthy, I couldn't believe my eyes. It was also, of course, hilarious. There was then a postscript he had added in caps.

"OR . . . ?"

My competitive instincts were beginning to tingle. To my segment I, too, added a foul and irreverent phrase. The postscript remained, "OR . . . ?"

This game went on for days, our obscenities becoming day by day more foul and more irreverent. What neither of us anticipated was that the stencil cutters in the studio typing pool could have been so numbed by their stultifying routine that they would dutifully type up every foul and blasphemous word without question. The stipulations under the Hays Office standards were blithely ignored. This game of ours had, without our knowledge, been getting its daily giggle from cast and crew alike.

What none of us had realized was that some fifty copies were also being shipped to New York for review by the top brass at RKO. This included a number of Wall Street bankers and industrial giants who sat on the Board of Directors. The chuckles that had greeted our little game in Hollywood were not echoed along the carpeted halls of the Manhattan offices. They were replaced by frowns of outrage; the Brass were not amused. In short order the phone lines were steaming. Who were these two writers, Benchley and Miner? This kind of irresponsible conduct, not to mention bad taste, did not belong on an RKO payroll.

Within twenty-four hours the roof had fallen in. Bob and I were quite certain, both of us, that we'd be out of a job before sundown. And so we might have been had it not been for one member of the Board slightly more canny and avaricious than the rest.

"What," he asked, "would firing these two do to our shooting schedule?"

Obviously it was going to cost money. It would take time to secure a replacement, and things were up against the clock as it was.

Once the penalties in dollars and cents had been calculated, the good name and high repute of RKO swiftly lost its compelling importance. Benchley and Miner were subjected to a tongue-lashing, nothing more. As a great concession we were kept on the payroll. There was one condition -- no more "OR . . . 's" were ever to appear.

SCHAFFNER: That was the start of your second summer at RKO?

MINER: Yes. And to make matters more unsettling, the head of the Studio in 1933 was no longer there. Merian Cooper had originally hired me. Up to the time I'd gone back to New York in the fall of '33, I was his "discovery." He had scheduled a number of choice properties for me to take over when I got back in February. There was one picture with Irene Dunne, whom I'd persuaded him with the utmost fervor not to fire; one with Katie Hepburn, and one with Jack Barrymore.

SCHAFFNER: Did you ever do any of them?

MINER: Only the Jack Barrymore show, but without Mr. Barrymore. That was the second incident. It's the one that mattered. It was 1934. The show was Hungarian -- A Hat, a Coat, a Glove. It was a better-than-average murder mystery, and with Barrymore it stood a good chance of being a box-office bonanza. Besides, I wanted like crazy to work with Barrymore. I went out to his house once before shooting began, and discovered to my great relief that he was on the wagon. He had been for weeks, ever since returning from a cruise to Baja California. He'd had a bad bout with some kind of Southern Fever, and hadn't touched anything since, not even a beer.

I was full of ginger when I reached the set for the first day's shooting. The scene was a department store in Budapest. Jack had just made a purchase and was about to charge it. It couldn't have been a simpler, more routine scene, except for one small problem; when the clerk came up with the bill, Jack couldn't remember his own name. Gradually, take after take, he began to forget more words, more pieces of business. By three o'clock that afternoon we hadn't put a single foot of film in the can. I finally called it off and began to shoot some silent shots at other locations. Jack came up to me, quite obviously chagrined and full of apologies.

"I'll have it cold by tomorrow, kiddo," he said. "I won't hold you up again."

And so, with a jaunty wave of the hand, he left the studio. Kenneth MacGowan, one of the original founders of the Provincetown Playhouse and a close friend of Eugene O'Neill, was the producer on the picture. Arriving on the set in answer to my call, he assumed that Jack was drunk. I assured him he was nothing of the sort, he was cold sober. I had gotten close enough to sniff his breath. So had the assistant director, who'd worked with Jack some dozen times before. This was something else, and possibly a lot more critical than a routine bout with the juice.

The following morning Jack appeared early, smiling and looking full of bounce. "Whenever you're ready, kiddo, I'm your man."

I breathed a sigh of relief, strengthened by his agent's assurance that these seizures were symptomatic of the fever he'd contracted; they were getting less frequent all the time. Jack's doctor had given him a pill of some sort, and a complete bill of health that morning before he started out.

And so, at eight o'clock I got ready to put the first bit of footage in the can. Jack appeared, clapped his hands and announced, "So, señor, avanti! Where do we start?"

"Same place as yesterday, Jack."

"Good. Have at it."

He roughed out his moves, skipped through his three or four speeches, and ended by pronouncing his name with conspicuous accuracy.

"You see, young fella," he said, turning to me with a rippling grin. "You thought the old man didn't have it anymore, didn't you? Don't underestimate us old-timers. We're tougher than you think."

The scene started with a lot of suppressed energy until his first speech came along. Suddenly, five words in, he dried. After a brief silence he burst out with a rush of profanity ending in a grin: "So let's start it again."

And so we did, and again he dried. We did it again and again and again, and still he dried. Each time his desperation became more intense and more painful. Finally I couldn't stand it any longer. I knew too well that if, by some miracle, he got through the day, all the gusto, all the excitement would be gone. This time there was no bravado as he started back to his dressing room. There was perhaps a trace of anger, but an intuitive mind could not mistake the fright and the shame that lay behind that facade.

After consultation with his agent and his doctor we agreed to shoot around him for the rest of the week and pick up with him on Monday morning. Before asking him to appear on the set he was to read through the scene with Kenneth MacGowan and me. So it was done. I still clung to the desperate hope that he'd be his old self again, but this optimism was tissue thin. Beneath was an icy foreboding.

Come Monday the amenities were brief and perfunctory. He scarcely looked at me as Kenneth and I came in. Almost at once, and at his urging, the reading began. Within thirty seconds my worst fears were realized. He could not remember a single speech, or, if he did, he read it in the wrong place in the scene. The sweat began pouring off his forehead, external evidence of the torture he was undergoing within. Suddenly, and in the middle of an utterly incoherent speech, he threw his script to the floor and turned to me in a towering rage.

"You're loving this, aren't you, you little son-of-a-bitch! You love it, being in on the break-up of the great Jack Barrymore. Well, go ahead, gloat, you little bastard, gloat until the spittle dribbles down your chin! But let me tell you this, you little snot-nose. All your greedy little life you'll never be big enough to shine John Barrymore's shoes. And don't think that John Barrymore is dead. He's sick. Yes, he's a sick man, but he's not finished, not by a long shot. I'm going to get well. And when I do, I'll enjoy telling you to go fuck yourself. I'll enjoy seeing you crumble just as much as you're enjoying seeing me fall apart this morning."

Those are not his exact words, but, believe me, they were burned so deep into my memory, I am not far from the mark. He had sunk into a chair, signalling his agent to call the doctor. His head was in his hands; I could not see his eyes. I looked at Kenneth; he nodded assent. In silence we rose and went down the stairs and into the burning heat of the RKO lot. We walked back to our offices, wordless and miserable. Kenneth finally asked, "Well, what do we do?"

"Personally, I'd like to shoot my lunch."

The picture went on with Ricardo Cortez in the lead. I began to hate the script, the production, even the cast. My work was pale and uninspired. To put it succinctly, it stank. Toward the end Kenneth MacGowan's assistant, who had a flare for camerawork, was called on to give what was there a pinch of style. He and the cutter worked long hours to try to give it some pace and distinction. Technically they succeeded, but it was all too late. Nothing could atone for the loss of Barrymore and the dispiriting effect it had had on me. I went to the first sneak preview and was heard to remark, in answer to an executive's smiling question: "Well, Tony, what do you think?"

"It stank at the beginning. It still stinks." It was an ungenerous and politically suicidal remark. My disappointment and misery ran too deep. Two days later I broke my contract, anticipating RKO's decision to fire me by a matter of hours. I never saw Jack Barrymore again. I never wanted to. I had suffered through his disintegration; I was unwilling to witness his further degradation on a New York stage.

SCHAFFNER: That's far more poignant than the other versions I've heard.

MINER: It cut me up pretty badly for a time, but frankly I hadn't expected it to move me so much, just talking about it now.

SCHAFFNER: You said a while back that you'd worked with Hepburn. When? It's not listed in your credits.

MINER: That's true. One, Jane Eyre, made a small for-tune, but it never came into New York. It was all on the road. The other, The Lake, was the first time Jed Harris gave me the royal finger.

SCHAFFNER: How could you have let yourself into something like that?

MINER: It wasn't quite that crazy. To begin with, the original offer hadn't come from Jed; it had come from Leland Hayward. He was Katie's agent at the time, and he had never wanted her to do The Lake. He disliked the play and distrusted Jed. But once he learned that Jed was at the same time going to produce and direct Yellow Jack, a large and costly under-taking built around Walter Reed's battle against Yellow Fever, his worst apprehensions began to fade.

SCHAFFNER: It was written by Sidney Howard, wasn't it? Yellow Jack, I mean.

MINER: Yes, and the insiders had it that it would be the first smash hit of the new season. To Leland that meant just one thing. Jed could still produce The Lake; he could not conceivably direct it. That was when I was called in, and why.

Fran and I were not only clients of Leland, we were the warmest of friends. I'd been his boy ever since I directed the California edition of The Front Page. He was my agent even before I did Five Star Final. I'd not done him proud in pictures, but in the theatre I still could do no wrong. And so, when he proposed I take over as director of The Lake, he all but guaranteed two things. One, that Jed would be nowhere around; two, that Katie would agree without question, which she apparently did. With Jed up to his you-know-what in Yellow Jack, I foresaw little danger in going along.

Leland assured me he'd been both tough and adamant with Jed. "If you so much as set foot on that stage, Jed, even once, I'll pull Tony Miner off that show so fast -- "

At that, according to Leland, Jed smiled his most winning smile. "Leland, baby, how could I? I'm going to have my hands full with Walter Reed."

That's how I got into it. Katie's attitude was a trifle cool toward me at the start. There were two reasons. She admired Jed inordinately; the only reason she had agreed to do the play was because he had assured her he was going to direct. The other? Fran had taken three jobs away from Katie a few years before. It was only human for her to view Fran's husband with some degree of suspicion. Despite this fact she began within days to develop a trust in my treatment of her and of the play. To begin with I was considerate. I had quickly recognized that Jed had cast her for The Lake precisely because she was totally unequipped to play the part. Few people ever recognized Jed's satanic compulsion to destroy female stars, particularly, though not exclusively, those who had shown no interest in him outside the theatre. The list was formidable: Helen Hayes in Mr. Gilhooley; Ina Claire in The Wench of Newgate (the following year it was an outstanding hit with Basil Sidney and Mary Ellis); Ruth Gordon in King's X; and a delightful little comedy with Os Perkins and Ruth to which both were absurdly unsuited. I've forgotten the title. Now Katie Hepburn. Later it was to be Lillian Gish, but that's another story.

In any case I felt my job was to find what Katie could do besides cry -- dear God, how she could cry! -- that would still fit the character she was playing. By the middle of the second week I'd found something that had begun to work; I could scarcely believe how well. I was once again enjoying myself; I had even begun to see The Lake as a thoroughly intriguing venture. This euphoria continued until the evening I got home to find a message to call Leland pronto.

The moment he came on the line I knew he had bad news to report. Jed had done something unforgivable to Sidney Howard, I never knew precisely what; there had been a colossal row and Sidney had stormed out the door, taking his script with him. If Jed wanted to sue, go ahead! Jed had at once got in touch with Leland to let him know that he, Jed, would be coming to rehearsals of The Lake the following day.

It was late afternoon before he arrived, taking a seat behind Leland toward the center of the house. We were just starting Act Two. He said nothing until the act was over. Kate had never been better. As the rest of the cast waited for some comment from him, Jed slowly made his way to the stage and began pacing along the footlights, his head bowed, a dour frown on his forehead. He spoke not a word.

I knew it was an act; the whole cast, especially Katie, had been too good to justify this melancholy response. I took it just so long; then I decided to forestall any scathing remarks he might be about to utter.

"O.K., kids," I said, "that's it for today. You were great. You can sleep easy. I have a few notes, but they can wait until the morning. If Mr. Harris has any comments to make, I'll pass them along to you when we meet."

With evident relief and a few scattered thanks they started to break up. Before they could get off stage, however, Jed spoke up.

"No!" he said. "I have some things to say I want you all to hear. The first is that you were not great. It was a dreadful performance. I'd like to speak to Miss Hepburn first, then I'll get around to the rest of you."

I butted in. "Just one thing, Jed, I'm still the director of this show. If you say one more word, I shan't be. Is that clear?"

"Well, somebody has to start directing this show, that's for sure."

"That's all I wanted to know," with which I turned to pick up my briefcase. Very softly, almost in a whisper, I heard Katie say: "Tony, don't, please."

Pleading was so unlike Kate Hepburn, I realized as I left the theatre that panic had already taken root. All her gay bravado had drained away. This wavering kept up for three days. One moment Leland would phone me to say Katie couldn't go on another day with Jed; the next he'd report she felt she had to go through with her commitment. For years she'd promised herself that, if ever she got the chance to work with Jed Harris, she'd drop anything else she was doing to grab it. In the end her pride won out. In genuine misery, according to Leland, she kept her promise to herself.

A week later Leland called to ask if I'd come to a run-through with him. He assured me he'd found a way to sneak me into the balcony so that Jed would never know I'd been in the theatre. With some misgivings I agreed.

What Jed had done to that girl in one week was as deliberately cruel, as sadistic, as anything I've ever seen. By insisting on her doing everything he knew she could not do, he had completely destroyed her. Sitting beside me Leland kept whispering: "What can we do, Tony? Is there anything you could do?"

"Not a thing. It's too late."

You can guess the rest. It opened and Katie took an unmerciful beating from the critics. Far worse was her own private humiliation. Her need for isolation was paranoiac. She even had a canvas passageway built from her dressing room to the set; she couldn't bear to be seen, or spoken to, even by her fellow actors. This was mighty close to a complete emotional crack-up.

SCHAFFNER: And Jed?

MINER: By firsthand knowledge? I've no idea. This much only I know. He was spreading the word far and wide that Katie Hepburn was a total bust as an actress, a hopeless amateur, that, indeed, she had destroyed The Lake, an otherwise touching and beautiful play.

SCHAFFNER: How long did she run the "gamut of emotions"?

MINER: Not long. A month? I couldn't say. Incidentally, I was there when Dottie Parker made that much heralded crack about Katie. It was 6:00 a.m. after a long night with Phil and Ellen Barry, the columnist Johnny McClain, Bob Benchley, Fran and me. We were breaking up for a few hours of sleep but the evening had been so spontaneous and unexpectedly festive, we had decided to meet at "21" for lunch. Phil Barry added: "And after? What are we going to do to round out this beautfiul day?"

"I know. Let's all drop in to the Martin Beck and watch Katie Hepburn run the gamut of emotions from A to B." Believe me, none of us felt it was more than light-hearted. We'd been drinking, we were all a little giddy, and that's the way it came out, clever but without venom. Nonetheless it lived on as the cruelest thrust of all.

I went on to a couple of other productions that year. Katie's performance faded from our minds. But she had to live with all that contumely, with all those snide remarks for a long time. She survived; Jed didn't. A few more years and he had become little more than a "Who?"

SCHAFFNER: You said you worked with her again?

MINER: Jane Eyre. It was some years later. I was doing it for the Guild. Katie was a wonderful Jane; it was her cup of tea, and she sparkled. But we had a dreadful Rochester and an even worse last act, which an opinionated and stubborn author refused to rewrite. Her name was Helen Jerome. We might have gotten a Larry Olivier or an Orson Welles for Rochester, if we'd been willing to wait, but we could have waited until doomsday before Lady Jerome would have changed as much as a comma of her beloved Act Three. As a result, we decided to book it on the road for a few months and not risk bringing it into New York. For weeks on end it battled the elements, storms and tornados, floods and disasters, without an empty seat in the house. Katie's name was already a prodigious draw in the hinterlands. Jane Eyre made a tidy profit, but the kudos was nil for any of us, even Katie herself.

118

SCHAFFNER: And you never worked with her again?

MINER: Never.

SCHAFFNER: And Jed?

MINER: Believe it or not, yes. And, it was a bitter experience, but the finest, the most sensitive, job I ever did. It was <u>Uncle Vanya</u> with Lillian Gish, Walter Connolly, Osgood Perkins and Eugene Powers. What has beset me for years is the fact that I cannot remember why I felt so serene about doing anything ever again with Jed Harris. God wot I knew from experience how untrustworthy he was, and yet, aside from insisting on his signing the roughest contract Howard Reinheimer could devise, I can no longer remember why I ever agreed to work for him in the first place. The one rationale I can offer is that I was so mesmerized by the prospect of directing Lillian Gish in her first stage appearance, I was willing to take an otherwise wild and unacceptable risk.

The toughest conditions I'd laid down were adhered to by Jed. Aside from Lillian, and Os Perkins as Dr. Astrov -- they were already set -- I was given a completely free hand with the casting. Jed never came into rehearsal without checking with me in advance. Moreover, when he did come, he refrained from criticizing any of the actors directly; he gave what notes he had to me to pass along. There was never a scene.

But one exception, vaguely mystifying at the time though vividly revelatory later on, exposed his insensate greed and dishonesty. One day about the third week of rehearsals, he came in early; he had had, he said, a most marvelous evening with Lillian.

"Oh, Tony, I just want to tell you -- ! Just watch that scene with Os and the Lermontov maps, you'll spot it right away. It's done something beautiful to her whole performance." My worst suspicions were jingling. That Lermontov scene was one of my favorites. If he'd -- ! Anyway, I decided to run it through before lunch. I was curious to see what he might have said to Lillian that could have made so vast a difference. When the scene was over, I was confounded. I hadn't been able to spot one move or gesture, not even an inflection, that varied in any way from what Lillian and Os had done at the last rehearsal. And yet there was Jed coming up to me, beaming and jaunty:

"See what I mean, Tony? Terrific, wasn't it? She's going to be sensational, just sensational!"

By that time this was no news to me; sensational she was, but for the life of me I could not see what Jed thought he had done for her. I can assure you it had made not the slightest perceptible difference. But so long as it fed his inordinate self-adulation, I was prepared to let it go. I simply said: "She's great, Jed. We've no argument there."

During the rest of rehearsals this charade was repeated some five or six times. Invariably it began with his claiming to have had "a most marvelous evening with Lillian"; always it had made "all the difference." I kept watching like a she-lion, but never could I spot so much as a comma that had been displaced. Whatever I saw was entirely attributable to her own marvelous invention which day after day kept building and enriching her performance. Everything was in response to something I had suggested the day before, or the day before that, or the day before that.

We opened in New Haven with Lillian giving an altogether breathtaking performance. Little wonder I was stunned when I got back to her dressing room to find her dissolved in tears. God damn, I thought. That filthy little son-of-a-bitch couldn't wait to get back here and say something to destroy her.

"Oh, Tony," she wept, throwing her arms about me, convulsed with deep and anguished sobs. "Oh, Tony, Tony, Tony -- I can't -- I won't ever be able to do it! That was my performance! I'll never be able to do it again!"

Suddenly I started to laugh, realizing I was no longer holding in my arms a mature and magnificent actress, but a child of twelve, for whom the word "print" was the only, and ultimate, sign of approval. Nothing thereafter would ever be more than an imitation, a cheap and worthless copy. Her life, her entire career, had been built about that one "take." My efforts to comfort her, to assure her, had carried no weight whatever. Only time was going to persuade her that she could do it again and again, and even again.

It entered my mind that I had falsely accused Jed of saying something to her that night to undermine her confidence. Yet one mystery remained. What in God's name had he said to her on all those other "marvelous evenings" they'd spent together during rehearsal? I was a long time finding out.

SCHAFFNER: How long?

MINER: Thirty years. Perhaps longer.

SCHAFFNER: So, after thirty years, what did you find out?

MINER: Nothing.

SCHAFFNER: That's impossible! He must have said something.

MINER: He couldn't. He couldn't, because he wasn't there. Outside of rehearsal he never saw, nor spoke to, Lillian from the first reading onstage to the opening night in New Haven. It was around 1968 or '69 that I learned the truth. I was driving her home after a late gathering at the Langners'. I'd bottled up my curiosity far too long. "Lillian," I said, "I've wanted for thirty years to ask you this. What was it that Jed Harris said to you on those evenings during Uncle Vanya rehearsals, those things that he insisted made 'all the difference' in your performance?"

She looked thoroughly nonplussed. "What did he say? Nothing. I kept calling him and begging him to give me some help, some kind of reaction, some advice. All he'd ever say was: 'Darling, stop worrying! You're going to be sensational. Just sensational!' I never saw him, I never met with him, not even once."

SCHAFFNER: So what happened after that?

MINER: Oh, he'd just begun. The notices came out Tuesday morning. Jed had been right; they were sensational. George Jean Nathan came up to see the show Tuesday night. He was enthralled. Bill Saroyan arrived for the Wednesday matinee. When, after the matinee, I came into the bar at the Taft Hotel, there were the three of them tucked away in the shadows. I was about to join them, when I heard Nathan say to Saroyan:

"I kept telling Jed, it's his greatest job yet. Did you notice that moment in the first act, Bill, when Lillian . . . ?"

"Of course I noticed," Saroyan said. "But there were touches like that all the way through."

And then I heard Jed's voice. "I hoped you'd noticed, particularly that love scene with Os over the maps. I think I'm prouder of that than of anything else in the show."

I was so stunned, so infuriated, I couldn't speak. I left the bar without their knowing I'd been there.

I was waiting for Jed backstage before the evening performance. He came in, wreathed in smiles. "Well, Tony, they loved it. Didn't I tell you? They both felt that Lillian was nothing less than magnificent."

When I get that angry, which has happened to me only three or four times in my life, I am utterly unable to say a word. I go a most dreadful shade of grey, a grey-green, in fact. My lips grow white; they tremble. I even lose my balance. This gave Jed the opportunity to go on.

"By the way, kid, I'll be dropping in on your rehearsals tomorrow. George and Bill had some wonderful suggestions to offer."

"Not -- not my -- rehearsals, Mr. Harris." It came out haltingly -- constricted and guttural. In a stiff, unsteady fashion I started for the exit.

After the evening performance, Walter, Os and Gene Powers came up to my room. I was all packed, ready to take the morning train back to New York. Jed had apparently called them together after the show to let them know he was planning to take over rehearsals the following day.

"I know," I said, "I'm going back to New York in the morning."

"Don't!" they said. "The show's too damn good as it stands." It was almost in unison. In the end they persuaded me to stay on in New Haven. They couldn't imagine what Jed had hoped to do in two days, but, if he were going to change anything crucial, they wanted me on hand.

I can no longer remember the details of what took place during the next few days. This much only: Jed did substantially nothing. Despite his efforts to humiliate me, the opening night performance in New York was, to all intents and purposes, identical with the performance they had given the previous Wednesday in New Haven. But hear this! For its delicacy, its poignancy, its humor, Jed received unstinted and exclusive acclaim.

SCHAFFNER: Exclusive? How?

MINER: I went to the theatre around six o'clock on opening night to deliver some personal notes to the various members of the cast; it was an old custom of mine. As I walked in I happened to pass an usher opening up a stack of programs for the evening. Jed had had my name excised. With no credit for direction, everyone assumed it had been Jed.

SCHAFFNER: I don't believe it.

MINER: Oh, yes. If you'd known Jed, you'd believe it. But time was running out for him. There was very little left for Jed before oblivion closed around him. He died only a few months ago, but the sound of applause had long since been stilled. What remained was a memory, not of the nastiness, the dishonesty, the vicious cruelty. No. All that was left was a legend the years have transmuted to a somewhat ephemeral snicker. Those he had hurt survived on the whole better than his own very real, but self-destructive, genius.

SCHAFFNER: What about the tough contract you had?

MINER: Oh, I sued him and won quite a sizable sum, but that was inadequate reprisal. The only true, and somewhat amusing, recompense came some dozen years later. Leland Hayward was doing a TV spectacular and had hired Jed to produce and direct it. Coming close to air, the show was in such dire trouble, Leland called to beg me to drop in to see if I could suggest anything, or any way, to salvage this unhappy turkey. It was far past the point of recovery, but Leland still felt Jed should hear what I had to say. After a disastrous run-through the absurdity began. Jed came up to us smiling and confident. After Leland's suggestion that he give me a chance to offer my experienced advice, Jed took off on an analysis of everything that was wrong with television. It was a profoundly philosophic Philippic. He even got into an outline of a way for me to give my work the stamp of professionalism it had so far lacked. Try as he might, Leland could not stem the flow. As a result, I saw nothing to do but get up and leave, which I did.

SCHAFFNER: How did Jed take it?

MINER: On the surface, serenely. Within? Who knows? A few minutes later he was fired. According to Leland, far from being chastened, he walked out as arrogant as ever. "Some day you'll remember this night. I have something better to give than this kind of commercial crap you and Tony have to offer." Such were his final words as he sauntered out the door. There was no grandeur to his departure; it was, at best, pathetic. When the great finally grow weary and fall, as Jack Barrymore fell, it is a time for awe and pain. There was neither for "Destiny's one-time Tot."

SCHAFFNER: Have you ever been able to explain his behavior?

MINER: Nothing that would stand up in a court of law. But I have believed for many years that I know the answer to the riddle. I believe it all began with George Jean Nathan. I believe he conceived the idea of launching Lillian on a new career in the theatre. He had felt for some time that Jed was the closest thing to a genius our theatre had produced. Ergo, Uncle Vanya landed on Jed's desk.

Jed faced a dilemma. It was, to begin with, a matter of fright. He could not afford to side-step Nathan's trust in him. If, on the other hand, he were to fail, it would be a catastrophe for him and his reputation. But, if he succeeded, ah then, then he would reap an unequalled succès d'estime. Yet, and here was the rub, he'd had an abysmal record of failure with female stars. I've cited a few of them already. To make the odds even more uninviting, Lillian had never set foot on a stage.

She was, of course, George Jean Nathan's protégée and publicly-recognized favorite. He would brook no excuses for anything less than her personal triumph. Jed was hungry for the kind of acclaim that Nathan could shower upon him. He was, at the same time, terrified by the threat of failure.

He knew me satanically well; he knew there was nothing I would more swiftly embrace than a challenge of this magnitude. He was, of course, right. I soon recognized that he was secretly convinced Lillian was inadequate. Were I the director, I, not he, would have to shoulder the blame and would, in addition, inherit George Jean Nathan's undying enmity. When it became evident that Lillian was not going to fail -- was, in fact, on the road to succeeding beyond his wildest anticipation, he panicked. He had never appreciated Lillian's hidden strength, nor had he ever envisaged the possibility of my creating an atmosphere in which Lillian Gish, and Chekhov, could be at home, in tune and instinctively responsive. What to do?

SCHAFFNER: I'm beginning to get the picture, and it's ugly. Could you give me a couple of explicit examples?

MINER: I'm not sure. I'll try. I'd always been convinced that, to grasp Chekhov emotionally, you had to go beyond the words, a little like Pauline Lord in Anna Christie.

SCHAFFNER: Go on.

MINER: This, for instance. At the end of Act One, Lillian had her first scene with Vanya. Knowing her stay was drawing to a close, Vanya was in despair over the wasted weeks when he'd never found the moment to let Elena know how desperately he cared for her. In the script it is written that he reaches out to touch her hand; instinctively, and somewhat harshly, she draws it away, speaking sharply: "Don't! Don't touch me, please."

For this moment I asked Walter to concentrate as hard as he knew how on touching her hand. Soon the desire became so intense, the sweat began to appear on his forehead and the backs of his hands. Just as he was about to risk the question, Lillian, with intuitive tenderness and understanding, spoke. "Don't!" she said. "Don't touch me, please." He had, of course, said nothing, made no move whatever. Her ability to perceive his thoughts with so much gentleness destroyed him more completely than any physical rebuttal could have done. This was one of the moments to which George Jean Nathan was referring as he called Bill Saroyan's attention to Jed's wonderful "delicacy of touch."

Another, in Act Two: Elena's scene with her gross and tyrannical husband. Lillian was on the floor, her cheek against

Gene Powers's hand. Gene was in his seventies, and his huge
hands were twisted and gnarled with arthritis. As Lillian
turned to look up at him, her eyes caught sight of this
grotesque claw clutching the arm of the chair. Suddenly, we
saw, as she did, this physical symbol of the horrifying price
she had had to pay, and was to pay again, for the miserable,
indecent protection he was able to offer her. Contrasted with
the delicacy of Dr. Astrov's long and tapering fingers, the
enormity of this enslavement sent a tremor of disgust through
her. And through us! There was no such gesture indicated in
the script; it was, nonetheless, Elena's entire story. I cannot
remember when the house was not, aside from a gasp or two,
completely still.

Last, the map scene that Jed had chosen to mention.
Mostly, as I have seen other productions, this scene has been
played as a tangential moment of awkward comedy. Astrov's
discomfort is based on the intensity of his caring for so many
things that matter deeply to him, and not one bit to her. The
audience's response has been one of amusement, a very thin
and uncertain laughter. But as Os and Lilian played it, it was
an agonizing and tortured love scene, culminating in a wildly
passionate embrace. After an early run-through I happened to
overhear Osgood whisper: "Dear God, that young lady kills me.
She's a burning icicle!" I could have cut his throat, I wanted so
much to have thought of those words myself.

It's not often anyone reaches a level of performance
that cannot be explained, nor often repeated. Uncle Vanya was
such an occasion. I felt I had achieved a level of emotional
sensitivity that would be hard to repeat in future productions.
Submerged passion, mingled with outbursts of rich and rippling
laughter, gave it the texture of a multicolored fabric. I hold
no warmer memory from my theatre years.

SCHAFFNER: Was this your swan song to the theatre?

MINER: No, I did some two to three shows after that.
But the end, I am sad to report, was unmitigated pain. What
made it so hard to bear was that my hopes had been so high.
The show was Jeremiah by Stefan Zweig. It was brought to my
attention by John Gassner, beloved teacher, beloved story edi-

tor for the Theatre Guild, and most beloved as a mortal man. The script was in literal translation at the time. Despite this handicap, I fell in love with it. The very next day John and I took it to Lawrence Langner and Terry Helburn, who quickly O.K.'d our spending $5,000 for a decent translation and adaptation. In 1938 that was a reasonable price for a job of this sort.

John and I spent the next six months getting the script we wanted; it took about as many days to get Board approval. This was the first time I'd ever seen the Guild give unanimous assent to any production. There had been few smiles around the Guild offices in recent months; for the next few weeks radiance ran high.

The fateful flaw did not appear until rehearsals were less than five weeks away. At the start every actor we'd wanted had accepted. Every major part was snapped up but one, Jeremiah. Don't misunderstand me, every star to whom Jeremiah had gone had been enthusiastic, but to their unhappy misfortune, and ours, they were one and all unavailable. We took this in stride for a long, perhaps too long, time. The first tremors of panic began the morning we discovered that our list of potentials had narrowed down to four nobodies and Kent Smith. Now Kent was a thoroughly competent actor: I used him on more than one occasion after that and he was excellent, but he was not by any stretch of the imagination an emotional tornado. Nothing less than an overpowering and inspired passion was going to bring Jeremiah to life.

It was, for me, a moment of truth, and I blew it. I should have stood my ground, I should have confronted the Guild, I should have insisted we wait until someone of stature became available. But the Guild was desperate. Two, or three, other productions had fallen apart; a fall production had become imperative. I was not just fond of Lawrence and Terry, I was deeply indebted to them. I was the good guy; I weakened. And so we went into rehearsal with Kent Smith in the part of Jeremiah.

I was out of step from that hour to the final sickening moment when Kent uttered his first cry as the prophet, Jeremiah. I had a letter in my pocket from Stefan Zweig, offering wholehearted approval of the adaptation John Gassner and I had made. He never, most happily for him, saw the Jeremiah I had allowed to desecrate his script.

It was not from lack of trying. I never worked so hard, before or after. I poured Niagaras of passion and spiritual fervor into the struggle only to be repaid in thimblefulls. I spent sleepless nights, I got drunk and got him drunk. I was beating my brains out against a mind of unyielding Teutonic heaviness. What added to the futility of my efforts was that, in my exhaustion and discouragement, I neglected and short-changed the other actors. They were eating their hearts out to help me overcome the engulfing mediocrity I could not transcend; I abused their trust. Even the crowds, with whom I had been able on other occasions to create a spirit of excitement, were listless and shallow. I'd given them all too little. The results were pale, hollow and painful.

Cecil Humphries said it best. Bumping into me after the final curtain on opening night, he said, "Ah, Tony, me lad, one thing no one can take away from you. It was the most beautiful production the theatre's seen in many a year."

The sets were indeed glorious; they'd been designed by Harry Horner and fully lived up to Cecil's unbounded praise. For the rest there was nothing to say. One gift from heaven; the show was not reviewed by Dorothy Parker.

This catastrophe forced me to take stock of my whole career. I'd had my moments of triumph, a thoroughly decent share of them, and I'd had my quota of failures and disappointments. But I was still a freelance. I had no regular income aside from my chosen vocation. I had also, as I have said more than once, gone into the theatre in response to a firm philosophic conviction that the theatre was a tardy art, flowering only after a time of war; at the very first hint of armed conflict, it shrivelled. I'd been convinced since 1936 that war was inevitable. After the Stalin-Hitler pact I was assured it could happen any day, possibly sooner. What insurance did I have to last out the impending drought?

It was then that I first drew up the following table. I had never, up until then, fully appraised the size and durability of my constituency. Frankly, this chart scared the hell out of me.

A Record of Broadway Productions by Worthington Miner

Name of Play and Author	The Author's 1st Production on Broadway	The Author Had No Subsequent Production on Brdwy	The Author Had No Subsequent Success on Brdwy
Jealousy Charles Walters	X	X	X

Up Pops the Devil
  Albert Hackett &
  Frances Goodrich
	X		

Week-end Austin Parker	X	X	X
Her Master's Voice Clare Kummer		X	X
Let Freedom Ring Albert Bein			X
Blind Alley James Warrick	X	X	X
Excursion Victor Wolfson	X		X
Bury the Dead Irwin Shaw	X		X
Father Malachy's Miracle Brian Doherty	X	X	X
200 Were Chosen Ellsworth P. Conkle	X*		
The House Beautiful Channing Pollock		X	X
Five Star Final Louis Weitzenkorn	X	X	X

*Mr. Conkle had had one W.P.A. production.

It's a thoroughly random and far from complete list,
yet I cannot think of any better confirmation of my statement
that the thirties was a time of desertion and flight. Too many
of those writers to whom I had given their first exposure, and
a goodly number of successes, thereafter and forever dried up
or disappeared, or both. Where was my stockpile of writing
talent, where was my backlog of creative friends to supply the
cushion against the lean and hungry years ahead? Where was
the action to be from 1940 on? Not in the theatre, of that I
was fully persuaded. So -- ? TV was beginning to beckon.

SCHAFFNER: One thing before moving on. How do you
sum up this period?

MINER: Can you bear a baseball analogy? I was not a
Babe Ruth. My hits were seldom home runs, they stayed within
the ballpark. I was more a Ty Cobb. The batting average was
reasonably high, but the hits were mostly singles.

V

SCHAFFNER: Tony, more than ever I feel we should go back to the start. There's so much we need to know before moving on to the final forty years.

MINER: Whatever you say.

SCHAFFNER: You were a child of the century, that much I know.

MINER: Right. November 13, 1900.

SCHAFFNER: You were born in Buffalo, New York --

MINER: North Street, just off Delaware Avenue --

SCHAFFNER: And across the way from Kit Cornell.

MINER: Father: Miner, Worthington C., C. for Cogswell. God, what a hideous name! Father's occupation: lawyer. Age at death: forty-two. Grandfather: Julius Miner, eminent surgeon, lost an arm operating on syphilis.

SCHAFFNER: I don't believe it.

MINER: Quite true. That is how the eminent Surgeon General of the United States George Brewer got his training. He lived in our home for many years acting as the great surgeon's right arm.

SCHAFFNER: Operated on syphilis?

MINER: That's the fact of the matter; don't ask me to explain how. Mother: Margaret (Greta) Willard. Age at death, ninety.

There are, I have found, a surprisingly few moments in a person's life that truly affect what he is, much less what he is to become. The first for me occurred at seventeen months. My family had rented a place for the summer in Athol Springs on the south shore of Lake Erie. A herd of cows that supplied our milk had broken into a field of rotten apples. After drinking a full bottle of that poisonous fluid I was on the verge of death. Legend has it that my mother repeatedly held me upside down by my heels during some seven hours until the last drop of that lethal potion had drained from my system. I survived, but not by much. I lived, but only as an invalid, until the age of eleven. That much you've already heard. Surely it has left its mark; far less, however, than the death of my father, a scant six months later. The impact of those two events was indirect -- I was too young to remember either -- but the latter had a far greater influence on my future than the former.

My father's death left us all but penniless; my mother was forced to leave Buffalo and return to Greenwich where my Aunt Louise ran an exclusive and, of course in that day, "restricted" hotel, named The Maples. There were a number of abnormal aspects to this life into which I was thrust at the age of two. To begin with, we were, as I have said, painfully poor; my father had died too young to leave my mother with much more than the funeral and burial expenses. My aunts --

there were four of them -- were equally destitute. Only one had married and she was dead; one of the remaining three was dying of tuberculosis; one was an alcoholic, between bouts with cocaine or heroin. My grandfather E.K. Willard was erratically active in the "Street," President of the Stock Exchange and a well-known participant in the wars and skullduggery of the railroading giants, Harriman and Hill. I've never been certain which side he was on.

He had, however, been enough of a bulldog to acquire a wide assortment of enemies. Late in the 1890s, while on a cruise in the Caribbean with his long-time friend, Commodore Benedict, a cabal of his more embittered enemies hauled him up on a series of "legal technicalities." That, at least, is the way it was presented to me as a boy. They not only divested him of the Presidency of the Exchange, but made it impossible for him ever again to operate on the Street. Right or wrong, it broke him. Commodore Benedict made it possible for my Aunt Louise to acquire the property and buildings which she converted into The Maples. Thus that old fighter, E.K. Willard, became the bookkeeper in his daughter's establishment on the Boston Post Road.

The one other male member of the family was my Uncle Jim. Unlike all the other Willards I'd ever known who were short, squat and bull-headed like me, Jim reverted to the aristocratic features of his great grandfather, Simon Willard. He was slight of build and ascetic, witty, graceful and irresistibly attractive to women. He was also a superb raconteur. Much of the lore and legend of the Willard clan I learned from him over the years. But Uncle Jim was a drunk. It destroyed him. I spent many a Christmas Eve in my later teens searching the Morgue, the Bowery and the main Waiting Room of the Grand Central Terminal in search of my charming, but besotted, uncle.

This created a most unnatural atmosphere in which I was enveloped throughout my childhood. My mother and at least two of my aunts took on the burdens of holding the family together -- one with The Maples, and one with a dress shop, Frances Willard, Inc., which my mother took over when her sister died. By 1906 my mother and my Aunt Louise were supporting not only my two sisters and me, but one sick and drug-ridden sister, their bankrupt father and an alcoholic brother. Thus, through all my youth I never saw a single responsible male within the family circle. I was surrounded by a colony of women, most of them highly capable and self-reliant. In addition, their friends were either teachers, sculptors, writers or extravagantly rich and loyal friends from school. They were, moreover, active participants in the most rebellious female community in New York. Remember, this was the turn of the century. Along with Ann Morgan, Mrs. August Belmont, Elsie DeWolfe, et. al., they were Charter Members of the Colony Club with its open bar, smoking permitted in every room and a Committee in support of Mrs. Pankhurst and Votes for Women. Such conduct was looked upon with disapproval and dire foreboding by the older members of New York's still-Victorian society. At the same time no one would have thought of excluding any one of them from the Social Register. After all, they were ladies. (a laugh) Seems pretty absurd, doesn't it?

Yet it bred in me certain abiding habits of thought that were not easily discarded. Living in Greenwich, one of the richest communities in the country, we were relative paupers. We were at the same time sufficiently secure socially to make me accept as unarguable the fact that I was a "gentleman" -- a large percentage of the nouveau riche residents of Greenwich were not. Living at The Maples I was surrounded by domestic service; my daily menu was fully on a par with that of Sherry's or the old Brevoort. I was, to my shame, forever wearing suits one size too large for me in the pathetic hope that I'd grow into them before they wore out. My sisters and I went to the most exclusive schools, made possible by the long-time friendship and generosity of Miss Caroline Rutz-Reese of Rosemary Hall and Dr. Something-or-other Austin, head of the Brunswick School for Boys. Dr. Austin also happened to be Clare Boothe Luce's uncle with whom she grew up. What that has to do with anything I can't imagine.

While I held men in generally low esteem compared with women, I also grew up with a lifetime fear of physical force, notably the masculine fist. The idea of being hit by a grown male, or even by an older boy, scared the bejesus out of me. My father's image had been that of a gentle, warm-hearted man, unabashedly given to laughter and tears. His gaiety had been infectious. Being a persistent invalid, I was timid. This bred a secret shame that persisted for many years, sad years, often lonely. Had I not been surrounded by a full and demonstrative amount of female love -- it helped to compensate for the courage I lacked -- I tremble to think of the hopelessness and ineffectuality it might have bred. The wonder is I didn't end up a queer.

SCHAFFNER: Were there no compensations?

MINER: A few. Forced to fall back on my own resources, I became abnormally self-sufficient. I asked for very little help from anyone. What I could not resolve for myself, I went without. By the age of five I had taught myself to read. This began with the First Chapter of Genesis which my mother had read aloud to me so many times I knew it by heart. This was superseded by the Stories of the Greek Tragedians, a series no longer available, I believe. Thus I became familiar with Hector, Achilles, and Ajax Minor well before I had ever heard of Jefferson, Adams, or Jackson. Beginning with my sixth year one of my mother's closest, and fortuitously, richest, friends began supplying me with sets of Greek and Roman soldiers, complete with glistening shields, helmets and chariots. I developed a fondness for, and familiarity with, the classics at an unusually early age. I should add that my fascination with Athens and Troy was only exceeded by the enchantment of jigsaw puzzles.

One of my most vivid and painful memories from those early days was my intermittent attendance at Brunswick School. Every attempt I made to be "accepted" was thwarted by my having to carry with me a large flask of beef juice. I was under doctor's orders to consume it before the lunch break. I did my best to sneak into a toilet, or hide behind the furnace, before going through this shameful ritual; it was futile. I never knew how, but the word was out within a matter of days. "Miner's mother's milk" it was called. I pleaded to be allowed to take it before I left home, or after I got back, but to no avail. It was the medical opinion of the day that, without this diurnal stimulant at 11:00 a.m., I would wither away and expire. Do you believe it? Nor do I. But it may help to reaffirm the frailty that so persistently threatened in my preteen years.

The atmosphere was unnatural: a mother, two sisters, four aunts and one of the first American nurses on record, part of Miss Maxwell's contingent that was assembled in Florida during the Spanish-American War. Her name was Thompy. She was attending one of those aunts of mine. Such were my well-nigh exclusive companions.

There were few exceptions. One was a young man named Jeremiah Robinson Beard who, once he caught sight of my Greek and Trojan legions, confessed to his own long-time devotion to the sons and daughters of Priam. His disdain for Achilles, for Agamemnon and the sly and untrustworthy fighting men of Athens was commensurate with mine. For some months we earnestly plotted an expedition to restore the walls of Ilium. Unhappily the one conveyance around which our entire venture had been built was my sister's bicycle. Once the globe at Brunswick School revealed the intrusion of the Atlantic Ocean between Greenwich, Connecticut and the shores of Asia Minor, our secret was interred without trumpet blast or roll of drums. As a tangential result, I became a whiz at geography. Never again was a plan of mine to be negated by an ocean outside my ken. I began to learn every body of water, sea, bay and major inlet from Tierra del Fuego to the Arctic Sea. By the age of ten I knew every state in the Union and every country in the world along with their capitals. I was to win a lot of bets on this arcane achievement over the years ahead.

One vivid memory out of my childhood was that of my grandfather. I silently, and I thought secretly, adored him. Three or four times a year he'd take me to New York. Inside my first ten years I cannot recall more than four, five, trips to town without him, and they were generally devoted to shopping for clothing at least one size too large for me. With Grandpa it was joyous, and an unalloyed adventure. It invariably began with a shave, a haircut and a manicure at the

Manhattan, luncheon at some expensive and relatively exclusive restaurant or hotel, and a visit to the Hippodrome. Small
wonder I remember so clearly the greatest clown alive, the
one and only Marceline. Nor would I belittle "The Fall of Port
Arthur." It was God knows how many years later that I first
recognized how much these junkets must have meant to him,
quite as much as they had to me, possibly more. At his salary
as bookkeeper for The Maples, he must have hoarded every
penny for months in order to pay for our lavish luncheons
alone.

He was a man of odd but adamantine habits. For him
they took on the dignity of tradition. He insisted, for example,
that spinach and guava jelly accompany saddle of lamb. When
lamb arrived with mint sauce and asparagus he would utter an
"Oh, God!" under his breath and push the plate aside. He went
on frequent diets of his own invention. They were somewhat
exotic. For three to five weeks he would take nothing but
roast beef at every meal, breakfast included. The next time it
would be mince pie. He firmly believed that every young man
of quality should be able to play bridge, which in his eyes
meant knowing the value and location of every card in the
deck. I became quite a bridge player at the age of nine.

On my tenth birthday we made a trip to town which
began as usual with a shave, a manicure and luncheon, but on
this occasion it was not the Men's Grill in the Manhattan, it
was Delmonico's. It was still at 28th Street I think, and 5th
Avenue then. The way the head waiter greeted E.K. made me
aware that not only had he been, but still was, a person of
consequence. It was the choicest table for Mr. Willard, a single
rose in a slight silver vase and a flourish as the menu was
opened before me. I went at once for the roast beef and corn
on the cob with a vanilla éclair to round it off.

"No, my boy. No! This is a special occasion. Henri," my
grandfather said with a summoning gesture. If the man's name
was not Henri, it was still a first name and French. "Henri, my
grandson here has this day reached the age of manhood. What
do you recommend as suitable for a young man on such an
august occasion?"

There is some rationale behind the Jewish bar mitzvah, but my grandfather was true enough to his age to spurn the slightest taint of Semitism. Thirteen was Jewish; ten was the age for a person of quality. "Well, sir," said Henri, "might I suggest -- to start with -- a dozen oysters."

"Excellent!" my grandfather replied. "Oysters it shall be."

"And for the main course, Mr. Willard, may I recommend the calves' brains vinaigrette. They are our specialité for the day."

"Right again, Henri. You are still a jewel, I see. And of course, a little champagne. Paul Roget, 1906?"

"Quite, Mr. Willard. Paul Roget, 1906," he smiled. "You have not forgotten, I see."

For E.K. Willard it was a moment of inordinate pride. May I add, however, as you may indeed have guessed by now, I was soon the sickest specimen of "manhood" you ever saw. I had, nontheless, outgrown my boyhood. I was now a grownup, a sort of man.

Fully aware of how unnatural an atmosphere The Maples was for a boy to grow up in, my mother, considering my still-persistent frailty, took a most courageous step; she enrolled me in Kent School. Lest anyone get the idea that this was a wildly extravagant move for her to make, earning as she was but $2,500 a year, it is important to understand that Father Sill was still adhering to his original purpose of starting a school where the sons of poor, yet worthy, parents could get an education. Tuition at Kent School in 1912 was $150 a year. My mother didn't even pay that; I was on scholarship.

And so at eleven years of age I set forth on a five-year stretch of boarding school. One might assume that I would have been assailed by constant and heart-rending attacks of homesickness. I've never quite been able to explain why this did not occur. Oh, I had a few bouts with tears and loneliness, but they were infrequent and surprisingly mild. It was in part,

I suspect, because of my active loathing for Greenwich. I knew
I was looked down upon because I was poor, and I returned the
compliment. As the years progressed I felt the same disdain
for all communities conforming to the same social yardstick of
acceptance, Watch Hill, Newport, Oyster Bay, Southampton. I
can now view with some amusement the violence of my childhood emotions, but, if honesty were to prevail, I would have to
concede that I still go a little white around the gills at the
prospect of a weekend in the environs of a Greenwich Country
Club or one of its innumerable counterparts from Shinnecock
to Palm Springs. Kent School provided the antidote for which I
had hungered too long.

Second, and this is almost inexplicable, after eleven
years of frailty and consignment to a sickbed, I went through
my five years at Kent without one visit to the Infirmary. I was
never ill. I was small and far from strong, but I was graceful,
resilient and whatever the opposite of accident-prone is, I was.

Above all Kent gave me the chance to get my hands
dirty without apology. Quite the reverse, I took pride in the
kind of work elsewhere reserved for mature men, farmers and
ditch-diggers: dumping ashes, unloading carloads of coal, building the baseball field and tennis courts, flooding the hockey
rink at ten below zero, etc., etc. Father Sill wouldn't have
been able to hold tuition to $150 a year without this kind of
help from each one of us. We all worked; we worked because
we had to, and we knew no shame. If anything, we became a
reverse sort of snobs. We held in disrespect the young lads
from Groton, Andover and St. Paul's who were presented with
posh and professional playing fields and hockey rinks; we had
two championship hockey teams while I was at Kent, but we
built our own rinks.

At Kent the hallmark of acceptance was the letters a
person won in athletics. Unfortunately through Fifth Form I
had never made a single First Team; I hadn't even made a
Second Team. I deemed it a humiliation. It represented a
constant and all-but-unbroken disappointment with myself.

The aristocrat among sports was football, and, as I saw
the bruises, cuts and broken limbs the older kids accumulated

during the season, my timidity turned into unspoken terror. I dreamed of being mauled and mutilated, a foot stomping on my face with the cleats tearing at skin and bone. My grades were high, often the highest in the school; I was Editor of the Kent News; I was Assistant Prefect; none of it lessened the ignominy of having spent five years without making so much as a Second Team.

Had it not been for a brief half hour on a September afternoon in 1916, I would not be here with you today. I've no idea who I'd be, nor where, but nothing we've discussed in all these hours could ever have happened.

SCHAFFNER: You exaggerate.

MINER: Do I? Wait! I had come back for the fall term of my last year of school. The football team had started practice some two weeks earlier, but, while they were getting the regular field in shape, the scrimmages were being held on the baseball diamond where patches of dirt and hardened clay replaced the usual cushioning turf. As I stood at one side, the Manager wandered over my way. One of the Second Team had turned up sick. Would I mind filling in? There was no way I could decently refuse.

A Second Team is made up of poor slobs willing to try to stop the First Team's most crushing offensives. I became the slob assigned to right end. The first couple of plays were up the middle, or around left end; I was not involved. But the next play started out toward me. The biggest and fastest back -- he'd been for me a terrifying figure for the last couple of years -- had the ball. I managed to duck the interference which was, in my case, fairly easy; they were paying me no mind whatsoever. Thus I found myself abruptly facing the monster one on one. At sight of me no grim set of jaw occurred, no sign of extra determination; he merely grinned and took off to run around me.

With the sight of that grin, something exploded, adrenalin no doubt, but I became in that instant a bundle of mindless fury. Regardless of cost, I was going to remove that grin from his face. Don't ask where the strength came from, but when I hit, I felt his 180 pounds rise in the air and land with a thud on the hard clay around First Base. The thud was accompanied by a loud and glorious grunt.

"Jesus, kid, you really mean it, don't you?"

As he rose to return to the huddle, I detected a slight, but unmistakable, limp. It was the most exultant moment of my boyhood years.

I continued to play out the rest of the scrimmage. Twenty minutes? Half an hour? I wouldn't know. I was, of course, peculiarly distinguishable. I was small, 5'8" tall, 139 lbs.; I was wearing a non-descript sweater along with a most inappropriate pair of linen plus fours. Obviously I had no helmet nor shoulder pads. When practice broke, the squad started back for the locker room; I had nothing to do but head for the bench along the sidelines to pick up my jacket. It was then that I caught sight of Bucksey, sauntering over toward me; Bucksey was the coach. There was a trace of a smile on his face.

"Hey, kid, where have you been hiding?" I couldn't respond -- I was strangled by too many warring emotions. "No matter, son," he said. "Just get yourself in uniform and report for practice tomorrow. O.K.?"

"Yes, sir." I couldn't even smile.

I was now facing a serious dilemma. I had no uniform; and even though prices were absurdly low compared with 1980, they were still far beyond my private cash account, a somewhat sophisticated word for a 15¢ a week allowance. At 15¢ a week I was within six weeks scarcely going to get more than a jock strap and pair of socks. I was reduced to begging, to which I looked forward with paralyzing misery. I was in for a swift awakening. It never occurred to me that so many kids would be only too eager to contribute, as loan or gift, any piece of equipment I asked for. It was the least they could do for anyone on the First Team. Did they resent it? Hell, no. It was for them an honor.

My first embarrassment came with the pants. Around the third play I heard a telltale sound; a rip is hard to mistake. Instinctively my hand went to my rear end. No luck. It was royally exposed to the wide, wide world. This was not too desperate a situation, so long as I stuck to right end, but it was a little tough on my cousin, John Worthington, when I was asked to take over at center. He was playing quarterback. I continued to inflict this indignity on him throughout the season. I made but one concession: for scheduled games with other schools I borrowed a brand new pair of pants from an eager young Third Former who happened to be precisely my size.

So -- there you have it! I was never anything close to a star, I wasn't even first string. I played right end when the regular right end was ailing, which fortuitously he was for better than half the season. I was also substitute center. Thus when all the best players were well, I was our official bench warmer. In point of fact, however, I played in all but one game, and was duly awarded my "K" after the final game with Choate.

But that was not the end; it was just the beginning. When hockey practice began, I put in an appearance. In past years I would never have dared to do anything so aggressive. And yet an hour or so later I was given a chance at right wing, which I continued to play as a regular for the entire season.

The saga rolls on. In the spring I was asked to fill in as catcher on the baseball team. I'd never caught in my life. Indeed, about the only baseball I'd ever played was One-o-Cat, and yet catcher I became, and on a regular basis.

One might have thought my appetite would have been assuaged by now. Weren't three letters enough? But in the spring of 1917 we were challenged by two schools, Berkshire and The Gunnery, to meet them in tennis. It was the one sport I had been allowed to play since the age of six. I was not very good, but I was Bill Tilden, Jr. beside the competition at Kent. I played, as I remember, twice, and lost both matches. Never mind, I got a fourth "K", the first and only undergraduate who'd ever been awarded that honor in the school's eleven-year history.

The effect on me was startling. I don't believe I, myself, knew how consuming my hunger had been to be among the select few in the school's athletic society. But for one who'd lived his entire childhood as an overprotected invalid, the effect was cataclysmic. Where before I had approached every opportunity as but one more chance to fail, I now walked with the assurance I would be among the elect, the chosen few, the winner at whatever I undertook. Infantile? Oh, yes, oh, yes!

SCHAFFNER: Fascinating, yes. And a little saddening.

MINER: And philosophically revelatory?

SCHAFFNER/MINER (together):   No! (a laugh)

SCHAFFNER: Aside from the reckless tackle, there must have been other experiences that left their mark.

MINER: There were two. My first Vespers Service in the Chapel at Kent. My father had been a Congregationalist. Returning to Greenwich, my mother, out of loyalty to him, I expect, attended the Congregational Church rather than the Episcopalian. The high occasion was communion. No filing to the altar, no wafer offered by a priest; communion was brought to the pews on two salvers, one for bread, the other for dollops of wine served in tiny shot glasses arranged in concentric tiers on a pyramidal silver salver. So enamored did I become of this enticing, if impersonal, ritual, I conned my mother into believing I truly wanted to join the Church. Arrangements were made forthwith. A few Sundays later I shook hands with a young man in everyday attire, and partook of my first communion. The bread was stale and the wine was vinegar. My disillusionment was so shattering I never attended service in the Congregational Church again.

Kent was high-Episcopalian. Father Sill was a member of the Order of the Holy Cross. Aside from the fact that the infallibility of the Pope was questioned and that the Mass was spoken in English, it was Roman Catholic in both form and substance. I cannot recall what special occasion was being celebrated at that first service I attended, but it was held in a converted workshed painted olive green. The service, whatever it was, possessed for me the solemnity of a high Mass -- crucifix, candles, incense, and above all, Plain Chant. As I knelt in mounting awe, I was transported to a state of wonder and disquieting mystery. I fell victim to the lure of Plain Chant as to no other music I had ever heard. What I had heard and seen in those few minutes lived with me, not for a day, nor for a year, but for the major burden of my life.

The second seminal experience occurred during World War I. In one fraction of a second I conquered fear.

I'd been asked to pick up a Lieutenant-Colonel and his Dog-Robber -- a military valet -- and drive them the final twenty kilometers into Château-Thierry, cross the Marne and rendezvous with our batteries at 1:00 a.m. It was the first time I'd driven at night without lights, and this one was a dilly. There was a driving rain, no moon, and the roads were alive with traffic in both directions. Inevitably we began running late. I was tense enough already, but when the Virginia-born Colonel beside me began complaining in a voice pitched somewhere between a whine and a police whistle, it was for me touch and go between rage and paralysis. "Faster, you little son-of-a-bitch!" he kept screaming. "Faster! Christ Almighty, we're an hour late already!"

No thanks to Col. Bishop we reached Château-Thierry without a crackup. In the main square an MP directed me toward the bridge which glistened with sulphur dust even in the enveloping downpour. The bridge was built in one high arc over the river, a type of construction favored by the Legions of Rome. I had stepped on the gas as we reached the upward incline when suddenly, unaccountably, my left hand did something involuntary, something it had never done before. It grabbed the handle of the emergency brake and gave it a colossal yank. We stopped. We stopped so abruptly, the jolt drove the squealing Colonel's head straight through the wind-shield. The squeals turned to screaming outrage as the blood began gushing from his forehead.

"Miner!" he yelled. "What the goddamn hell are you trying to do?" It was but the start of a torrent of abuse and blasphemy. As for me, I was paralyzed, not figuratively, liter-ally. I could not move. I was still under some supernormal influence over which I had no control. When at last my motor nerves began once again to function, I got out of the car to look. I could not yet discern any visible justification for my having pulled up to so abrupt a stop. As I came level with the radiator, the mystery was hideously revealed. Eighteen inches in front of my front wheels there was only blackness and the waters of the swollen Marne racing thirty feet below. The Germans had expertly blown up the bridge before retreating to safer ground. You ask, do I believe in the intervention of Providence? The answer is yes, I do. Do I believe our span of years is ordained? Yes, I do.

SCHAFFNER: All because of this one incident?

MINER: I'm not sure, but I began gradually to realize that I was no longer afraid. If I were not intended to die, what reason had I to fear death? For I'd long believed that the conquest of fear was a sign of courage, yet now I had got rid of fear, but the cowardice remained. Without fear there is no bravery; without threat, there is no gallantry.

SCHAFFNER: By a monstrous stroke of luck you became fearless. You went back to Yale and hated it. You won a Phi Beta Kappa but never wore the key. In fact, you deliberately lost it. You went to England and fell in love with it, and, to a degree, it appears to have fallen in love with you. How much did any of this contribute to your career in the theatre?

MINER: Had it not been for my two years at Magdalene College on the Cam, my career in the theatre would never have been. I might have become a teacher, I might have imported woolens and worsteds from Verviers, I might have built mousetraps, but I would never have known the feel or the smell of a Broadway stage.

SCHAFFNER: You mean you had no hint whatever before you arrived in England?

MINER: None, not even the vaguest. This is odd in its way, because I had always acted, from the age of three when I played a page in Romeo and Juliet. At nine I played in The Man Without a Country at the Brunswick School for Boys. At Kent I was in every play we put on during my four years at the school. At Yale I'd been a messenger in Rhesus -- that you know -- and I played a Park Bench Bum for an unpretentious and short-lived group known as the Playcraftsmen. Each contributed some measure of delight, especially the Bum. After the show was over, and on a bet, I got myself arrested as a vagrant. It was a glorious feeling. But the two events that wrought a sea-change in my life were utterly unpremeditated and unpredictable. It was a case of serendipity, pure and simple. One, I went to a performance of Henry IV, Part I at the Old Vic. Two, I got a letter from my mother.

SCHAFFNER: Pretty obscure!

MINER: Not really. Acting had always filled me with a certain delight, but it was an amusement quite apart from anything "important" one might do with one's life. It was delicious, but trivial, like licking the dasher after making ice cream. Those three hours at the Old Vic were anything but trivial. I had lived so intimately within a community of human beings of varied tastes and varied moods, I'd been warmed by their laughter and shaken by their defeats, their agonies and their deaths. I'd matured more in that one evening than in any year I'd known before. I had gone alone; I came out alone. I walked alone across Waterloo Bridge all the way to my digs above Marble Arch. I was at once stunned and exalted. This was no casual event; it struck me at the roots of being. Never before had I seen the theatre in this light.

SCHAFFNER: It must have been a pretty stupendous production.

MINER: I rather doubt it. There wasn't an actor in it who ever moved on to the West End or Broadway. But little people gain cubits when the words they speak simply and well take wing. No American child should be allowed to reach his teens without experiencing the supreme eloquence of our language as his heritage, for it belongs to us quite as much as it does to the Brits. Our lingering envy is absurd. We have so much better reason to rejoice.

SCHAFFNER: And then your mother wrote a letter.

MINER: She did. And though for years -- at Kent, in the Army, at Yale -- she had written regularly every week, no letter of hers had ever left any permanent mark. This one changed my life. Early in the fall I'd met up with a member of the History Department at King's College, a man named Frank Birch. Frank had for some years produced, directed and played the Cockney lead in the Christmas Pantomime for the Amateur Dramatic Club (ADC). I didn't even know what a Christmas Pantomime was when Frank asked me to take over as stage manager. I could only laugh, "Me? Why me?"

"I need someone efficient. You're an American. All Americans are efficient."

I went into it as a lark; it ended a shambles. Ten days before the opening Frank came down with influenza. There being no one else available, Miner took over as director. Twenty-four hours before the opening night Frank lost his voice; Miner took over the Cockney lead with something like six major singing numbers.

You may recall that four weeks before I had not even known what a Christmas Pantomime was. I spoke not one word of Cockney, and I couldn't sing "Happy Birthday" on key. The disaster of that opening night must live "in infamy" in the annals of the ADC. The British audience responded in pity, but with little spirit. I knew the worst. The night of the last performance I wrote a dutiful letter home, fully exposing my humiliation.

The next day I left for a six-week "Mid-year Vac" in Switzerland. It was a form of racket, a semi-pro junket for hockey teams from Oxford and Cambridge, exhibition games in Antwerp, the Palais de Glace, Montreux and Switzerland. Christmas was in Mürren, New Year's in St. Moritz, with side events in Pontresina, Gstaad and Davos. The last thing on my mind during those "hot chocolate and croissant" days was the theatre. But the night I got back to Cambridge I found a letter from my mother. I remember only one statement; it was enough.

"At last, Worthy," -- she even used my father's diminuitive, unconsciously, I'm sure -- "you seem to have found something you want to do with your life. Well, son, you have my blessing. It's a far cry from anything I had ever dreamed of for you, but, if it excites you this much, you'll do it, and do it well. So go to it."

It hit me hard. To begin with I couldn't credit my own stupidity. How could something have been so obvious to her without arousing some trace of suspicion in me? And it hadn't, honest to God, it hadn't. It had been for me an anecdote without deeper implications. That my life was to be in the theatre? How absurd and how obvious!

VI

MINER: From that moment there was never a doubt in my mind, nor has there ever been in all the years. It's been a love affair with all the bruises and hurts that love exacts, but no other world has ever taken up more than transient occupancy in my heart. I felt the enchantment of a pioneering adventure, but it's been a theatrical unknown that has cast its spell. The thousand little steps I learned to take in order to transmit an elusive mood, a personal excitement, into a million homes via a six megacycle band was thrill enough, reward enough, for me. Few know nor remember how much sweat and imagination, how many hours and days, how many failures and disappointments, were endured by the dozen or so of us who fashioned the tools in such common usage today. Alas, how painful it is to see how many have never yet learned to use those tools as they were designed. Why should they, when they get paid indecent sums for their ignorance and desecrations? But they will never know the delight we derived from seeing those tools used well, and as they were meant to be used.

SCHAFFNER: And who in television uses them best?

MINER: One above all the rest -- Dwight Hemion. He's towered over the musical field for a long time. I'd dearly love to see him try his hand in the dramatic realm. In the interval I'd have to grant the palm to Ingmar Bergman and Scenes From a Marriage.

If you'd asked about opera, I'd say Kirk Browning. But if you'd asked about sports, I'd have been stuck. They're all pretty bad. They all subscribe to the cult of the extra camera. It never seems to occur to them to ask, "How can I use, and better, the cameras I have?" Holy Cow! That's the proper phrase now, isn't it? I saw better coverage of football in 1950 with three cameras than any Super Bowl broadcast in recent years using how many? Seventeen?

SCHAFFNER: You'd throw out the replay cameras?

MINER: No. They're great. The fault lies in what's done with the basic cameras. Until they learn to cover a run, a pass and a punt effectively, they'll get no applause from me. . . .

Back in 1941 I wrote a White Paper for CBS. I under-took to explore what made television unique, what was its peculiar and most impressive capacity, and I concluded that television's supreme capacity was as a reporter, that this aspect of the medium must never be forgotten, even when it was operating in as remote an area as dramatic production.

SCHAFFNER: And so?

MINER: So, covering a football game is reporting. It is using television to do what it should do best, but too often doesn't. That's what saddens me.

SCHAFFNER: I won't argue the point. One of your finest achievements was The Iceman Cometh, right?

MINER: Right. By me it was the finest.

SCHAFFNER: That was theatre; how do you relate it to reporting?

MINER: There's a fine point at issue. The design of The Iceman was to set an action into motion with such validity of detail it would seem as if the cameras were reporting the incident, as though we were recording a man on the ledge of a roof. That's why it moved so fast, why its casting was so vital, why every camera angle was measured by its reportorial effectiveness, not by some meretricious reach for the "unusual."

SCHAFFNER: Give me the facts behind your leaving the Theatre Guild for television.

MINER: As early as 1937 I was on the alert for any chance to make a get-away from the Big Stem. Jeremiah supplied the final impetus. But even sooner a loss of assurance, of self-belief, of gaiety had begun to set in. The signal was given, I was more than ready.

SCHAFFNER: So the gods took over.

MINER: It was in the spring of 1938. Fran and I were having dinner with John and Carly Wharton. John was at the time Advisory Counsel for Philo Farnsworth, one of the early pioneers in television engineering. He had just returned from a long stay in London, observing and consulting with the BBC and the British television industry as a whole. I was an eager listener from the start. Even though 1936-37 had been a bumper year for me, and 1937-38 was holding out equal prospects, something deep inside me had begun to whisper: "Look out, kid! There's war in the air. It's a-coming. And when it does, the theatre has no foxhole to offer." So here was John, holding forth about a medium that fitted the times ahead as the theatre never could.

Before we left I took him aside. "John, what you've been saying excites me; I want to know more."

"I thought it might."
"So! What do I do? Is it time to move?"
"No. Not yet. Give it a year."
"O.K. But will you let me know?"
"You have my word."

A year went by. One Friday evening in late August, 1939 the phone rang. Fran picked it up and handed it to me.

"It's John Wharton," she said.

He came directly to the point. "Tony," he said, "you remember a year ago you asked me to let you know when I thought television was going to take off? Well, I think it's here."

On the spot I made a date to meet with him early the following week to map out a plan for landing a job.

We were spending the weekend with Ilka Chase and Bill Murray. Bill was a high officer in MCA. Late Sunday evening he asked if any of us wanted an early ride into town. Fran and I accepted. And so, at 7:00 a.m. Monday morning the three of us set off in a driving rain.

We were about halfway to town when, for no apparent reason, our car went into a most ghastly skid. It swerved around broadside into the oncoming lane, then slithered first this way, then that, until it finally slewed into its proper lane and continued toward New York. There was understandably a moment of deadly silence, at which, and in a most casual tone, Bill Murray said: "Tony, have you ever thought about going into television?"

I know, I know. You feel it's naive and sophomoric of me to proclaim a purpose to our human condition. But had you been in that car at that moment, I would dare you to insist there was no power above dictating the next stage of my destiny.

At 3:00 p.m. Wednesday afternoon I was in Gilbert Seldes's office in the Grand Central Terminal. At 9:30 Monday morning I left my office in the Theatre Guild to take up residence at 15 Vanderbilt Avenue. Television was to supply my working home for the next twenty years.

The first ten of those twenty years might appear a time of well-nigh unendurable frustration. Indeed, nothing that television had seemed to offer came to be. Less than a week after I moved into 15 Vanderbilt, England declared war; within the hour, the BBC's transmitter went off the air. Competition with Britain had supplied the major incentive for NBC and CBS to go forward with television programming; now that the competition was withdrawn, lurking disputes over technical standards broke into the open. The major warring parties were RCA, General Electric, DuMont, Philco, McDonald at Zenith, Phil Farnsworth and Bell Labs; CBS was not yet a challenger in the technical field. By October the FCC issued a paper known as "The Brown Light Before the Green Light," the net result of which was to block all television broadcasters from securing commercial licenses until the various manufacturers could agree on a set of engineering standards. In effect, television broadcasting was as dead as a duck for another year and a half.

In the spring of 1940, Peter Goldmark's development of a mechanical form of color broadcasting set in motion a vicious corporate battle between CBS and RCA that would defer television's flowering for another eight years. Much of this was foreseen by the knowledgeable and the wise; I was neither. For a decade I believed in every tomorrow.

SCHAFFNER: Have you ever regretted those wasted years?

MINER: No, because they were anything but wasted. I could, in fact, never have done what I did when the time came, had I not learned what I had in those irreplaceable years. One example: had we been forced to go commercial with the equipment we had on hand in 1940-41, television might never have got off the ground for another twenty years; it was the advances made by Dr. Vladimir Zworykin and others during the War years that made Milton Berle and Ed Sullivan possible, not to mention the World Series of 1947. If it hadn't been for Peter Goldmark's incompatible color, we might not have had compatible color for another thirty years. It was a dark decade with a bright silver lining. To add to the glow I built a house in the country. It was our home up to 1974.

But let's stick to television. The decade divides itself into two halves, prewar and postwar. Each was, to some degree, affected by color. For me, the postwar period came close to being a disaster. If Bill Paley had not returned from England precisely when he did, Tony Miner would have been drummed out of CBS and into oblivion.

SCHAFFNER: When did color happen?

MINER: Spring, 1949. The first presentation to the FCC was in the fall and on film. There were no live color cameras yet.

SCHAFFNER: So six months had intervened since that fateful skid. What had you done in that time?

MINER: I prepared a "Shakespearian" adaptation of Burlesque.

SCHAFFNER: What did Shakespeare have to do with the Burlesque Wheel?

MINER: Nothing. But after a lot of study and thought, I'd reached the conclusion that no form of play structure was better suited to television than the Elizabethan framework. The Three Act form was surely the worst, the least suited to the new medium. The wide outdoors was a luxury only pictures could afford. And it scarcely seemed feasible to return to the chorus and masks of the Athenian stage, much less the stylized traditions of the Oriental theatre. What else? And believe it or not, it worked rather well. Miraculously well, in fact, aside from one small miscalculation. The first draft of Burlesque would have taken three hours of playing time. While structurally effective, it would not have appealed to the money-boys.

SCHAFFNER: Is there a copy around?

MINER: I'm afraid not. I wrote "A Guide to Writers" for CBS. It defined all the major principles I'd used in adapting Burlesque aside from one thing -- it never mentioned the name Shakespeare. It was widely circulated for a time. Now? Who knows?

SCHAFFNER: I never saw it.

MINER: Few did.

SCHAFFNER: There must be a copy somewhere.

MINER: If CBS could lose the 450-page "History of Television" I wrote for them during the war, what chance does a 22-page memo have? You see, before it could be distributed and studied, color had captured the minds and the imaginations of the high brass at CBS. Everything else was deemed irrelevant.

SCHAFFNER: How much did you have to do with color?

MINER: A lot. I shot the original film for FCC presentation; I devised every show CBS put on in the next three years. In fact, my recurrent involvement with color has been rather strange. Long before television I had been asked to shoot a critical test of Technicolor for Merian Cooper at RKO.

That was back in 1934. Merian had had a feeling that Technicolor had some secret flaws that Natalie Kalmus had been concealing; he wanted me to spot as many as I could and expose them. To lend importance to the assignment he gave me Joel McCrea and Dolores Del Rio as talent for the test.

I listed a great many of the most critical flaws some week to ten days in advance of our shooting date. A roster of my suspicions, along with a schedule of shots to reveal them, was submitted ten days ahead of time to Merian Cooper and given official approval before shooting began. As a result, while winning the undying enmity of Natalie Kalmus, I was for a time in high good favor at RKO. This test saved them a tidy sum by supplying them with the ammunition to insist that Technicolor correct a sizable list of faults before RKO would move forward with its production schedule.

So much for film and color. But my involvement with color in television persisted. After moving to NBC in 1952 I was asked by General Sarnoff to prepare RCA's presentation of its compatible color system to the FCC. It was a far more complex and expensive program than anything I had done for CBS, but for RCA it was worth it. On the basis of that one presentation RCA won FCC approval for its color system which automatically eliminated Peter Goldmark's mechanical system which CBS had so ardently supported. But for me, while color served as an intellectual stimulant, my emotional allegiance was to television itself.

The date that generated the most excitement for me was July 1, 1941. That was the date when, with FCC approval, NBC and CBS went on the air under commercial license for a minimum of fifteen hours a week, black-and-white.

SCHAFFNER: That was before my time. Fifteen hours of what?

MINER: News, sports, variety, ballet. Our first show was a fairy story read by a Mother to her Child (the Child was Anne Francis) while a cartoonist illustrated the narration. Then there were discussions and interviews, quiz shows with contestants that would bankrupt any network today. Everyone who was anyone in the theatre, the arts, business and government in 1941-42 was sooner or later to be seen on one of our CBS Quiz Shows. Our MC was Gilbert (Gil) Fates, later the producer of What's My Line?

SCHAFFNER: And the cost?

MINER: Cheese and crackers, sometimes a casserole, and liberal beakers of wine and whiskey at the Miner ménage.

SCHAFFNER: And how much of a hand did you have in it all?

MINER: (a laugh) Conservatively speaking, everything! I produced and directed the entire fifteen hours for the first ten weeks that CBS was on the air. Little by little I began to delegate some of the simpler shows, but I still handled some eight to ten hours a week up to the fall of 1942. That was when we closed down "live" operations for the duration of the war.

Most people imagine that the greatest strain in live production came during the programs themselves. Oh, no, oh, no! The worst tension occurred during the thirty-second station breaks. You see, in those primitive days, the director had to handle everything for himself; he had to call all the takes for each of the three cameras plus the film channel, if used. In addition, he had to prepare the other cameras for their next set-ups. As a sheer vocal exercise, just getting the words out clearly and succinctly within a span of thirty seconds was a stunt. For the first six months the most prodigious foul-ups occurred, not during the course of a program itself, but between the end of one program and the start of the next. Some measure of the strain is certified by the fact that computers make the same hash of it today. In truth, they do somewhat less well than we did.

It's impossible to exaggerate the paralyzing grip that took hold of one's viscera. NBC subdivided the strain by allowing a good part of the responsibility to be taken over by the technical director. This was but another confirmation of General Sarnoff's short-sightedness as a showman, of his inability to appreciate the loneliness an artist must be granted at such moments of decision. Bill Paley seldom erred in this area. He was a superb businessman, but he was also a supreme showman. He recognized the impossibility of creativity by committee. The technician was there to give technical and electronic life to the director's dreams. To evade the danger of having a director ask too often for the impossible, General Sarnoff gave the technical director the right to veto the director's commands; Bill Paley's blunt response was: "Get another director."

So fundamental was this principle to CBS that, long before television was ready to move into high gear, the bitter jurisdictional battles had been fought and won. As a result, little blood was spilled by CBS or IATSE in hammering out a television agreement. Only people like Fred Coe or Max Liebman or Arthur Penn can truly appraise the hurt and the handicap the General imposed on his best creative talent throughout these early years.

By the late forties I had been granted so many privileges, my conduct had become somewhat high-handed. While I never presumed to tamper with the electronic aspects of the equipment, I was allowed to adjust picture quality in the control room and to handle any of the cameras on the floor. Many union members, moving over from radio, deeply resented this conduct on my part and complained bitterly to their shop stewards.

One incident in particular got pretty hairy, and to avoid further trouble a meeting was called -- 1949? 1950? somewhere in there -- as a result of which certain privileges were informally granted to me "without prejudice" as to the limitations formally imposed on directors as a class. It made it possible for me to train new directors and new camera crews with a minimum amount of friction or ill-feeling; it made it possible for technicians to establish their areas of authority without complaint from new, or even "old," directors.

How often do we find an entire organization, even a large and sophisticated organization, reflecting the strengths and the weakness of the boss-man at the top? Seldom have I found this more apparent than at CBS and NBC. While General Sarnoff, as an engineer, was a visionary and crusader, as a showman he was inept and spendthrift. Compared with William S. Paley he was a tyro. With one exception -- and let us swiftly give the General his due -- Bill Paley never evidenced any aptitude, nor taste, for classical music, particularly opera; for the General that type of music inspired a native and genuine enthusiasm. Small wonder, therefore, that Toscanini was one of the top artists in the NBC roster of radio stars; Bill Paley ran second with the Philharmonic. In television the pattern was followed again. It was the General who initiated and supported the NBC Opera Series; it was the General who commissioned Gian Carlo Menotti to write Amahl and the Night Visitors.

SCHAFFNER: When you finally went on the air in July 1941, what audience were you reaching?

MINER: On a big night? 150. It was, let's face it, a thoroughly meaningless exercise. Fran used to laugh at me -- how could she help it? Night after night I'd come in full of piss and vinegar to ask with teenage intensity: "Did you catch that window shot on Tamara?" or "Did you realize that for the first twelve minutes of Men at Work" -- a variety show -- "I stayed on one camera?" or "Watch the ballet tonight. I'm going to be cutting halfway through a series of pan shots. That's something pictures can't do." Can you credit it? A reasonably mature showman, forty to fifty years of age, making such a scene night after night after night about a camera angle that could be seen by 150 people at best? How could we get that worked up over some bit of routine photography? You'd think we were taking another step on the moon.

SCHAFFNER: Wasn't it that kind of caring that made the age "golden"?

MINER: Maybe, maybe.

SCHAFFNER: Is there any one principle that you devised that has played a critical part in the future of the medium?

MINER: One. Vertical composition.

SCHAFFNER: As opposed to horizontal composition.

MINER: Of course.

SCHAFFNER: That was so solidly accepted before I even came to CBS I'd almost forgotten that you proclaimed it. Come to think of it, it's about as pivotal as D.W. Griffith's invention of the close-up. How did you arrive at it?

MINER: In the theatre I'd prided myself on my ability to "people" the stage in a consistently interesting way. Such compositions were, perforce, horizontally conceived on a single plane imposed by the shape and form of the proscenium arch. In the theatre it is often effective to have two characters confront each other at a distance of thirty feet, thus putting the full width of the stage between them. But let two characters face each other at only half that distance in television, and the stature of a man is automatically reduced to that of a horsefly. Facial features become indistinguishable, reactions are without meaning or impact. You know all that. But what if it be essential to the power of a scene that the varied reactions of four or five characters be observed at one time? Vertical composition, arrangements in depth, offered the only solution. That's scarcely an arcane observation, is it?

SCHAFFNER: No, but didn't pictures once suffer from the same handicap? Didn't the aspect ratio of the screen in the average theatre impose an unnatural and unattractive constriction on the composition of the picture?

MINER: Yes, but nothing to compare with television, and for one controlling reason, size. The home screen is measured in inches, the theatre screen is measured in feet. And although the technicians assure us that the subtended angle of the image on your 19-inch home receiver at eleven feet is identical with the angle subtended by a Music Hall picture from the twenty-sixth row, it isn't true. To so ardently discount the psychological factor is stupid!

SCHAFFNER: No argument.

MINER: Once I'd resolved the pivotal issue of vertical composition, television was ready, I thought, to take off and girdle the globe. But massive pitfalls remained. In 1941 the very existence of television was so awesome, few of us were ready to admit the hopeless inadequacy of the iconoscope cameras. The images they were able to render were limited to shadings of grey -- there were no blacks whatever -- with a depth of field of roughly three feet. Thus NBC, which had gone on the air as early as 1938, continued to present dramatic programs with characters maintaining a straight, horizontal line at a three-foot remove from the back wall of the set. I insisted on using our entire studio with a depth of field often exceeding eighteen and twenty feet. Technically speaking, we were not sending out very good pictures. Indeed there was no such thing as a good picture in 1941-42, which probably explains why no one at the time seemed to recognize how far CBS had gone toward establishing a series of basic principles governing camera usage for television. All we needed was the equipment.

SCHAFFNER: And when we got it, how many ever thought to say: "We're using Tony Miner's form of camerawork now"?

MINER: (a laugh) No one! Ever! I could only wish that all of the other principles established in those years, especially the "no-nos," were as widely accepted today as the basic principle of vertical composition.

SCHAFFNER: So there were others?

MINER: You know them as well as I. I drummed them into your heads ad nauseam for three years. Does this ring a bell? "Always arrange cameras so that, in any cut to a tighter lens (close-up, medium close-up, over-the-shoulder shots), the two characters will still be facing each other."

SCHAFFNER: (a laugh) And it's still ignored. Why? Have you any idea?

MINER: None. And most grievously on some of the most prestigious shows. Another! "Once the audience is oriented to any space, internal or external, the angle --"

SCHAFFNER: "-- angle of view should be retained at the opening of each succeeding scene in order for the viewer to recognize the area as rapidly as possible."

MINER: Precisely. Thus a door is a door, but what establishes whether that particular door leads to the kitchen, the bedroom or the bath is its position in the initial orienting shot. A confused audience is an audience whose attention has been partially, if not totally, lost.

SCHAFFNER: And that's one I found hard at the start, maintaining orientation, I mean.

MINER: I know, but it became easier once it got to be a habit. And an audience's attention is too precious a commodity to ignore.

SCHAFFNER: But it can become monotonous, if you don't watch out.

MINER: Only if the director uses the same orienting shot each time, something of which you were never guilty, of course.

SCHAFFNER: Only because you were such a caustic bastard when you caught us at it.

MINER: (a smile) I know, I know. But this you'll have to admit, I showed you so many ways of avoiding visual monotony, your imaginations began to flower without further assist from me.

SCHAFFNER: And, if they didn't, the days with you were numbered.

MINER: Right. How many other of Miner's Laws do you remember?

SCHAFFNER: More than I intend to recite. After all, I'm here to listen. It's for you to talk.

MINER: If you insist. "When cutting from a wide two shot to a tighter two shot, retain the same focal depth of field."

SCHAFFNER: "The distance between the characters should remain constant."

MINER: Right. When it is abruptly reduced from twelve feet to three feet, or vice versa, it will inevitably result in a visual shock.

Oddly enough this principle was repeatedly violated in motion pictures long before television came into being. In fact, it is still observable today. For television it often represents both a hazard and an inconvenience; the wide angle camera may have to move in so close to secure an over-the-shoulder shot, it will intrude on the outside line of the establishing lens. For the experienced director, this presents no insuperable hurdle, but some infractions are to be expected from sheer annoyance. In pictures, however, there is no danger, and need be no annoyance. Why then does this sloppiness persist? I have no answer.

SCHAFFNER: "In framing a head in profile, the line of vision should occupy roughly one-half the width of the frame. When horizontal motion is called for, the same ratio should be maintained."

MINER: "When cutting during a pan shot, both cameras must be at the same height and moving at the same speed." These, of course, are rules to be broken by the experienced director, not by the novice.

SCHAFFNER: But when a director ignores these principles, does the audience notice?

MINER: Consciously? Probably not. Subconsciously? Yes. And repeated infractions breed a loss of concentration which, as I've said again and again, is a cardinal sin.

SCHAFFNER: How then can we recognize good direction?

MINER: Good direction attracts the least attention, and the better the work, the less we should be aware of the style.

SCHAFFNER: Hear, hear!

MINER: That does not mean that there should be no unforgettable visual moments; if they are true and advance the story, hurray! Witness the wedding scene from The Deer Hunter, the best example I have seen in a long time.

SCHAFFNER: How much more had you discovered before 1948?

MINER: Ah, that's hard to say. More than a little, some of it important, some not. Mostly it was a question of taste and judgment. I was a nut on the subject of dance, for instance. Keeping the lens at chest height was a custom that infuriated me. I equally deplore the indiscriminate cutting in of heads, arms, facial expressions and feet. In shooting Billy the Kid in 1945, for example, I kept the camera as low as possible, showing the full figure at all times. It set a pattern that I still can't fault, unless a dance piece is specifically choreographed for television -- Twyla Tharp for example. Close-ups then become a part of the pattern of the dance and are quite acceptable. Other principles were also explored; when to use a low angle camera, when a high; how to establish visual rhythm --

SCHAFFNER: How?

MINER: I've no idea! I don't know how to explain nor teach it. I tried for years with signal lack of success. Bergman has it, never more effectively than in Cries and Whispers. Hitchcock has it. Dwight Hemion has it to his fingertips; Kirk Browning has it. Robert Altman, for all the critical acclaim showered on him, lacks it to the point of unintentional obscurity. I dearly trust it is "unintentional." If not -- (a laugh and a shrug). Chaplin had it to the point of choreographic wizardry.

SCHAFFNER: Did you have it?

MINER: Of course! Wait! That's not as candid as it should be.

I had it, but since I am not a musician, I didn't have it to the degree I admire so much in others. My outstanding skill was in three-dimensional composition; and, if only I'd had the musical capacity, I might have been a whiz of a choreographer, a Jerry Robbins or an Agnes De Mille. I could handle motion, but it was, too often, in the rhythm of prose.

SCHAFFNER: What more?

MINER: Not something I learned, not something I either devised or taught, only a corroboration of my conviction that when television gets a decent chance to report an event it is able to rise above any inherent shortcomings and establish a triumphant record. I suspect you'd cite John F. Kennedy's funeral among such events.

SCHAFFNER: I don't see how it could be excluded.

MINER: The incident that I have in mind faded so swiftly into obscurity, no one remembers it. Few even remember that television was there. It was the occasion of Wendell Willkie's nomination in 1940.

SCHAFFNER: How bad a picture was it in 1940?

MINER: Gruesome. It was nothing but black and white, by which I do not mean black-and-white as opposed to color; I mean black and white and nothing else. Snow! Periodically it totally obliterated the picture. Regardless, the tension and the restlessness kept building, until that explosive moment when the final votes that put Wendell Willkie over the top were recorded.

SCHAFFNER: Are you sure that's all? Wasn't there some last, final principle you instituted during this era?

MINER: Not really, except to clear up one point. The vast majority of the basic standards of good camerawork I assembled for television had long been accepted in pictures. I was not a pioneer on every front. It was when I discovered new techniques, or new emphases on old standards, that my contribution became significant.

One conviction of mine was that the most essential difference between television and motion picture photography lay in the fact that, in pictures, actors for the most part moved in and out of a fixed frame; in television actors often remained still, while the frame around them moved. The very usual use today of the telescopic lens -- something we didn't have in the early days -- reveals the distinction in simplest terms. Moving from a waist shot to a close-up in motion pictures is normally accomplished by cutting and either moving the camera or putting on another lens. In television the lens closes in at any speed the director may specify, while the actor remains immobile.

After fifty years I am still unsure which is the better technique for television. Indeed the use of a moving frame is so common in TV today, I often long for a sudden instantaneous cut. On the other hand, to achieve its full effectiveness, a picture director must call for the proper lens after the cut is made. Again and again, to my extreme discomfiture, he does not. It is then that I cry for a telescopic lens to protect the director against his own ineptitude.

SCHAFFNER: And the critics seldom notice.

MINER: Sadly enough, no. Too much sloppy and sleazy picture-making has won approval -- fad acclaim, I call it -- through critical applause. Fortunately it shall not last. The best will, in the end, prevail.

SCHAFFNER: Over the past three decades, do you believe that the television "style" in camerawork has affected technical standards in filmmaking?

MINER: Yes, profoundly. A good many directors with a background solely in film will dispute that statement. They may even resent it. Yet as early as A Streetcar Named Desire I was aware that, aside from a handful of exterior shots in the streets of New Orleans, the rest of the picture might very easily have been shot in Studio #42 at CBS or 8H at NBC. Since then a wide assortment of directors has moved from television to films, many of them utilizing ideas and techniques they acquired here in New York. You for one. In fact you might quite well head the list.

SCHAFFNER: Besides me. I need names.

MINER: George Roy Hill, Sidney Lumet, Arthur Penn, Bob Mulligan --

SCHAFFNER: Fred Coe, up to his untimely death. But there is a difference. Good film direction is seldom the best for television, and vice versa.

MINER: Yea and yea! It was one of the fatal flaws in Playhouse 90 -- I can't think why I failed to point it out at the time. Originating in Hollywood -- which was no part of my original idea, God wot -- more and more of the directors were seduced into a belief that a picture approach would give a sophisticated sheen to the series as a whole. Maybe Marty Manulis, himself, agreed -- I don't know. But exactly the reverse occurred. It was a dismal failure. I was so distressed by those unhappy efforts, I became adamant that Play of the Week should be shot precisely as though it were "live," one act at a time without a break. If any part of the performance were sub-par, we'd reshoot the entire act. Oh, once in a while, when a mike dipped into the shot, or a camera, or a stage-hand, we'd reshoot from thirty seconds, or a minute-and-a-half, but this was rare -- very rare indeed.

SCHAFFNER: I'm confused. You weren't with Play of the Week at the start, were you?

MINER: No. It wasn't my invention. Necessity was the mother of that invention; so long as the material was theatrical there was no other way to handle a three-act play. But what if Play of the Week began to use scripts written for television? What then?

SCHAFFNER: Did you ever?

MINER: One. Reggie Rose wrote Black Monday for us. But he also wrote it as a film script. We either had to use our cameras as film cameras or not do the show at all. I voted for turning it down. But the pressures were mounting too fast. I was outvoted. It was time for us to "graduate" to film -- such was the byword of the day. It was a form of insecurity, of kindergarten maturity, but once the disaster was there for all to see, my insistence was never challenged again. I had maintained that television was television in its own right; it was not a poor man's version of motion pictures.

SCHAFFNER: With so many credits to your name, why is there scarcely one for you in pictures?

MINER: Well, I told you my troubles with Jack Barrymore, but, more important, during all my years in the theatre, I looked on pictures as a secondary art. I had disdained those who fled to Hollywood, or was saddened by their treachery. That is, I expect, the major reason for my signal failure with a motion picture camera. No workman can earn his salt in a craft he denigrates. And absurd as this prejudice may appear to you now -- and to me now -- take my word for it that absurdity was commonplace during the twenties and thirties. A director in the theatre was generally regarded as an underpaid artist; a director in pictures as an overpaid cowhand.

Look at the record of the top directors and producers of the early century. David Belasco, Henry Miller, the Theatre Guild, Guthrie McClintic, George Abbott, Phil Moeller, Billy Rose, Schwab and Mandel, Sam Harris, Dwight Wiman. But the two film directors who did best had unimpressive Broadway records -- George Cukor and Gar Kanin. As a result, they were ready and eager to learn, and did.

SCHAFFNER: Why, when so many other talents have moved in relative glory from television to pictures, have there been so few producers?

MINER: Simple numbers. There weren't that many dramatic producers in the early years of television. I had four shows, Fred Coe had three -- between us, just he and I alone, we must have used some twenty directors in the course of a year. And don't forget -- the great mass of television producers did nothing to equip themselves for pictures. What have Goodson and Todman done to warrant entrusting them with ten million dramatic dollars? Does Captain Kangaroo prepare its producer for Mutiny on the Bounty?

SCHAFFNER: I have a feeling you're holding back, taking less credit than you deserve.

MINER: Heaven forefend! I'm a pushover for praise, I eat it up. But you'll have to be more specific. At the moment I'm in the dark.

SCHAFFNER: The other day, I ran into Franklin Heller.

MINER: Erstwhile of What's My Line?

SCHAFFNER: The same. When he heard I was meeting with you, he couldn't wait to warn me. "Whatever you do, Frank, don't let Tony try to duck the job he did setting up the crews for every type of show television was ever likely to do. And not just predicting how many would be needed and what their assignments would be, but writing job descriptions for every damn person in the studio, or working with a mobile unit, for CBS." Did you?

MINER: You want the God's truth? I don't remember. I do know that I trained just about every crew CBS took on for a period of two years -- camera operators, sound men, cable pushers, grips and electricians. I did most certainly invent the job of Assistant Director. And, if Frank says I wrote job descriptions for all of them, I guess I must have.

SCHAFFNER: He said a lot more. He said those job descriptions were so clear and farsighted no one has ever had to change them to this day. Considering television's primitive condition at that time, that's a pretty astonishing achievement.

MINER: I'd had ten years to think about it.

VII

MINER: Let's move on, shall we? What's next?

SCHAFFNER: Pearl Harbor, December 7, 1941. Where were you when that fateful news arrived? Do you remember?

MINER: Did you ever meet anyone who didn't remember? I was casing a drain pipe in our bedroom closet in Kent. We still didn't have a phone. Allen Grover of Time, Inc. was our next door neighbor. It was a little after three when he appeared to announce: "Well, kids, put down your tools. We're at war." He was mad as a wet hen.

SCHAFFNER: Why?

MINER: A top officer at Time, Inc. having to learn about Pearl Harbor from some office boy at CBS Television trying to reach me? What could be more humbling?

SCHAFFNER: (a laugh) Nothing! But for you? What then?

MINER: I'd like to say I set down my hammer and saw and went to war. I didn't. I drove to New York that afternoon. We were on the air by 8:00 p.m. that night.

SCHAFFNER: Did you ever go into the Service?

MINER: No.

SCHAFFNER: Why not. Had the "music of the barrage" begun to fade?

MINER: (a smile) You are a stinker! No, there were problems too personal to discuss in a public forum. Suffice it to say we had one child that wasn't supposed to live. That just about says it all, doesn't it?

SCHAFFNER: Yes. But what did the next years hold in store?

MINER: I finished building our house in Kent: five rooms, three baths, plus, later, a two-car garage with guest quarters above. I wrote that 450-page "History of Television, 1932-1942." And I came perilously close to being fired for proposing a practical solution to the color impasse. Color very nearly buried television in a technical graveyard, you know.

SCHAFFNER: Let's take these activities of yours in order, shall we?

MINER: So be it. House and home? Against a great many bets by the local gentry, I finished what I had started. On May 1, 1942, we moved in, bag, baggage, three children and a mother-in-law. To say the place was "finished" is a euphemism. There were no interior doors, no flooring for the back bedroom, no door from the cellar to the outside world and no screens. Let other errant home-builders take heed. For a mother with three children eleven and under, life without screens is a diurnal hell. Bugs and bees and bats and birds have

174

no place in the castle of one's dreams. But a wider truth is here revealed. No matter how charming, how warm and inviting, let this be engraved above the door: "A house is a never-ending torment. If it weren't, it would no longer be a home." You know, you've seen the place.

SCHAFFNER: And could never quite believe it. You say you were earning a meager salary during these unsettled years?

MINER: $250 a week. (a smile) And we were living at the Dakota.

SCHAFFNER: And you surely weren't building a shack. How could you afford it? How much did it cost you?

MINER: The estimates of three architects consulted in 1940 ran between $30,000 and $35,000, and that was without well, pump or landscaping. Fran kept scrupulously detailed accounts of our outlays, even including gas, rental of a cottage for the summer, food and $10 a week to my loyal helpmate, an apprentice from CBS-TV, named Gray Lockwood. From the day the barn contractor started to lay the foundation to the day we moved in, the total cost was $9,330. I kid you not!

SCHAFFNER: But you just mentioned a contractor. How much did he do for you?

MINER: The house was made up of two barns, as you know. One I bought with the land, but it was located a half mile down the road. It had to be dismantled and put up again on a new foundation. The second was bought off the back of a truck. For this, plus two chimneys and a roof, we paid $3,410. For plumbing, including furnace and fuel tank, we paid $2,600. For all wiring and outlets we paid $285.

SCHAFFNER: That's not possible.

MINER: It really does seem unbelievable, doesn't it? And there was not one other time in my entire life when it could have been done. If ever I'd had the time, the prices of everything we used would not have been at rock bottom. When prices rose, we could never have afforded it. I learned a couple of important lessons along the way, caveats for any presumptive carpenter undertaking to build his own home. Do not start with the foundation or the frame. Leave that to others; they are the most difficult and the most exacting parts of the entire venture. Start where we did, with the sheathing. It's the easiest part of the whole undertaking. Each step thereafter becomes more sophisticated and more exacting. Thus, by the time Gray and I got around to laying the random-width oak floor in the living room, building redwood cabinets for the kitchen and a couple of Dutch doors, we were pretty damn good carpenters.

SCHAFFNER: And pretty proud of yourselves.

MINER: What else? I developed an abiding pride in craft. It taught me to honor a person's hands, to recognize how much they are able to add to a man's sense of accomplishment and self-respect.

SCHAFFNER: I get the feeling that, for you, the implications run deep.

MINER: You're right. They do. I know no way to explain it, but along with an increase in a man's facility with his hands comes an exactitude of thought, a disaffection with easygoing and unquestioning acceptance, a need for certitude. The rewards are measured in dignity and in mind's content. . . . Enough of our home in the country -- except that it was so damn beautiful.

SCHAFFNER: So, you also turned out a 450-page "History of Television" --

MINER: -- "1932 to '42" --

SCHAFFNER: -- for CBS.

MINER: Like Topsy, it grew. And I had fun. The process of learning carries, for me, an irresistible allure. Did you know, for instance, that scientists in the 19th century were exploring the transmission of electronic images -- that is, television -- well before they turned to the transmission of sound -- that is, radio?

SCHAFFNER: What stopped them?

MINER: No one came up with the type of phosphors that would both accept and discharge an electronic signal in the necessary micro-seconds. Still pictures they could handle, but, when the trolley-car began to move, a small parade of trolleys would cross the screen. I got a kick out of such arcane facts, even though they could advance my career not one cubit.

SCHAFFNER: How far is that?

MINER: Seventeen inches.

SCHAFFNER: I don't believe it.

MINER: It's true. The distance from the tip of your middle finger to the elbow. (he demonstrates) That is generally seventeen inches.

SCHAFFNER: Let's move along another seventeen inches.

MINER: Your whim is my command. When would you think CBS began television broadcasting? Many might answer 1941; some might add July 1; very few recall that CBS instituted a Television Broadcast Schedule as early as 1932. It was a primitive system known as the "Flying Spot." It was abandoned in a matter of months, but what I found fascinating was not that the same critical flaws that had baffled so many scientists in the 19th century were still the bêtes noires of engineers in 1932, but that in a mere six years RCA, or more accurately Zworykin, had gone so far toward resolving this elusive riddle that NBC was able to set up a regular schedule of broadcasting from Studio 8H.

SCHAFFNER: And the year?

MINER: 1938. It could have been '37.

SCHAFFNER: Something else you said a while back, and correct me if I'm wrong, you said that, if television had ever tried to capture a commercial audience with the equipment you were given in 1941, iconoscopes as I remember --

MINER: Right.

SCHAFFNER: -- that television might well have folded and faded away for another twenty years.

MINER: Right.

SCHAFFNER: So, something earth-shattering must have happened in the interval. What?

MINER: War and its technological prompting. It wasn't just a little bit here, and a little bit there; it was one earth-shaking event. In the fall of 1942 we were still using iconoscope tubes in our cameras. To render a picture of acceptable quality, 525 lines of definition, the acting area had to be flooded with 1,250 foot-candles of incandescent light. The heat was so intense an actress with sensitive skin could receive severe burns even through a none-too-sheer cotton blouse. It happened at NBC. While we experimented with lower intensities at CBS, and with modest success from the point of view of the creative personnel, our own engineers still endorsed RCA's insistence that 1,250 foot-candles were the minimum needed to produce an acceptable image. But unacceptable in wartime. What was needed was a wartime miracle.

On an afternoon toward the end of 1943 or the early part of '44, I, along with other representatives of the television industry, were invited to a demonstration in the old Madison Square Garden, 49th Street and 8th Avenue. First we were shown a man on horseback using the customary iconoscope camera. Then, at an appointed moment, all lights in the Garden were extinguished. We were left in total darkness. Suddenly the man on horseback struck a match and lit a candle, after which he started moving slowly around the arena. And all of this we had been able to see by the light of that single candle. One foot-candle! One against 1,250! It was my first introduction to the Image Orthicon tube.

At that moment I knew that, when the War was ended, television was going to become an insistent part of our everyday lives; I also knew that it was going to be well worth waiting for, color or no color. From that moment there was never a doubt in my mind that, if any one man should be held responsible for this awesome miracle, it was Vladimir Zworykin.

It is to the undying shame of our industry that the recognition extended to this remarkable man has been, at best, perfunctory.

Now on to how I was almost fired. It all began with color and the man who held things together at CBS during Bill Paley's absence abroad. His name was Paul Kesten. Did you ever meet him?

SCHAFFNER: No, never.

MINER: Your loss. He was one of the most able, and surely one of the most beguiling, men I ever met in the halls of broadcasting. That's what led me down the garden path. I simply could not believe that anyone so brilliant and so imaginative could not only have devised, but actively pursued, a policy so devious and so shortsighted.

SCHAFFNER: How does color fit in?

MINER: He used color to buy a few million dollars' worth of publicity for CBS Radio. He had no intention ever of advancing Columbia's competitive position in television; he would have killed television once and for all if he could have. It took a long time for me to learn, even longer for me to accept, that it had become Kesten's covert policy to cripple television in order to enhance CBS's primacy in radio.

SCHAFFNER: Did he ever articulate this policy to you?

MINER: Never. This I could only deduce from his conduct. In fact, I've never been certain that anyone at CBS was privy to his intentions with one exception.

SCHAFFNER: Who? Or don't you want to say?

MINER: At this point, what harm can it do? Moreover, this is only a conjecture. Frank Stanton. How else can one explain Frank's meteoric rise up the hierarchical ladder? I cannot accept that it was his facility with statistics alone.

SCHAFFNER: But the main source of my concern remains with Tony Miner. Where did you fit in?

MINER: Right behind the eight ball. I was a prime patsy. As Johnny went off to war, Tony Miner remained behind. This led to my being assigned to write the "History of Television." It was a forbidding assignment, but it was given out of sympathy. Generally such make-work assignments end up in severance, and so it might have in my case, were it not for the fact that a carbon of Sections I and II had somehow reached Mr. Kesten's desk. Paul was a victim of virulent arthritis; the pain was often so agonizing, sleep was out of the question. In such a moment he'd happened to pick up these draft pages of my manuscript. Some of my facts and deductions had aroused his curiosity. On the following day I was asked to meet with him for the first time.

SCHAFFNER: And this was?

MINER: 1943. In October 1942 live broadcasting had been suspended for the duration; we were limited to fifteen hours a week of film. The best of it was supplied by the British Information Services; "One of Our Aircraft is Missing" was the high-water mark on our schedule. The rest of my time was spent trying to pick up enough mathematics to grasp, I hoped, the basic principles of our electronic medium. My bible was Mathematics for the Million. Having been an abysmal student of math, I was delighted to find how much I could attribute to the inept and puerile system under which I had been taught.

        I return to the track. Paul had a mercurial imagination. His tangential flights were a source of recurrent delight over the next few months, but the pressures of immediate demands were too often too exacting. At such times he demanded of himself, and others, the utmost economy of thought and speech. It was during this period that I began to denigrate the role of the creative artist and to assign to the executive function an exaggerated degree of reward and security. In a nutshell, I began to envy the administrative posts at CBS that led up to Frank Stanton. I deluded myself into believing I was "sitting pretty," that with Paul Kesten's stimulation and assistance I would one day be placed in command of Television itself at CBS. I was even seduced into believing I would prefer the life and the power such a responsibility would entail. Now, today, I can scarcely believe that I could ever have been such an idiot child.

SCHAFFNER: Were there any signs to encourage this belief on your part?

MINER: Too few by far. I was living in a fool's paradise. Being substantially alone in my 15 Vanderbilt Avenue sanctuary, I occupied an enormous office with furniture considerably more attractive, if somewhat less expensive, than Bill Paley's at 485 Madison. The assumption of visitors was that this was with Paul Kesten's approval. To reinforce this illusion I was little by little assigned to represent the broadcasting interests of CBS Television in meetings of greater and greater importance, meetings with NBC, Philco, DuMont, General Electric, and, of course, RCA.

Such gatherings were all-but-exclusively concerned with the engineering standards that were to obtain once commercial broadcasting resumed after the war. Inevitably the most persistently disruptive element was color. CBS was the defender of the Very High Frequencies, since its mechanical color process was designed to operate within a six megacycle band; at the time no one had found a way to carry RCA's compatible color system on so limited a band width. As a result, RCA was advocating standards suitable for black-and-white only, with standards for color to follow if, and when, the industry should move into the Ultra High Frequencies. Time after time in Chicago, in Detroit, in Princeton, in Schenectady I was the fly in the ointment. My insistence that the industry agree on technical standards for both color and black-and-white to be carried on a six megacycle band was bitterly opposed by RCA and every other engineering operator in the business. I, representing CBS, stood alone. I represented a stubborn attitude that no one else could tolerate politely, or only with the greatest effort. I did not, I suspect, fully appreciate the billions of dollars at stake; I only knew I was growing more and more unhappy in my role as spoiler.

182

A sidelight on this situation reveals the extent to which I had become Mr. Kesten's "boy." When I voiced my unhappiness at the effect my position was having on television he appeared thoroughly sympathetic. His position struck me as valid and perceptive. "Thanks to Peter Goldmark, color is here," he was saying. "Whatever its shortcomings, the public will never accept black-and-white on a scale large enough to justify its gargantuan cost. I want television as much as you do, Tony, but I will not allow RCA to cripple it with a set of self-serving and specious standards. When television takes off, it's going to be in color, or it's never going to take off at all." In retrospect, it doesn't seem too illogical, does it?

SCHAFFNER: It sounds persuasive.

MINER: Such was the background as the FCC began putting pressure on the industry to forget its intramural haggling and come up with an agreement on some set of workable standards to get television off the ground. The meeting was to be held in Schenectady. In doing my homework I had found myself asking a crucial question again and again: What is so sacrosanct about the Very High Frequencies? What about the Ultra High Frequencies? In that area of the spectrum there was ample room for both black-and-white and color, compatible or incompatible. This cut the ground out from under RCA's most formidable objections, or so it appeared to me.

The following day, after listening for over an hour to the same old futile arguments, I decided to pose a hypothetical question. "If all of television were to move to the Ultra High Frequencies with enough band widths for black-and-white, RCA color and any other other future developments, would the short-term delay in launching commercial broadcasting outweigh the long-term advantages?" DuMont moved in like a Sherman tank. Before I recognized what was happening, my hypothetical question had been transmuted into a formal motion, voted on and passed. I believe I abstained.

The uproar it caused throughout both the Press and the 20th Floor at 485 Madison was not to be believed. As reported to me, Paul Kesten's rage was unbridled. I never saw him again. The man I had revered for so long had turned ugly. It was both an unpleasant and a disillusioning experience. Television was taken out of my hands by noon the following day. A short time later I was moved from my courtly offices at 15 Vanderbilt to a dust-closet on the top floor of a building opposite CBS on 52nd street -- the number eludes me, 49 I think. A few friends persuaded Paul to keep me on the payroll. I was given the meaningless title of Director of Program Development, but others were hired to take over all my prior authorities, and I was forgotten.

I was forgotten until a day in early winter, 1948, when Bill Paley, having recognized the inescapable mandate of the World Series of 1947, ordered a full-scale resumption of television broadcasting. I was released from my humble isolation for the very simple reason that there was no one else at CBS who had any idea how to go about putting on a Television Program Schedule. Thus I found myself in my old office, considerably reduced in size by now; I was given a reasonable budget to work with and was even authorized to hire an assistant of my own choosing.

It was only through a friend, however, that I discovered what Bill Paley was expecting from me, that within six months I was to come up with a prestigious hour-long dramatic series, an hour-long variety show, a half-hour situation comedy and a children's show to rival Nila Mack's Let's Pretend.

SCHAFFNER: Where are we now?

MINER: Spring, 1948.

SCHAFFNER: Was it solely the World Series that set Paley off? Or was there something else?

MINER: There was something else. Milton Berle.

184

SCHAFFNER: Of course! Mr. Television! How could I have forgotten?

MINER: Easily. It was as unpredictable as snowflakes in August. Berle was a third-rate comedian, full of energy, but tasteless, obvious and "tired." His jokes had been heard too often on other lips. The unequivocal fact remains, however, that his success was explosive, spontaneous and genuine. In less than a week word came down to me that there was to be a Program Department Staff meeting the following week. I was expected to come up with an answer to Milton Berle. That was like asking for an answer to Vesuvius. The one thing in my favor was the fact that I had pondered this problem for close to ten years and was ready to present a sober, if untested, conviction.

SCHAFFNER: And it was?

MINER: Ed Sullivan.

SCHAFFNER: Where are we? April?

MINER: May, I believe. Once I got the word I called in Jerry Danzig -- he was my assistant at the time -- and presented him with my idea. I was interested to find out how he might respond. These were the essential elements.

One: no performing MC could do in television what so many stars had done in vaudeville. Ed Wynn and Cantor, Fred Allen, et. al., had been great precisely because they had spent so many years perfecting their acts. Thus it was fair to expect that the first show any of them did would be dynamite; but with each succeeding week they'd have less and less time to polish and refine their acts. Gradually the glitter would erode. Soon, and far too soon, they'd be left with a big name, a monstrous salary, and a third-rate show. I predicted that this high road from raves to rejection would last a little under thirteen weeks.

Two: radio had provided a long-time home for Jack Benny, Fibber McGee and Molly, Burns and Allen, Easy Aces, and enough good writers had been found to maintain a decent standard of comedy. But all a star had to do in radio was read the words. If he were forced to memorize an hour-long script, he would, I believed, fold.

Three: topnotch stars were a rare and precious commodity. They would demand, and were entitled to get, exorbitant salaries, far too rich for television's blood in 1948. As a result, producers would start to compromise, to unearth stars from another day. They would never be able to set an audience on fire, even with their first performance.

Was there an answer to this grim prospect? I had long since contended that there was, provided:

a. You began looking for a non-performing MC with a proven flair for spotting talent.
b. The show must make its reputation from presenting the stars, not of today nor of yesterday, but of tomorrow.
c. The title I had chosen for the show was Top of the Town. A legal conflict forced us eventually to change "Top" to "Toast." Its host: Ed Sullivan.

Years of observation had persuaded me that no one in the business came close to matching Ed's instinct and imagination as a talent scout; Winchell was an irresponsible and spurious second best.

SCHAFFNER: And what was Jerry Danzig's response?

MINER: He found the thinking behind it interesting, but he seriously doubted that anyone in the Program Department would buy it. I must, he felt, have an alternate suggestion to offer. "Remember," he said, "that Berle has knocked the hell out of your argument that no performing star can be found."

SCHAFFNER: Tough to refute.

MINER: True. But I was convinced that Berle was a freak, the exception to prove the rule. "Name me another." He couldn't, nor could I. Feeling none too sanguine about my solution to the Berle challenge, not to mention my future at CBS, I set off for the meeting ahead with little optimism. One wildly improbable incident offered the only break in my pessimism.

SCHAFFNER: What was that?

MINER: As I arrived in the anteroom of our meeting hall, I was given a message, asking me to call my office at once. I did. It was Jerry Danzig.

"Tony, you won't believe this," he said, "but not two minutes after you left I had a visitor."

"Who?"

"Ed Sullivan's agent. He's in my office now. Ed wonders if this might not be a good time for him to break into television."

"You must be kidding."

"Wild? I just thought you ought to know."

My head was spinning. "Keep him talking. I'll call you as soon as I see how things go."

SCHAFFNER: Was Bill Paley there?

MINER: I had thought he would be, but when I arrived Frank Stanton was in the chair. Fortunately there were next to no amenities. Within five minutes Frank had called on me to present my programming response to The Texaco Star Theater. I outlined my proposal almost precisely as I presented it to you just now. When I was through there was a thick and baleful silence. The few sly looks I had spotted spoke to a polite, but final, requiem for my career. Frank Stanton had just started to move the meeting along to the consideration of other matters, when the door opened and Bill Paley walked in. As he sat down, he wasted no time.

"Well," he said, "where do we stand with Berle?"

Frank Stanton explained that I had just reviewed my one suggestion. I had no other proposal to offer.

"So, I'd like to hear it."

His hands were folded in front of him, his eyes fixed on the interlaced fingers. As I concluded I looked for any sign of approval, or disapproval. His only response was a still and painful silence. When at last he spoke, it was startlingly abrupt.

"I like it."

This was a stunner, to me as much as to anyone. No one had expected this reaction. At that point Bill turned to me for the first time.

"One thing bothers me, Tony. You make a good case for Ed Sullivan. Have you any reason to believe you can get him?"

"It happens I have. His agent's sitting in my office at this moment. He's waiting for me to tell him what chance Ed has of breaking into television this summer over CBS."

For the first time, Paley smiled. "Well, I'll be damned," he said. "What made you so sure I was going to say yes to this hunch of yours?"

Bill turned to the head of Building Operations. "What space do we have for this show of Tony's?"

There was another moment of hesitancy. Again I was able to step in; that "show of Tony's" had given me a new lease on life. "There's the Maxine Elliot," I said. "I had a couple of shows there in the twenties. It's not ideal, but it should be adequate."

Paley turned back to the Department Head. "How quickly can you have it ready?"

"Well, I'd have to look it over, Mr. Paley. Three months?"

Paley: "Too long! What about five weeks?"

The man started to falter. "Well, I don't know -- That's pretty --" His eyes met Paley's. "Yes, sir, we can make it."

"Good. We'll shoot for a Sunday toward the end of June. So, you'd better get out of here, Tony. We don't want to give Ed a chance to change his mind. But let us know how you do."

The deal was completed in record time. The date for the opening: June 20, 1948.

SCHAFFNER: That's not the way Marlo Lewis has been telling it.

MINER: (a laugh) He has reason to forget. From the start the thorn under the saddle was Marlo Lewis. It came to a showdown at one of our earliest meetings. Marlo and his sister, Monica, were outlining the first program as though it were a fait accompli, with Ed's approval thrown in. He hadn't gone far when I realized he had Ed taking part in every act on the bill. I blew my top. I pointed out that this show was not his, nor Ed's. It had been created by me, CBS owned it, and I had Ed's signature to the agreement confirming his acceptance of those terms and conditions. I further pointed out to him that the entire agreement was built around the premise that Ed was to be a non-performing MC. I wanted it to be clear to both of them that I was objecting to his appearing in any act at all, even one! Never, ever! And if in the future an exception were to be made, it would be with my specific approval, or not at all.

I had assumed that Ed was a man of his word and so, indeed, he turned out to be. Once recognizing how far Lewis had gone in ignoring the central theme of the show, he pulled back, confirming the validity of everything I had said. The meeting went on without further interruption.

Despite this explicit understanding, some days later I received a copy of a memo from Marlo to Ed presenting a list of potential performers for Show #1. It lacked the one ingredient on which the entire series was to be built. Within the hour I had called Ed and set another meeting for the following day. I reminded him that the agreed-upon theme of The Toast of the Town was a salute to the stars, not of today, much less of yesterday, but the stars of tomorrow. Anyone who could misunderstand this enough to send out the memo I had in my hand could not be trusted to produce the series. As a result I had decided to put Jerry Danzig in as producer to protect my interests and those of CBS.

I had expected Ed to explode. I was wrong. I think for the first time he began fully to understand the challenge that this show afforded him. His attitude reflected a zest and enthusiasm I had not seen before. Within another ten days he had the big headliners to give us a smash send-off. Do you remember who they were?

SCHAFFNER: I don't.

MINER: Martin and Lewis. That alone justified my belief in Ed. It also became my answer to Berle.

SCHAFFNER: And yet Berle continued to inherit the preponderant share of critical applause and public approval. Why?

MINER: It's true. Of course his public was built around a teenage and pre-teen audience and a big bar room constituency. It was enough. With little or no competition, he was able to drive his ratings through the roof. The critics of the day were hesitant to throw brickbats at the darling of such a vocal majority. Ed, on the other hand, got dreadful reviews. It took two years and more for people to learn to "love" him. But Toast of the Town was sold to Emerson within three weeks and to Ford in another week. And the series lasted upward of twenty years, twenty-three if memory serves.

SCHAFFNER: I hope you had a piece of the action?

MINER: Not one thin dime. Remember, at this point I was on the verge of getting bounced; I wasn't exactly dealing from strength. It was eventually one of the reasons for my leaving CBS, but not yet. The Columbia Broadcasting System was known for paying its top creative people less than they deserved; NBC was equally well known for paying second-rate talent a whale of a lot more than it was worth. Look at Berle. He lasted a bare decade, yet NBC underwrote him for life. Ed Sullivan also made a fortune, but he worked hard for it. Berle has been sleeping on a gilt-edged featherbed for a long, long time.

SCHAFFNER: You mean you had no part in any of the shows you created for CBS?

MINER: If I had, I'd be a lot richer man today, which it's easy to see I am not.

SCHAFFNER: Not for Studio One? Not for The Goldbergs? Not for nothin'?

MINER: Not for nothin'!

VIII

MINER: The Goldbergs, of course, was another story. It
was Gertrude Berg's baby from the start. I created a style of
camerawork to make Molly and her people come to life, but
the characters themselves were hers. She was a great woman,
no soap opera hack; she was a true writer. Her people's behavior dictated the words she gave them to speak, and when at
last Red Channels drove Phil Loeb off the air, she tried but
once to replace him. The moment she saw how shallow this
substitution was, she put up no further resistance. She closed
the show. There were so many things she might have done, so
many compromises she might have made, but for Gertrude
they would have been tantamount to a betrayal. Phil Loeb had
become Jake. They were inseparable; no other would do. No
post-mortem papa would ever be allowed to replace him as
pater familias. Phil ended by taking his own life; Gertrude
ended by letting The Goldbergs die in dignified silence.

SCHAFFNER: You were genuinely fond of her, weren't you?

MINER: I was indeed, and much more than she ever
knew. You want to know why? It was the kind of thing she'd
do that could bring a lump to my throat.

        When we first sold The Goldbergs to Sanka it was late
winter, 1949. The first Jewish feast day thereafter was the
Seder Supper. I got a supplementary budget to allow Gertrude
to honor the occasion in an appropriate fashion, with a choir
of cantors. As it turned out, it was, for me, a deeply moving

and spiritual occasion. I tried to convey to her the impact the show had had on me, but even as I spoke, I sensed the words were pedestrian and inadequate. Her intuition must have compensated for my inept maunderings more fully than I knew, since some six weeks before Christmas she took me aside and said, "Tony, you gave us a most beautiful Seder last spring. Now it's our turn. Here!"

What she handed me was an altogether charming Christmas script. But, in addition to its charm, it was economically a whopper. One item alone was a sizable choir, sixteen to twenty voices, as I recall. For this I selected the choir from the Church of the Blessed Sacrament on West 71st Street.

The program was less than half over when the phone began to ring. A segment of New York's Jewish community was incensed at our singing "Adeste Fidelis" in a Kosher home on Christmas Eve. When the program was over and Gertrude learned that the CBS switchboard was still jammed with complaints, she flew into a rare but awesome fury. A production assistant was just picking up the receiver in the Control Room. Gertrude's 240 pounds swept through that door like an Avenging Angel.

Grabbing the instrument out of the youngster's hand, she announced: "From now on all calls on this phone are mine. No one else is to touch this receiver, is that clear?"

With that she lashed out at that poor benighted caller with an invective born of Biblical outrage. In essence she was saying: "This is Gertrude Berg. This call of yours makes me ashamed of my own people. If our good, Christian producer could give us a lavish and profoundly reverent Seder, what right have you to tell me that I, a Jew, cannot be equally generous on one of his holiest feast-days?"

Her words were incandescent, her anger was of the ages. I learned the following day that it was 2:30 a.m. before she put down that phone for the last time. She was a big, a very big lady, and I loved every pound of her.

SCHAFFNER: But The Goldbergs was not the next thing you did after Toast of the Town? Or was it?

MINER: I'm not sure. You see we shot the pilot a long time before we first went on the air. Gertrude had a lot of rewriting to do after the try-out; in addition we had a rough time finding a replacement for Menasha Skulnik as the Uncle.

SCHAFFNER: Was that Eli Mintz?

MINER: That's right. And what a sweetheart he was. That was Gertrude again. I couldn't understand why she was so hell-bent on getting rid of Menasha. He'd been funny as hell, I thought. "I know," she said. "Funny but false. I need someone true."

SCHAFFNER: And was Eli ever true!

MINER: To the marrow. He deluged the show with warmth. She was intolerant, that Molly. Tricks she would not have. In any case the next show to hit the air was Studio One, November 7, 1948. Is that what you've been after?

SCHAFFNER: Yes. What prompted you to select a slick-paper potboiler to launch so dignified a series?

MINER: Showmanship! A master stroke of intuitive show-manship.

SCHAFFNER: Stop pinning laurels on yourself. It was a bust, and you know it. Why not admit it?

MINER: It was not. It was smart as hell. What made Frank Capra? Hamlet? Never no how! What made Frank Capra

194

was It Happened One Night -- and, if that wasn't a slick-paper potboiler, I don't know whereof the "walls of Jericho" were built. But there was a more profound compulsion that made me select The Storm. It was the only psychological mystery I'd been able to find that offered no solution to its quandary.

SCHAFFNER: The one flaw that every critic cited in that production was the fact that at the end The Storm left the audience dangling.

MINER: And talking as they dangled. Right? Like "Lucky Strike Green has gone to war." No one knew what the hell it meant, but it made George Washington Hill an everlasting fortune. This much I'll confess. I didn't expect Harriet Van Horne to get so apoplectic. But it was a small price to pay for all the free publicity she gave us.

SCHAFFNER: And you expect me to believe it was delib- erate, that this was the decisive reason for your selecting this story?

MINER: In all candor, yes, it was. And this for proof. The continuing mystery was an integral part of the original story. I did not invent it, but it caught my fancy. I knew at once it was the show I wanted to do, not in spite of the fact that, but precisely because, it would cause people to talk. One thing I'll concede. I'd have given my shirt to open with an original. It was a sign of weakness to have had to open with an adaptation.

SCHAFFNER: What was wrong with Julius Caesar?

MINER: Nothing aside from an empty house. I was not content to open with a succès d'estime.

SCHAFFNER: But you had all of literature to draw from.

MINER: That's what everyone expected. That was not for me. And even though there seemed to be a plethora of classic material, I'd long since discovered that this was a delusion. How much dramatic material has the Western World produced in the last 2,500 years? Let the three networks schedule three dramatic hours a week and they'd chew up a little over 1400 hours in one year. By the middle of the second year, they'd be scraping the bottom of the barrel. Oh, I know all right! I know I was being a spendthrift at one a month, but in those carefree days we shed few, if any, tears for the pains of the morrow. But this argument applied to the series, not to the opener. For the opener I wanted an argument.

Yet the threat remained. How long, I kept asking myself, how long is it going to take for us to discover, nourish and develop a school of recognized creative writers?

SCHAFFNER: Was recognition necessary?

MINER: No. It was a bad choice of words. Let's say "skilled." And then there was my tandem concern, or better, "consuming" concern. What good would it be, I kept asking myself, to turn out a goodly stockpile of sensitive and witty scripts, if there were no one on hand to give those stories a visual life and a zing? -- which led to a clarity of purpose on my part. With Studio One, with all my productions in fact, the accent was to be on direction, on laying down the road bed, the ties and the rails, to carry television's some-time Super Chief. And so, The Storm. It was a director's holiday. It would have to hold the fort until television's own Aeschylus could spring to life.

SCHAFFNER: Was Paul Nickell the first director you took on?

MINER: That's right. I'd seen his production of The Medium.

SCHAFFNER: Out of Philadelphia, wasn't it?

MINER: Right. I'd signed him by 11:00 a.m. the following day. As you remember, Studio One did not operate on a weekly schedule until 1949. We began with The Storm, which I directed. Then there was a light comedy with John Conti which Paul and I directed together; then The Medium which Paul directed alone; then an original by Joe Liss with Katherine Bard --

SCHAFFNER: Mrs. Martin Manulis --

MINER: You joined us right after the start of the new year. Do you remember the date?

SCHAFFNER: Not exactly.

MINER: Nor I. You and Paul were my sacrificial lambs. You were there to create a style of visual storytelling for the industry. You had only to trip and your heads would have been on the block. It was a risky business for all of us, but we were saved by two wholly unpredictable happenstances. While you and Paul were creating a style of camerawork, Fred Coe over at NBC was supplying the other essential ingredient. He had had one early production, Bedelia, which he had written himself, but admittedly he was no writer. From the start he had made it his business to find and train a school of writers. I was no writer either, but I was literate and relatively expert in structural craftsmanship. As a result, the Studio One schedule was composed almost exclusively of adaptations made by me, but its reputation was made by its quality of direction, by the principles and practices it introduced, and by the technical flexibility you and Paul displayed.

Philco meanwhile lived on the growing imagination and effectiveness of the stable of writers Fred Coe had assembled: Paddy Chayefsky, Robert Alan Aurthur, et. al. It was only after I'd left Studio One that it began to develop its own roster of creative writers, beginning with Rod Serling and Reginald Rose.

SCHAFFNER: You did most of the adaptations for Studio One. That we know. What did that mean in a year?

MINER: A silo-mix of drudgery, slavery and exuberance. We were putting on forty-four shows a year at the start. The first year I wrote thirty-nine. I continued to write upward of thirty shows a season until the spring of '52 when I moved over to NBC.

SCHAFFNER: And you produced, often directed, The Goldbergs?

MINER: Yes, but I gave up the direction after ten to twelve weeks. Walter Hart took over after that.

SCHAFFNER: And you created and produced Toast of the Town?

MINER: Yes, but that could be misleading. I launched the show; Jerry Danzig kept things in line over the summer, but the whole thing was back in Ed's hands well before Studio One first hit the air.

SCHAFFNER: And you produced a children's show that won the Peabody.

MINER: Mr. I. Magination. I had less to do with that than with any of the others. Paul Tripp, an old friend from my theatre days, brought it to me. I saw it through its opening; thereafter the Pincus Brothers took over. (a smile) That's why it did so much less well than my other ventures, I expect.

SCHAFFNER: I've asked you "How?" a couple of times already. I'm embarrassed to asked it again.

MINER: So let's just agree it's not humanly possible and move on.

SCHAFFNER: One further mystery. How were you able to con Margaret Sullavan into doing the first (Studio One) show for you?

MINER: Ineffable charm! O.K., O.K. -- you want the truth? It was half a matter of gall on my part; half a series of unhappy events altogether unbeknownst to me in advance; and, of course, timing, the most exquisite and inspired timing. It began with the fact that Fran and I had been unusually close to Maggie and Leland (Hayward) ever since Fran and Maggie had been together in Stage Door. We were living in the Dakota then; Maggie and Leland had an apartment directly across the Park. Night after night the four of us would don roller skates and spend an hour or so exploring the paths and by-ways between their place and ours.

It was a carefree and joyous time; we felt, and acted like, children again. It was the kind of association that breeds a lasting intimacy that even years of separation can do little to tarnish.

What I knew about Maggie in October, 1948 was this:

a.   She was a wonderful and loyal friend.
b.   She had had a rough time in England with The Voice of the Turtle. The British press had had little time for the play and had been cruelly critical of Maggie. The run had been cut short, and she was on her way home. She was, I imagine, more receptive to my offer than she would have been at any other time.
c.   Maggie had one of the most inquisitive minds I ever encountered. It was, for me, one of her most irresistible charms. This much I foresaw. If

any proposal of mine were to win her approval in the fall of 1948, it should be the one that offered her the prospect of a daring adventure, of playing a part in a new and untested medium. Television would be fighting my battles for me.

And so I sent her a wire, saying I had a show for her when she got back. Within twenty-four hours I had her answer: "Yeah, yeah!" And she hadn't even seen a script. It was that simple.

SCHAFFNER: There were rumors around that she behaved badly during rehearsals of The Storm.

MINER: Calumny. She was no half-assed amateur. She was a professional. She worked like a dog and without complaint. There was one moment during the dress when she blew up, but for a compelling reason. More than half the last act of The Storm was a soliloquy, during which all her actions had to conform to the words that were spoken. Since these "words" were, in fact, thought, we had cut a record in advance to which Maggie could listen and do as her thoughts prescribed.

At the dress all was going well until I saw her hesitate. She started in one direction, then stopped; started in another direction and stopped. Suddenly she let out a frightening sound, beat on the piano with her bare fists, and raced out of the studio to her dressing room, screaming: "I can't do it! I can't do it!"

I was stunned. So, I discovered, was everyone on the set -- with one exception, the stage manager. Seeing me start toward Maggie's dressing room, he caught up to me.

"You know what I think, Tony? I think Miss Sullavan is going deaf."

"Deaf?"

"Yes, sir. The sound on that recorder was too low, but not all that low. It was still audible. But for a deaf person it would have been incomprehensible. That could scare the hell out of anyone."

Maggie had never said a word. But, as I arrived at her dressing room, she threw herself into my arms, sobbing, "Oh, Tony, forgive me! Forgive me! I just can't do it! I can't do it! I can't hear one word. Not one!"

"Listen to me, Maggie," I said. "Is it true? Are you going deaf?"

She loosened her grip on my arms so abruptly it startled me. I was unprepared for the sudden quiet and practical tone. "Yes. I've got to have an operation. But I didn't think it was going to catch up with me this quickly. Now look what I've done to you."

Her voice had begun to quaver again. "But I can't do the show, Tony dear. I'd just louse up everything for you. Can you ever forgive me?"

"No!" This came like a slap in the face. "No, I can't forgive you, because you haven't gone deaf at all. The recorder wasn't working correctly, that's all, and they probably have it fixed by now."

"I don't believe it!"

"Come and see."

Five minutes later the panic had gone, and we were ready to start the last act again. So much for her bitchery during rehearsals.

SCHAFFNER: How did Bill Paley react to your success with Studio One?

MINER: That's hard to say. We never became intimate; I met with him perhaps a dozen times in the next three years. On the other hand I never again hesitated to pick up the phone when my autonomy was threatened.

SCHAFFNER: Did that happen often?

MINER: No -- two or three times, perhaps. How could it have been otherwise? My post-Schenectady demotions had occurred less than three years before. For those who had been granted the authorities I had once held, I was an object of corporate inconsequence; I most certainly was not a threat. Some of them were slow to recognize the sea-change that had taken place between me and the 20th Floor in a scant six months. When they awoke to the realities, their resentment of me was swift and abiding, but so long as Bill Paley supported my judgments there was little my intramural detractors could do. In matters of policy, CBS and Paley were interchangeable.

SCHAFFNER: I won't argue.

MINER: Some of the incidents were ugly; some were merely absurd, like the Lamp Division of Westinghouse refusing to sponsor The Light That Failed. What made it so ridiculous was the fact that they'd had our schedule for a good six weeks. Can you imagine what mileage a smart advertiser could have got out of such a windfall?

SCHAFFNER: "Kipling's light may fail, but never a bulb from Westinghouse!"

MINER: A noble opportunity! But after wasting six full weeks of precious time, they waited until the Saturday run-through before Air to blow the whistle. And can you believe this? They had the crust to take it all the way to Bill Paley.

      It began quietly enough with a call to me from Al Scalpone at the agency. Al wanted me to know that, since by the Westinghouse system of rotation this week's production was allocated to the Lamp Division, we'd have to find another title for the show. I got out of it by saying I didn't have the authority to make such a change, particularly with a semi-classic author like Kipling. I referred him to Hubbell Robinson, then Program Director for CBS Television. From then on everything came to me secondhand.

Hub, I was told, passed the buck to Jack Van Volkenburg, President of CBS Television.

Jack in turn passed the buck to Frank Stanton, President of CBS. Frank is purported to have said no one but William S. Paley could rule on such a matter. He suggested that Harry Ommerle, Assistant Program Director, might make the arrangements. A short time later Harry was on the phone.

"Oh, Tony, Tony, Tony, why can't you ever cause just a little trouble?"

I began to laugh. "Have you been burning your fingers on a light bulb, Harry?"

"It isn't funny!"

"So where do we stand? Has it gone all the way to Paley yet?"

"It has! And do you know what? He won't talk to anyone but the President of Westinghouse."

SCHAFFNER: And did the President of Westinghouse comply?

MINER: Yes. No -- wait! I shouldn't say that. To be thoroughly honest the final outcome is very possibly apocryphal. But for what it's worth, here it is. The President of Westinghouse was so worked up he threatened to cancel the entire series. Paley was not impressed. Why should he have been? By that time he could have sold Studio One any time he wanted to for twice the $8,100 Westinghouse had paid for it.

"Go ahead," he is reputed to have said. "Do what you feel you have to. But the Kipling title will remain."

SCHAFFNER: And so it ended?

MINER: So it ended. No, not quite. There remained one more sardonic twist, and at my expense. The Light That Failed had been a favorite of mine as a boy. The moment I thought of it for Studio One, I didn't even bother to re-read it; I simply shipped it off to Joe Liss, one of our best writers, for adaptation. When some two weeks before rehearsals the first draft arrived, I pounced on it eagerly. I was in for a shock. Imagine my fury on discovering that Joe Liss, for no reason I could fathom, had so jazzed up the end that the whole thing had become sleazy and salacious. Into Kipling's tender and beautiful love story, he'd introduced a Lesbian theme. Lesbian? Kipling?

I was still so angry when Joe got to my office I lit into him before he had a chance to speak. I lashed out at those bloody little schoolboy pranks he thought were funny. I tore him apart unmercifully, and I meant every word of it.

"Tony," he said gently as I finally gave him an opening. "Tony, baby, when did you last read The Light That Failed?

"What's that got to do with it?" I said.

"Read it, baby. Read it! I didn't add that Lesbian angle. Kipling did. I just softened it a little."

I re-read The Light That Failed that night. Joe was right. Kipling hadn't even minced his words. That was the story Kipling had meant to tell, and he'd told it. I never again scheduled an adaptation without re-reading the original.

SCHAFFNER: And what did Westinghouse do? Blow its top again?

MINER: No. They were so consumed with anguish over that failing bulb, they had no time to notice that they had, at one and the same time, given their stamp of approval to a blaringly homosexual love story. Lord, we mortals!

SCHAFFNER: Didn't John Crosby take you apart for taking unforgivable liberties with Kipling?

MINER: He did. He, too, had failed to re-read The Light That Failed.

SCHAFFNER: And Paley?

MINER: His conduct had been enough to assure me that his trust in my judgment had not been corroded. This became doubly evident when we met with Jack Benny.

SCHAFFNER: Why were you meeting with Benny?

MINER: He was planning to branch out into television. It was a short meeting, but, from my point of view, assuring. Bill had called to ask if I'd sit in and listen to what Benny had to propose. For nearly an hour Jack outlined the kind of show he and his staff were considering. One thing seemed to cause him the greatest concern: Fred Allen had tried television and failed, dismally.

SCHAFFNER: Whoa, whoa! When did Fred ever try television? He emceed The Colgate Comedy Hour -- I think that's what they called it -- but it was only a quiz show.

MINER: Right you are. Only this. As early as 1944 I was asked by Jim Seward --

SCHAFFNER: Arthur Godfrey's mentor?

MINER: -- and a love of a human being, to see if I could find a way to introduce Arthur and Fred Allen to television. Godfrey taught me one thing: there was such a thing as a "professional amateur." If he went into television, he'd have to make them accept him on those terms, or not at all.

Arthur had to be spontaneous at all costs. He could never tell a joke a second time. As a result he could never learn a script, because each word had to be spoken on the air for the first time. That's a little hard on the other actors trying to pick up their cues. It was why Arthur went as far as he did in radio, but could never really make it in television.

SCHAFFNER: Professional amateur! Now I've learned something. And Allen?

MINER: I never worked with Fred, but we made two all-out efforts to re-create Allen's Alley. One I did myself; one was done by Ben Feiner, Dick Rodgers's brother-in-law. Both were abysmal failures. Fred saw them with Jim Seward and was, as I've heard, all but sick at his stomach. This I assume is what Jack had got from Fred. How was he to make sure the same thing didn't happen to him?

At this point Paley turned to me for the first time. "Well, Tony, what answer do you have to that?"

"I don't believe Mr. Benny has as much to worry about as he seems to think."

Jack was immediately on the attack. "Why not? Fred's a great comedian. His failure gives me every right to be uneasy."

"I can't agree with you, Mr. Benny. Fred Allen failed, and Norman Corwin failed, and so will a lot more of the best people in radio."

"That's what I'm saying! I'm out of radio too, you know."

"But they were pure radio, Mr. Benny. You were not. You were pure vaudeville. They relied on fantasy; that was the way their minds worked. What was Allen's Alley? What was

Fibber McGee's 'closet'? What was Curly's caterpillar? Rich, delicious fantasy! And none of it, none of it can ever be re-created in television. It defies translation. I know, I tried it. But you and Rochester could walk onto the stage of the Palace tomorrow, and they'd still be laughing."

Bill was smiling. "Hear that, Jack? That's why I asked Tony to join us."

"I hope he's right. God, do I hope."

"His batting average has been pretty good so far. He predicted that Ed Sullivan would outlast Berle."

"That I'll have to see."

Paley laughed. "You will."

And that was the sum of my contribution to The Jack Benny Show. I never saw, nor heard from, him again. But this brief encounter had done something beneficent to my peace of mind. It had assured me that Bill Paley's support was not going to be transient, as I had too often feared. He had a reputation for infidelity.

SCHAFFNER: And you were having a great time, right?

MINER: The best! Oh, the theatre had meant a lot, and its rewards had been tremendous, but television was allowing me to do so many things I would never have had a chance of doing had I spent my full eighty years in the theatre. Turgenev's Smoke, Coriolanus, The Ambassadors, The Wings of the Dove, Waterfront Boss, Eudora Welty's Shadowy Third, The Medium. Those are but random selections from a roster of thirty-five to forty plays a year. And so long as we remained among the top ten shows on the air, and we did, who was to say me "Nay"? Not all our productions were of the best -- some made my skin curl -- but there was enough excitement, literary stimulation and audience applause in my four year tenure to make it a richly rewarding part of my life.

SCHAFFNER: How may young actors did you discover
during those years? Do you remember?

MINER: A sizable number. There had to be; without
them we'd have starved. Our budgets were pitifully small. I
think I've mentioned that Studio One was sold to Westinghouse
for $8,100. We'd been forced to adopt a top salary of $750 a
show, including two full weeks of rehearsal. That wasn't going
to buy us Cary Grant or Humphrey Bogart, or Lauren Bacall
even. At that price we had to discover our own "stars of
tomorrow" just as much as Toast of the Town.

SCHAFFNER: Some of whom being -- ?

MINER: Anne Bancroft (she was Anne Italiano then, and
more often Anne Marno), Chuck Heston, Grace Kelly, Don
Murray, John Cassavetes, Yul Brynner, Felicia Montealegre,
Maria Riva --   Felicia was, as you remember, a concert
pianist from South America; she became Mrs. Leonard
Bernstein. Maria Riva was Marlene Dietrich's daughter. They
were good, very good, but they were both victims of their own
successes.

SCHAFFNER: Overexposure destroyed them.

MINER: And what a loss. It's criminal to throw away
talent that rare.

SCHAFFNER: But how did "The Red Director of New
York" escape the clutches of "Red Channels"?

MINER: Pure accident. And it could have been a pretty
gruesome decade. You may recall that the original production
of Bury the Dead was a benefit for a far-left magazine raising
money for Loyalist Spain. That put me on every sponsor's list
for radical and Communist causes. They were springing up like

toadstools in the middle thirties. These solicitations were nothing to me but junk mail, one glance and into the trash-basket. One, however, caught my eye; there on the masthead, big as life, was Worthington Miner's name as Honorary Sponsor. I was outraged, and I let them know how I felt in an extremely stiff and abrupt letter. I did not know them, I knew nothing about their cause, I recognized no other name on the masthead aside from my own, and I wanted my name removed at once. A few days later I got a reply asserting that, since I had raised no objection to their original solicitation, they had understandably assumed my acceptance. They never mentioned removing my name, which was still being carried on their letterhead.

I started to throw it out, when some small voice began whispering: "Don't. Call a lawyer."

SCHAFFNER: And you did!

MINER: And I did. And thank God! When I showed this missive to Howard Reinheimer, my then attorney, he was quick to let me know I'd been well-advised to come to him. Their next step would probably have been to present me with a bill for $1,000 as the recognized contribution expected of an Honorary Sponsor.

To settle the matter Howard wrote two letters. The first was to the specific organization which had been using my name. The second was a form letter of refusal to any other solicitation I might receive in the future. The first did what it was supposed to do; I was harassed no longer. Copies of the second letter were used by me in response to every solicitation I received for the next twenty years.

SCHAFFNER: I'm not sure I understand why that was so important.

MINER: Nor did I, not until the fifties came along and Joe McCarthy's hounds began to bay. Then I knew, and well. Do you have any idea how many innocent people were blacklisted for no other reason than that their names, or their husbands' names, or some aunt's name in Walla Walla, had appeared on the masthead of some so-called "anti-American" organization? It was only then that I began to appreciate the lethal nature of those letterheads. In Joe McCarthy's hands they had become the precursors of the cruel and senseless character assassinations of the early fifties. In fact, had it not been for Howard Reinheimer's legal foresight, I, too, might have been riding the tumbrils.

SCHAFFNER: What did you do?

MINER: I did nothing as courageous as Ed Murrow's <u>See It Now</u>, nor as effective as Eisenhower's use of the Army and Joseph Welch to stifle that inane giggle. But I did speak out against the absurdity of CBS's position.

SCHAFFNER: The loyalty oath?

MINER: The loyalty oath, no less. And I did hire a sizable number of actors, actresses and writers whose names adorned the pages of "Red Channels."

SCHAFFNER: How did you get away with it?

MINER: I cheated. When faces were known, Margo's, for example, I could do nothing even though I knew for certain that she was totally innocent of the charges brought against her. But when people's faces were not well known from either pictures or television, I would call them in and offer them a part, provided they were willing to appear anonymously or under an assumed name. With writers I'd let the wives sign the contracts for the property, using their maiden names. It was sleazy and shame-making, but the alternatives were a little too ugly to tolerate.

SCHAFFNER: And what was CBS's official posture?

MINER: Indefensible. They continued, as I've said, to ask everyone to sign a pledge stating that he was not, nor ever had been, a member of the Communist Party nor of any other organization sympathetic to the Communist cause. The minute I got wind of this decision I hied me to Joe Ream's office. Joe was Executive Vice-President of CBS at the time. I had a warm spot in my heart for Joe; certainly nothing in our past association foreshadowed such absurdity on his part. I pointed out the futility of CBS's position. The first to sign a pledge of this sort would be the hardcore card-carriers. I'd ridden up in the elevator with two of them that very day. The victims would be the innocent, the ignorant and the kind of heart, those whose humanity had been stirred by the cruel injustice of the thirties, those to whom our brand of freedom meant the most.

SCHAFFNER: How many were eventually caught in the dragnet? Five? Six?

MINER: One! She was, as I remember, one of the Typing Pool. She was also a member of a rock-ribbed Republican family from New Jersey. She had refused to sign as a matter of principle. "No decent American," she was reported to have said, "could ever sign a document of this sort." Soon thereafter CBS's insistence was withdrawn.

SCHAFFNER: A female David! That's nice! And you? Did you ever get caught?

MINER: Once. I thought for a time I was about to be bloodied. I was scared to the marrow.

SCHAFFNER: (a smile) You were scared?

MINER: I was that! I was over fifty. I was just beginning
to reap the harvest from ten years of patience and reluctant
anonymity. With three children of our own, and two more we
had undertaken to raise, we were barely skimming by on my
weekly paycheck. We had not one penny of savings. To be
blacklisted at that moment meant destitution. To have acceded
would have demanded the surrender of every decent instinct I
had inherited. Fortunately the crisis lasted a scant forty-eight
hours.

SCHAFFNER: Tell me.

MINER: It began by my being summoned to give a depo-
sition respecting the "personnel and policies" of Studio One. I
was to report to the offices of a man whose name I can't
recall just now, a former agent with the FBI, who was heading
up the investigation of the New York theatre by the Sub-
Committee on Un-American Activities. His Bible was, of
course, "Red Channels." When I brought word of this to Joe
Ream, his response was simple and direct.

"Get down there tomorrow morning, Tony, and be ten
minutes ahead of time. Keep your mouth shut, and your eyes
and ears open. If you get stuck for an answer, plead ignorance
and get out."

My interrogator turned out to be ideally cast -- tall,
dark, handsome with a gracious smile and enough charm to
disarm any unwary victim. Fortunately I'd been through enough
ugliness with Phil Loeb and The Goldbergs to be acutely alert.
What did stun me was to discover how little homework he had
done. He never associated my name with the Phil Loeb affair,
much less with Bury the Dead, Let Freedom Ring, or my other
left-wing excursions in the theatre.

In the first hour he did a great deal of talking; I said
virtually nothing. Quite inadvertently, however, I had confessed
to having spent two years overseas in World War I. This was,
for this fellow, the best character witness I could have produced. "Regular Army, huh? Man!" His grin was as wide as a
whale's yawn.

212

SCHAFFNER: How wide is that?

MINER: More than seventeen inches. And you're interrupting. Grin, or no grin, my service overseas was scarcely
relevant to the Hollywood Ten, the loyalty oath, or the wholesale blacklisting that was taking place then, that moment, in
New York.

When at last he recognized that he was going to get
nowhere with a simple interlocutory approach, he decided to
bring things to a head. Reaching into a drawer of his desk, he
brought out a piece of paper on which there appeared a list of
names. At a glance I knew precisely who they were. First of
all, they were, without exception, ardent supporters of Senator
McCarthy; second, they were all, with possibly three or four
exceptions, actors of mediocre ability.

"Mr. Miner," he was saying, "you're obviously a good
human being and a good American. We don't want to cause you
any unnecessary trouble, and I'm sure you don't want to have
any trouble with us. So, just glance over this list of names.
Most of them will be familiar to you, I'm sure."

"Yes," I said, "I think I know all but a couple of them."

"Good! So you know they're first-rate performers, the
kind it would be advantageous for you to use."

He was looking at me searchingly, but I remained
silent, my eyes still intent on studying the list.

"Now then," he continued, "I can't imagine that you
would arbitrarily refuse to use any of these people in one of
your productions. I rather think, moreover, that, if you did find
work for, say, a dozen or more of these people in the next few
months, we'd have very little fault to find with Studio One's
operations. What do you say?"

I offered no swift response; my mind was churning.
When I did finally respond, I followed Joe Ream's advice.

"Well I'll tell you, that would involve a policy decision beyond my authority to make."

I began to fold the paper. He reached for it, but I was too quick for him. I'd slipped it into my pocket before he could get hold of it.

"I realize you'd like a prompt response, so I'll be in touch with you as soon as possible." I was on my feet, my hand extended. "It's been good meeting you."

He was far from happy as I left, but far happier, I imagine, than he was a half hour later. The tongue-lashing Joe Ream administered, once I'd given him my report, was a masterpiece. It was the last I heard from "Red Channels." It was surely one of our country's most shameful hours.

SCHAFFNER: Sickening. But what effect did any of this have on television and you?

MINER: Who can estimate? The theatre, in the broadest usage of the word, always reflects the changing fashions of its time. But revolutions that have in the past taken millenia to achieve, have taken no more than decades in our lifetime. From such a perspective the McCarthy era is no more than a bubble of foam. What will live are those events in whose maturing our standard of morals, our system of values, and our day-by-day conduct have been restructured.

SCHAFFNER: Such as?

MINER: The automobile, the telephone, the airplane, relativity, and the voyage to the moon. But perhaps more cataclysmic than all others -- television. McLuhan's warning should be ignored at our peril. The breakdown of linear thought may, in the long run, have a more radical effect on the workings of our minds than any event since the invention of speech.

IX

MINER: During the fifties I became obsessed with the growth of television; I failed to appreciate how compelling a sense of futility had begun to infect the thoughts and philosophies of our Western World. There had been such energy, such optimism, such raging impatience among the few of us sharing the birth pangs of this new medium, we had become more and more isolated from the society around us, more and more out of harmony with the drumbeats of the day.

During the McCarthy era, escapism offered a major inducement for moving West. The East, specifically New York, was more receptive to Ed Murrow and See It Now or You Are There with Walter Cronkite. Studio One, Philco and Play of the Week fared better with more mature, more thoughtful themes. Hollywood's highest boast was I Love Lucy. This is not meant to demean Lucy as a series. Indeed, it represented a very high order of farce that well deserved both the praise, and the popularity, it achieved. But if I had cited My Mother, the Car, the stultifying influence that the hegira to Hollywood entailed would be more clearly understood.

It wasn't until the sixties that I began to appreciate how firmly the cults of permissiveness, self-depreciation and negativism had taken hold of young people's minds. The pattern of their lives was being cast in disillusionment and self-disgust. The young were beset with insecurity and loss of faith. What they did not appreciate -- and too few of them yet do, even today -- what they failed to see was that a large measure of the hideous mistakes we, our government, that is, had made were spawned from a very high order of selfless and idealistic

214

intentions. The clarion call of John F. Kennedy's inaugural was a bellwether to the ghastly stain of Vietnam and My Lai. This was the miasma that I, as an educator at the American Academy of Dramatic Arts, felt obligated to expose and dispel.

Fury and violence were brought into the home primarily by our network newscasts. Reporters did not describe the war; they showed it. Aping the actualities, the producers in television began to introduce more and more spurious and hyped-up violence in the prime time entertainment hours. While the honest writers became sullen, inarticulate and mute, the hacks and opportunists in television enjoyed a heyday of popularity with the cotton bullets, tomato juice and synthetic smoke. By that time it no longer mattered whether you were in Burbank or New York, no one dared touch the truth, it was too hideous and too saddening. That was left to the evening's news. For drama, television's daily diet was a flight from reality. Yet in so doing, it was not holding up a false mirror to our age. It was simply saying that our life had deteriorated to a masquerade.

SCHAFFNER: And what became of your one-time liberal ideas?

MINER: I was lucky; I had shed them well before. Oh, not all. I still hold by a number of iconoclastic convictions. But for that ironclad pattern of thought and feeling I long since had lost the taste. . . .

Now we are in 1980, and when in all of television's history, Golden Age and all, have we been offered as much maturity, passion, eloquence and music as we have over the last year? Martha Graham, Twyla Tharp, and Mummenschantz; The Philharmonic with Isaac Stern, Ytzak Perlman, Pinchas Zuckerman and Zubin Mehta; The Naked Civil Servant with John Hurt; Bill Moyers's interview with Max Lerner; the American Hockey Team in the Winter Olympics; Shogun and Playing for Time; and perhaps the top of them all, the remarkable science series by Carl Sagan.

216

SCHAFFNER: Sagan has been harshly criticized.

MINER: Would you prefer I go back to Kenneth Clark?

SCHAFFNER: It would still be eighty percent PBS.

MINER: Of course. Anything good will always flourish where the advertiser is least in evidence. Give it time. The wonder is that so sizable a public has already been garnered. Soon there will be a crop of sponsors as well. Why? Because the anathema of today is often, and happily, the kiss of success tomorrow.

I left television because I felt I had fulfilled my aspirations with The Iceman. But television is a long way from fulfilling its potential. And naive as my faith may have seemed in 1939, it hasn't lessened, only changed.

SCHAFFNER: But in the beginning, before any of the caveats were discovered, where did you find, and how did you choose, the story lines for forty-odd shows a year?

MINER: Good man! Up to now, no one has ever asked that question. And that's odd, because I have long felt it to be one of the most vital reasons for the success of Studio One under my four-year tyranny.

I spent many a restless night debating an answer to the question: What must a dramatic series have to make it both prestigious and popular? The first part of the answer was simple, good writing. There I was lucky. I had the best product of the ages to choose from, everything from The Iliad to Catcher in the Rye. There were two bugs in the cookie mix, however. Would such a schedule be popular? And how many of those stories could be told in fifty-two minutes and thirty seconds of playing time? In both cases the answer was the same. Not "None," but "Very few." I knew from the outset that we could never do <u>Hamlet</u>. All else aside, it was about two hours too long. I did think I could do <u>June Moon</u>, however. It was a sad awakening. We had an all-but-ideal cast of players to which we added two fabulous youngsters.

SCHAFFNER: Jack Lemmon. Who else?

MINER: Eva Marie Saint. Nonetheless <u>June Moon</u> was the saddest flop of our entire first season. Why? Because by the time we had cut the script to <u>Studio One</u> size, it was no longer a hit show, it was a louse. I should have known better; I should have known that by the time Ring Lardner and George Kaufman had finished with a script there would not be a word left that wasn't essential. The very few Broadway shows that made first-rate television were scripts that ran out of steam by the end of Act II. We got some pretty good shows that way; simply by cutting Act III we were halfway home.

SCHAFFNER: How then do you account for the success of <u>Julius Caesar</u>?

MINER: That was both rare and fortuitous. My reason for choosing <u>Julius Caesar</u> as our first bout with Shakespeare was in response to a long-time conviction of mine that there was an egregious flaw in the manuscript as it had come down to us. I got an inordinate kick out of this chance to expose Mark Antony for the hypocrite he was, or the one that Shakespeare, I was convinced, had meant him to be.

SCHAFFNER: What flaw?

MINER: A single line. "This was the noblest Roman of them all." In all the texts that have, to my knowledge, come down to us, this line has always been spoken by Mark Antony, thus revealing a generosity of spirit and nobility of mind that could only befit a man of royal stature. For this, and for no other reason I can imagine, Mark Antony has been cast and portrayed as a hero. I don't believe it. I don't believe it's what Shakespeare intended, and I don't believe it's what Shakespeare wrote.

SCHAFFNER: What, then, did he write?

MINER: Oh, he wrote the line all right, but he wrote it to be spoken by the future Emperor of Rome, not by the traitor of Actium. It was written for Octavius. In the pragmatic operations of the Globe Theatre, however, Octavius was a bit part, played almost certainly by a young apprentice. Mark Antony was quite as surely played by a star. That line was too juicy a plum to give to an underling, but what it could do for Mark Antony was inestimable. Villain he may have been, but at the last we were granted a glimpse of the nobility that lay beneath. Because of his recognized stature in the company, he simply purloined the line and made it his own. (a laugh) The dog!

SCHAFFNER: Did you give it to Octavius?

MINER: No, that would have been a little too high-handed. I did something more subtle. The actor playing Mark Antony recorded the line, but in performance his lips never moved. A moment later, however, and with a nudge of his boot, he kicked Brutus's body, rolling it down a slight incline into a mire of mud. Thus it became an epitaph from a man of cowardly instincts and a loathsomeness of mind. This is what lent excitement to this production for me. It was, incidentally, a point I could never have made in the theatre; it was a gift from television.

SCHAFFNER: And the fact that it was one of the few of Shakespeare's plays you could cut without critical harm had nothing to do with its selection?

MINER: Not a thing. That was sheer accident. It was one block cut of forty minutes. The rest was trimming.

SCHAFFNER: Accident or not, it must have been gratifying to get the kind of recognition you were accorded by Jack Gould.

MINER: Who doesn't like a review that good?

Yet unlikely as it may seem, my own appraisal of Julius Caesar was far less sanguine than its critical acclaim might seem to warrant. The production had one colossal flaw. To add bitterness to the pill I could never pretend it was inadvertent nor beyond my control; it was deliberate. I had sacrificed too much to achieve clarity. I believed most ardently that an audience had to understand Shakespeare before it could reasonably be expected to embrace Shakespeare. To this extent I achieved what I had set out to do. Lillian Ross of the New Yorker declared it was the only play of Shakespeare's she'd ever fully understood. But along the way I'd allowed the poetry to get lost. And therein the bitterness. I can no longer bear to look at it, I want to vomit. Too much of the eloquence and beauty was sacrificed. It's one show I would I might do over.

SCHAFFNER: That's a far cry from The Storm. No lofty aspirations there. Pragmatism pure and simple.

MINER: Exactly. The easiest and most reliable type of story for its day and time, with one unheralded bench mark of its own. It was black-tie. There were no dark alleys nor kitchen sinks on Studio One. There were evil souls and dangerous people, but they dressed for dinner. If they were raped, it was in satin. (a smile) You hadn't noticed that, had you?

SCHAFFNER: Frankly, no. Do you feel it was a selling point?

220

MINER: With our then-audience, I feel sure it was. They felt more at home with bloodshed in a duplex.

SCHAFFNER: And there was one moment when you came close to giving them real blood.

MINER: No. I was a little crazy, but not that far off my rocker.

SCHAFFNER: Weren't you going to take a pot shot at Grace Kelly?

MINER: Dear God, it's beginning to come back. But it wasn't Grace Kelly.

SCHAFFNER: That I'll concede. It wasn't Grace Kelly. It was the lady sitting next to her.

MINER: Millie Natwick. Or was it Ann Shoemaker?

SCHAFFNER: I'm a little hazy about this, but it was Grace's first show. Of that I'm sure.

MINER: That it was. She was one of the many Fran sent us from the American Academy of Dramatic Arts.

SCHAFFNER: And the show was The Rockingham Tea Set.

MINER: Correct. And the set was a duplex. The climax was brought on by an occult event. The guilty party was exposed by the shattering of a teacup she was holding in her hand.

In preparing the script I had assumed we would cut to another camera focused on another cup with some contraption rigged to shatter cup and saucer through the table-top. During the first run-through that contraption was a complete bust -- no pun intended. There was nothing mysterious about it, nothing shocking nor, God knows, occult.

SCHAFFNER: (a laugh) It not only didn't work -- it was visible even in long shot. In close-up you could see nothing else.

MINER: After the third try the stage manager came up to us and said --

SCHAFFNER: Not the stage manager -- it was Johnny DeMotte. He came into the Control Room and announced: "One thing's for sure, gents. This thing's never going to work unless it happens in mid-air."

MINER: And I think you were the first to say: "But how?"

"I'll shoot it out of her hand."

I thought he'd gone off his rocker. "Four inches from the lady's face? Not likely."

"Why not? I'm a pretty good shot, you know."

I remember your laughing. I didn't.

SCHAFFNER: But you were thinking.

MINER: It has begun to come back to me. As a boy in Colorado, Johnny had won every kind of sharpshooting medal they had to offer. I heard myself saying: "How close in can we get?"

SCHAFFNER: I realized you were beginning to give the idea some thought. And then I heard Johnny saying: "I can come in early tomorrow, and we can give it a try." And you had a smile on your face.

"How about it, Frank? Are you game?"

With more than a little reluctance I finally agreed. I was praying like crazy it wouldn't work.

MINER: But it did work. When we got the camera in close enough, the barrel of that gun was less than two feet away. Johnny smashed that cup ten times without a miss.

"So that's it! We'll give it a whirl."

SCHAFFNER: "But we'll have to get the lady's consent first. We just can't spring it on her."

MINER: "Never, never, never! She'd never agree. If this thing's going to work, no one but us can know anything about it. Let anyone begin to shake and we will start spilling blood."

With some reluctance you agreed.

SCHAFFNER: Remember, the show was "live."

MINER: One take only!

SCHAFFNER: That's all we needed to kill the lady.

MINER: True. All went well up to the climatic moment. The actress lifted her cup toward her lips, hesitated as she'd been instructed, then spoke her fateful line. At which point -- Wham! -- the teacup shattered, tea sloshed all over her blouse, and from her lips there came forth a shrill, and

unmistakably genuine, scream. The other actors were so unnerved it was some time before they were able to get back
into the script again. It was a supreme example of the unpredictable excitement a live performance can generate.

SCHAFFNER: I was petrified.

MINER: It was the kind of risk that only "live" television
could countenance. Risks were our daily diet, and we took
many more of them than we should have. We knew it endowed
what we did with a thrill that neither film nor tape could hope
to equal. It accounted for much of the eagerness with which
audiences tuned into Philco and Studio One each week. And in
comedy the unexpected exerted an equal appeal. There was a
loyal audience for Your Show of Shows, too, you know.

SCHAFFNER: Weren't there ever any sobering aftermaths
to your unconscionable behavior?

MINER: One. The man died. It was black comedy at its
blackest, but that didn't stop the temporary hilarity. The
closer we come to unendurable pain, even to death, the deeper
and more unrestrained the laughter. Why does a pratfall invoke
such immoderate hilarity? Precisely because it comes so close
to a shattered spine and total paralysis. The pain of adoles-
cence is delectably funny to the adult, until the child is driven
to suicide. We seldom appreciate how closely laughter is linked
to catastrophe until the one who slips on the banana peel fails
to scream, or even to move. The sudden snickers are smothered in shame.

        Such was the case with Henry Stephenson. He died
because of my arrogance in being so certain I could not be
wrong. But this did not alter the fact that, at the time, it was
collapsingly funny.

        During the twenties Henry Stephenson was one of the
entrancing character actors the British seem to produce in
such recurrent abundance. I had been captivated by his wit and

his warmth, and was sorely saddened by his joining the parade to California. Hollywood had become painfully adept at misusing such distinctive talents. It offered extravagant salaries in return for stereotyped casting, boredom and anonymity. In Henry's case age and a serious loss of memory had caught up with him and forced his retirement. He had returned to New York but with too little income fully to enjoy the city he loved. When I heard that he might be available for a small part I jumped at the chance.

Bob Fryer, who was then working as my assistant, tried to warn me. "Of course he'd be great for the part, but the memory's shot, Tony. It could be a disaster."

"But the part's so small," I argued, "only that one scene in the last act. He's the one person that might make that saccharine slosh bearable. With Henry it could be genuinely moving."

"So be it."

And so it was. For the first week Paul Nickell was utterly entranced; by the second week he'd begun to bring up the matter of cue cards. I hit the ceiling.

"Over my dead body! This is theatre, goddamn it, not radio. You might as well have the actors come on with scripts in their hands. They could read the whole damn show."

This was the era before Teleprompter. To use cue cards, or not to use cue cards, was a burning issue. No one had yet dreamt of an hour-long soap opera five days a week. It was a war between those with a theatre background, and those from radio. My reaction was both over-emotional and irascible. "Nobody reads on a Tony Miner production! Nobody!"

Up until then no one had made a dent in my conviction. I was adamant in my belief that acting only began after memory was secure. But toward the end of the first runthrough there had been one speech where Henry became so befuddled, the stage manager had to walk onto the set and show him the script before we could go on. Henry was on the verge of collapse. It was so pitiful and heartrending to behold, my vaunted stubbornness melted to a mush. I gave orders for cue cards to be made up before the next run-through. The relief was widespread, topped by Henry's overwhelming gratitude.

His confidence seemed fully restored by the time we went on the air. Imagine my consternation when the time for that critical speech arrived to find Henry beginning once again to panic. His voice started to tremble, his gestures became both random and desperate.

I could not fathom why. The boy was holding those cards just as he should, but, as Henry stared at them, his face became contorted, his eyes filled with anguish, and no articulate sound came forth from his lips.

I was about to go out into the studio when I realized that the other actors had invented some words to cover the crisis and the action was again under way. A vital element in the resolution of the story was still unresolved; as a result our audience would remain forever bewildered. My gratitude to the actors who had saved us from utter disaster had failed to dissolve my fury at the hurt I, albeit without intention, had caused Henry to suffer.

Before I could get out onto the floor of the studio the stage manager appeared at the door. My rage was intemperate. "Christ Almighty," I shouted, "what happened?"

"You won't believe this, but the kid -- "

"Don't try to shift the blame to the kid!" I said. "He was holding the cards the way he was supposed to! I saw him. So what happened?"

"He held them upside-down."

"Oh, my God!" I had seen too much pain in Henry's eyes to see anything very funny in this revelation, but the utter absurdity of it was more than one of the technicians could bear.

"Upside-down?" he repeated, struggling to suppress a vagrant snigger. The briefest pause, and the entire Control

Room broke into uncontrollable laughter. My response was only momentarily deferred -- then I broke into laughter along with the rest. But a sense of latent guilt soon stilled my reluctant gaiety.

Recapturing my composure I made for Henry's dressing room. He was still shaken, but, once his sense of humor was able to reassert itself, he, too, began to laugh. Though somewhat less unrestrained than it had been in the Control Room, it was a relief to discover that even for him this agonizing incident had become less than a lasting tragedy.

Some five days later at ten o'clock in the evening Henry Stephenson suffered a massive coronary. On arrival at the hospital he was declared dead.

SCHAFFNER: And the guilt still pursues you?

MINER: How could it not? I have not often told the story.

———————

SCHAFFNER: How did you select your stories? I was right there with you for close to four years, and still I never knew.

MINER: In cycles of four. One classic, one mystery, one comedy and one catchall, the sole stipulation being that it be well-written -- anything from Pontius Pilate to The Medium. Comedy was, by far, the most difficult.

SCHAFFNER: Isn't it always? But I'll have to admit it never occurred to me you were using a regular pattern of story cycles.

MINER: You were in good company. I kept it secret far back in the fastness of my brain. You didn't know? Neither did the people who took over when I left. They had good shows and bad in the ensuing years, as you know.

SCHAFFNER: Some were better than good.

MINER: Right. But it was hit or miss. There was no sense of structure, of a guiding hand, to establish a continuity and a momentum. I can't explain why, but with no fore-knowledge on the audience's part, this awareness of structure seems to lessen the sour taste of failure, and enhance the impact of success.

One of our problems was that a sizable number of properties, and often the best, refused to conform to any one of our specified styles. The Horse's Mouth, for example, was basically a comedy, yet it was surely literate and modern as well. Eudora Welty's Shadowy Third was seriously concerned with the occult, yet it fitted equally well into the pattern of a psychological mystery. No one, I suspect, is going to deny that The Taming of the Shrew is Shakespeare, yet it is equally difficult to deny its being a pratfall prank, an outrageous farce. Despite these shady areas of nonconformity, these four categories guaranteed a variety of moods that encouraged a healthy curiosity amoung our regular audience.

As the third season was drawing to a close, however, I had begun to sense a number of critical flaws in the hour-long dramatic form itself. I had begun pressing CBS to initiate two new concepts of dramatic programming: an hour and a half to a two hour frame for Studio One, and an hour-long dramatic form extending over a variable number of weeks as dictated by the length and complexity of the story to be told.

If Westinghouse were unwilling to extend Studio One to an hour and a half, such a concept, I contended, should be launched as a new series on its own. The eventual outcome was, of course, Playhouse 90. And while CBS contributed little to that hour and a half series aside from its title, it didn't hesitate, once I'd gone over to NBC, to claim the format for its own.

My other proposal was a series made up of stories too big to be told in any existing production schedule and too good to be hacked to bits to squeeze into a commercial time frame. The solution, as I saw it, was to present such productions in a serial pattern of widely varied durations. Along with being my favorite, it had two built-in advantages.

One: It made possible the production of stories, great stories, that television had previously been unable to touch.

Two: By using a production schedule of anywhere between three to thirty weeks, it gave the audience a chance to build up an allegiance to specific actors as they had before in repetitive series.

This met with little more than cursory interest on the part of CBS; NBC dismisssed it out of hand. Eventually, as you know, it was adopted by the BBC as a framework for some of the most effective, and often most popular, productions of recent years -- The Forsythe Saga; Henry VIII and His Six Wives; George Sand, one of the best; etc. We soon joined the parade with Roots, Holocaust and Shogun. Some have been failures, dismal failures at that, but the number of successes runs well ahead of the flops.

Here is a sample of the kind of production I was advocating in 1952. Though the casting is now dated, the concept remains as valid as it was then.

Kristin Lavransdatter -- with Ingrid Bergman. Thirty weeks.

The Dwarf -- with Laurence Olivier and Michael Dunn. Ten weeks.

Life and Love of Ulysses S. Grant -- with Spencer Tracy. Thirteen weeks.

SCHAFFNER: That's pretty high-powered! Did CBS really give this the brush?

MINER: Substantially. Certainly they had no time for Kristin Lavransdatter. That was predictable. I don't think any of them had ever read it, and the six hundred pages terrified them. As for The Dwarf, they just pretended there was no such thing as a dwarf.

SCHAFFNER: This was pretty close to your departure for NBC, wasn't it?

MINER: A matter of weeks.

SCHAFFNER: Did you offer them the same suggestions?

MINER: I hardly had time. For one brief moment I thought Pat Weaver might be my salvation. He had the chutzpah and the creativity that television sorely needed. But it was the kind of chutzpah and creativity that scared the bejesus out of the Sarnoffs, père et fils. They couldn't wait to kick him upstairs and out the window. Kristin Lavransdatter? The soul of a woman coming close to the soul of a saint. The Dwarf? The lure of pure evil in the texture of a nobleman's secret desires. U.S. Grant? The power of a single passionate love affair to turn a future President into a drunkard or a hero. This was scarcely Sarnoff country.

SCHAFFNER: (a laugh) But before your departure from CBS, were there any incidents that added to your maturing?

MINER: Yes, one thing. But it was scarcely an incident, it came about too gradually. The more writing I was forced to do, the more assuredly I knew I was never meant to be a writer. I had the technical skill to do a literate job swiftly and effectively, but the spark of individuality was not there. At the start writing was perhaps the most rewarding and exhilarating part of the entire chore. I thrived on it. But month after month my shortcomings became an increasing disappointment to me. For a time my structural skill continued to bring a certain satisfaction; my capacity to design the set before I put a word on paper; to visualize the camerawork for climactic moments before attempting an outline of the script. All this gave a sense of assurance to a show's development; the story lines seldom got muddy or unclear. But by mid-year of the second season I began to sense a personal plagiarism. I began to see that I was borrowing from myself; my sense of structure had become more and more repetitive. I began to envy Fred Coe for developing a Paddy Chayefsky, for coming up with <u>A Catered Affair</u> or a <u>Marty</u>.

When some two months before I was to depart a young copywriter for the P and G station in Cincinnati sent me a script entitled <u>Buffalo Bill is Dead</u>, I felt a great burden being lifted from my shoulders.

SCHAFFNER: Rod Serling came to you?

MINER: And I sent him to you. Had you forgotten?

SCHAFFNER: I certainly had.

MINER: I had just come up with a new play and was about to go into rehearsal with it. That was <u>Pontius Pilate</u> by Michael Dyne. It made my departure for NBC a most dubious cause for celebration. Just as I was beginning to glimpse the reality of a writing stable, CBS became so niggardly in its financial dealings and Pat Weaver was so generous, I had no choice but to make a move, a move I'd have given my eyeteeth to turn down. It brought me what little financial security I have today; it also brought me eight years of meager gratification, brief and transient moments of exhilaration and no satisfaction whatsoever. I knew no genuine happiness again until I bought off my contract with NBC to take up Ely Landau's offer to produce <u>Play of the Week</u>. Midas was a touch I had not.

SCHAFFNER: But before we leave CBS for these years of misery, I want to be sure there were not some memorable moments you've left out.

MINER: (a smile) Perhaps we should call this a series of digressions with intermittent intervals of logical sequence.

SCHAFFNER: (a chuckle) An editor's privilege. Now -- what memories have you forgotten?

MINER: Two I can think of. One in which you play a pivotal part.

SCHAFFNER: I'm in the dark.

MINER: It was in the course of the 1951 season. Someone on our staff first suggested that the saga of Cockeye Dunn might be made into a story for Studio One.

I was at a loss; I'd never even heard the name. He began to fill me in on the life of the cocky little Irishman who, at an improbably early age, had made himself absolute overlord of the New York waterfront. His roster of crimes was grotesque and pitiless. For a time he was stunningly successful; in the end arrogance was his undoing. Caught and convicted of Murder One, he had been sent to the electric chair just about a year earlier. I was hooked by the story from the start. "But how," I asked, "could we get the rights?"

"What rights? It's all in the transcript of the trial."

To make it simpler, I could be put in touch with the detective who had brought Dunn in. He could give us anything we'd ever need, including some wonderful snatches of dialogue that had the unmistakable smell and rhythm of the waterfront. Within twenty-four hours I'd hired a writer, Joe Liss, to do the script; I had spoken to Don Hollenbeck of the CBS News Staff to act as Narrator, and had picked a title for the show: Waterfront Boss.

The next few weeks were a little hairy. It began after Joe Liss had had his first sessions with our contact in the Police Department. Within a week Joe's office was broken into, his typewriter smashed and his papers strewn to hell and gone. Since you were planning to shoot some film along the waterfront --

SCHAFFNER: Right.

MINER: I decided we were going to need police protection. I got off a letter to the Commissioner citing some ten areas of concern.

SCHAFFNER: You listed the dates and locations of our shooting schedule, requesting secure parking for our film truck and crew; you asked permission to shoot inside Pier #39 -- I think it was #39; you requested the right to use a quote from a recent statement of the Commissioner's that you had found both passionate and moving. He had railed against the criminal justice system in New York, asserting that gangsterism was becoming more firmly and ruthlessly entrenched with each passing year. You even suggested that he might appear on the program, giving it his stamp of approval. There were a number of other points. And you never got an answer. Or did you?

MINER: For nearly a month, nothing. Then finally, the day before shooting was to begin, a letter arrived. It was a terse, one-paragraph note acknowledging that the Police Department of the City of New York had been alerted to the fact that CBS was shooting parts of a television program outside certain unspecified docks on the date I had mentioned.

SCHAFFNER: But police protection and secure parking were completely ignored.

MINER: As was our right to shoot on Pier #39. He didn't even deign to acknowledge his appearance on the program, or the use of his speech respecting the waterfront.

SCHAFFNER: What was he so afraid of? After all, Dunn was dead.

MINER: Ah, yes -- very! But the real waterfront boss was not! He was very much alive.

SCHAFFNER: Why were we so foolhardy? We knew the risks we were running, just putting the show on the schedule.

MINER: Risks had become quite usual by then. Not long after that you set out for your first day of shooting. As you and the crew started down the ramp toward Pier #39, three squad cars were stationed outside, right?

SCHAFFNER: Right. Once they spotted the CBS truck approaching, they scattered, two southward, one to the north. No sign of an officer of the law was anywhere to be found for the next twenty-four hours.

MINER: So for a time our shooting schedule seemed in considerable jeopardy. The entire venture was rescued by an absurd, and scarcely credible, incident. You're going to have to help me out on this. You were there.

SCHAFFNER: The thing I remember most was the quiet. No one seemed to be moving outside the pier, or speaking. Once inside I asked someone if I could speak to the foreman. I don't remember his saying anything; he just pointed to a figure way down the pier. By the time I got there he and the three men he was with had spotted me. The greeting was chilly. I handed him a list of the shots we wanted to get. He had begun to study it, when I noticed one of the men tugging at his sleeve. When he turned, he went stock still. The color drained from his cheeks, and the paper in his hand started to shake.

MINER: Had you any idea why?

SCHAFFNER: All I could see was that Kent Smith and Roy Hargrave had come onto the pier to look around.

MINER: What had they seen?

SCHAFFNER: Let's be clear about this, because no one ever said anything specific, but you remember how much those mug shots you had looked like Roy Hargrave?

MINER: Do I not? Roy had played the kid for me in Blind Alley, but ten years had passed since I'd so much as heard his name.

SCHAFFNER: So up to then his appearance had seemed to be a small plus, nothing more. But this was the first day he'd got into costume and makeup to match the snapshots we had of Dunn. Now in snap-brim hat with a plug of tobacco in his mouth and the collar of his trenchcoat turned up, he was the walking image of our Waterfront Boss.

MINER: And the foreman? Did his manner change?

SCHAFFNER: He sniggered. The frozen face that had greeted me now suddenly softened with welcoming smiles.

"Anything you want, young fella'. Just let us know."

There was nothing I could ask for from then on that I didn't get, except for one thing. None of them would go anywhere near Roy Hargrave. Not by twenty feet! We kept

Roy off the pier as much as we could; when he had to appear, we kept him in the shadows. It was like walking a high wire for two days.

MINER: Did you ever disabuse them of the ghostly presence you'd brought along?

SCHAFFNER: Do you eat concrete? No. I told you that night. I told no one else. It's left me with very little perspective on the show itself. Now, in retrospect, how do you feel it rated?

MINER: High.

SCHAFFNER: Compared with On the Waterfront?

MINER: Well, obviously we had no Marlon Brando and no galaxy of stars such as the picture assembled. We could never match the popular appeal of Gadge Kazan's production. But with the help of Don Hollenbeck we had a far more adult and devastating story to tell. There was a certain catharsis in our bringing Dunn into court and sending him to the Chair; the kind of satisfaction that On the Waterfront achieved was based on a contrived survival of the good and a punishment of the bad. There was no reward for nobility in our final statement. Don's summary was matter-of-fact, yet devastating:

"This year, two years after Cockeye Dunn's conviction and death in the electric chair, the take from the New York waterfront was . . . " -- and he quoted a figure fifty percent higher than Dunn had ever skimmed off the top in his heyday.

I'd never encountered such insensate cruelty as the Cockeye Dunn episode revealed. He was as emotionless as a phone book; life and death were no more than entries in a ledger of profit and loss. Killings were a dismal, yet diurnal, way of doing business. I was learning there was a part of our world I could never love nor forgive. I was learning an angry intolerance. At fifty years of age I was still growing up. What a dope.

SCHAFFNER: And when do you expect to stop maturing?

MINER: God knows. I don't.

SCHAFFNER: One other incident during the fifties left a mark.

MINER: I was made to feel deeply ashamed at the start. It was a religious issue.

SCHAFFNER: A conversion?

MINER: No. It was a matter of sudden revelation; it was a matter of unpardonable ignorance. It was also memorable for allowing me to meet one of the wisest and most lovable of men. By coincidence the show also marked my farewell to Studio One. That it should have caused more fury and turmoil than any production in four years made it a fitting epitaph to my unsettling tenure.

SCHAFFNER: What was the show?

MINER: It was the Easter show for 1952, Pontius Pilate by Michael Dyne. Sometime during the fall the script had arrived, unsolicited, from the West Coast. Normally I did not read unsolicited scripts, but it happened I was looking for an Easter program and the accompanying letter from Michael displayed enough wit and humor to intrigue me. It hadn't been written for television; it was a three-act play. Five pages in, and I was seduced; by the end of Act Three I knew we had not only found our Easter show, but had also discovered a new writer of unmistakable quality.

I was still suffering, however, from my June Moon syndrome; I was unsure whether a play script could be cut down to size without destroying its impact. Since winter was fading fast, I began to tackle the job a day or so later. All went smoothly; by the following Monday, I was ready to pass my handiwork along to the typist. On discovering that the mimeoed version not only read well, but ran well within the time frame for one of our productions, my relief was unbounded.

The joyous days were short-lived. I'm not sure whether I mentioned that, following The Light That Failed episode, I'd persuaded CBS to hire someone as a buffer between the Agency, the Sponsor and me. The two-cocktail, three-hour lunches had long since begun to pall. My assigned bodyguard for a little over a year had been Bill Dozier, one-time husband of Joan Fontaine, and a master at coping with the trivialities and mindless apprehensions of those $50,000 a year watchdogs for Westinghouse and McCann-Erickson. For months Bill had handled this tedious chore without incident; indeed, no grey-flanneled figure had even tapped on my door.

Bill appeared one morning in my office to announce: "Well, Tony, me lad, we've got some real trouble this time, real and nasty. Rabbi Eisendrath doesn't like Pontius Pilate. He's appealed, as I understand it, to the B'nai B'rith. He wants us to cancel the show."

I was sick. I knew enough about the B'nai B'rith to know this was no trivial matter. But what in the script had got their backs up I couldn't imagine, unless, of course, it was the Crucifixion itself, which I could scarcely be expected to chop.

"What do I have to do?"

"They want to meet with you in the morning."

When I arrived at the Commodore, my reception could not have been more cordial and complimentary, but the moment I displayed the slightest restlessness, the amenities were cut short, and we got down to the matter at hand. I could kick myself for never having found out who their spokesman was, because he was good -- God, was he good! -- but I never saw him again after that one meeting. He began by making it clear how unhappy he was, how unhappy all of them were, at having to ask for this meeting, but there was a problem they could not ignore.

"You are speaking about <u>Pontius Pilate</u>, I assume?"

"Yes." They'd read the script and all of them understood why I'd wanted to do it. "It's an enthralling document" was, I believe, the phrase the spokesman used. Anywhere you'd schedule it, there'd have been a problem, but in Passover week it was a mortal threat.

He went on to enlighten me about the history of Jewry over the Passover season, the fact that some eighty-five to ninety percent of all pogroms, since pogroms began, had occurred within ten days of Passover -- in Spain, in Russia, in Poland, in Germany, it mattered not where.

"We cannot," he said, "treat this matter casually; it is too persistent a part of our history, persistent and persistently implacable. It is a haunting legend."

Though he spoke in a voice both quiet and faintly academic, his eloquence was like a white-hot iron. I found myself in a most untenable position. Having been brought up in an atmosphere of casual, but nonetheless inexorable, anti-Semitism, I fully understood, I thought, the apprehension of any Jew toward the mention, no matter how oblique, of their 2,000-year persecution. For many years, moreover, I felt I had shed all childhood prejudices, had, indeed, built up so much respect and caring for Jewish customs, Jewish religion, Jewish music and vocabulary, it came as a stunning shock that I had yet failed to recognize the monstrous threat this script presented. They had been my friends, my workmates, my companions. How could I have understood so little about their hearts?

First the shame, then the anger.

Ignorance, I thought. Inexcusable ignorance! Why had I never been taught? That was the indictment I could not forgive. How could we have been taught so much about religion and political history without ever being given a hint that our Feast of Easter had directly induced this ghastly amount of bloodshed and hatred over so many years?

I was, in fact, so distraught I very nearly offered to cancel the show without further discussion. One television production seemed a trivial matter in the shadow of such inhumanity. Yet I could not imagine any compromise or change I could make that would not wholly emasculate Michael's script. Further discussion seemed futile and indecent. With an offer to get back to them in a couple of days, I started for the door.

As I did so, I must have projected an image of such abject misery that the speaker for the group edged over toward me and placed a hand on my shoulder.

"Don't give up so soon. We've dredged our way out of worse than this." And then in an almost casual tone he asked: "Have you ever met Moses Jung?"

I'd never even heard the name.

"Well, you should," he said. "Here's his address. Give him a ring. He might be able to help."

I mumbled some inadequate thanks as I slipped the scrap of paper into my pocket and made for the door.

"Good luck," he called. Again I'd forgotten to ask his name.

I met with Moses Jung within the next forty-eight hours. I fell in love with him on the spot. He was built on a diminuitive scale. His eyes were alight with a tragic twinkle that was altogether disarming. I soon discovered that he was not only an eminent scholar, but unique. He had just returned from Boston where, on alternate days, he was allowed to conduct seminars at both a Jesuit Seminary and a Rabbinical College. His flexibility of mind made things far easier for me than I had expected. When I mentioned Pontius Pilate as the title of the piece, I was prepared for a scowl; Moses Jung grinned.

"Oh, ho!" he said. "So you would re-enact the Crucifixion at Passover, eh? You are a reckless man. And our
Protective Fathers have threatened to name our next blood-
bath after you -- Miner's Pogrom, is that it?"

"Something like that," I said. I wanted to respond to
his smile, but I was still too unnerved for humor. "Only I can't
really find it very funny," I said.

On the instant the grin was gone. His voice was gentle
and infinitely sad. "Nor I. Nor I. Only this," he added. "There
may yet be an answer. Perhaps if I could read your script, we
might meet again."

It's scarcely necessary for me to say that I jumped at
the chance. "Of course," I said, reaching for my briefcase. My
eagerness was so undisguised, he began to smile again.

"I am no Savonarola," he said. "My mission is not to
torture, but to soothe."

Our next meeting was most painful for me. It was
humbling to have him expose my lack of knowledge and comprehension respecting Our Lord's last hours on earth. Not all
the details he cited were part of the account presented in the
New Testament, but he gave them the stamp of authority. He
was, as a matter of fact, in the best of humors for the simple
reason that he had, he believed, found a solution to our
dilemma.

SCHAFFNER: What was it?

MINER: The problem lay with Caiaphas and Annas. So
long as they were treated as leaders of the Jewish state or
religion, we were, by implication, accusing the Jewish people
of everything these two had ordered or condoned. And this was
precisely the attitude portrayed in Michael's script. The moment they were depicted as Quislings, they became at once
the enemies of the Jewish people and the Jewish state. There
was, moreover, historical confirmation for this accusation.
Within a decade after Christ, both Annas and Caiaphas were
put to death by their own people as traitors.

Moses Jung had gone further than finding an answer for the B'nai B'rith. He had stippled the script with notes, pointing out specific places where a different accent could turn rejection into approval. I was abashed at the amount of what should have been common knowledge yet came to me as revelation. The pinnacle of shame was reached toward the end of the session.

"And, of course," he said, "you realize, or perhaps you don't that both Pilate and his wife, Procula, ended up saints, one in the Eastern Rite, and one in the Coptic Church."

I thought he was closing out the day with a light-hearted hoax. "Oh, of course, sure, that much I know." I'd worn the Dunce Cap long enough. His misery at having inadvertently inflicted one more humiliation on me was a measure of his delicacy of feeling. I'd deserved no such consideration. A goy who didn't even know his own saints!

SCHAFFNER: And were they saints?

MINER: Yes, and highly revered at that. Can you imagine what a fool I felt?

SCHAFFNER: And did that end it?

MINER: Not quite. I still had to rework the adaptation. One thing I soon knew; it was far more effective dramatically than it had been before.

The final twist was happily a laughing matter. The first reaction from both CBS and the B'nai B'rith had been good, but one powerful rabbi in Washington, D.C. had yet to be appeased, Rabbi Eisendrath, the original complainant. The job of contacting him was given to Harry Ommerle, Assistant Program Director at CBS, as you know. I was in his office for the final confrontation. The moment the Rabbi came on the phone he began to berate Harry, protesting loudly that he could not understand how we could present him with a script that had totally ignored the original objections he had made on behalf of the Jewish people. After absorbing a heavy amount of abuse and sarcasm, Harry suggested he put me on the line. The Rabbi was still steaming, when I broke in.

"Excuse me, Rabbi Eisendrath, but do you know Moses Jung?"

He was insisting that no Jew could let this string of vicious calumnies go without challenge, when the name Jung seemed to penetrate his consciousness.

"Jung?" he said. "Moses Jung?" There was for the first time a trace of uncertainty in his tone.

"Would you accept his approval of the script?"

"Why -- well, yes -- I suppose. Moses Jung is a very brilliant man. One could hardly brush aside anything Dr. Jung had to say."

"Excellent. Then you should be interested in a note I received from him yesterday." I had a copy with me. It was not long, but it was an almost unstinted tribute to the script changes we had made, to the show's dramatic impact, and to our dispassionate fairness in dealing with such delicate subject matter. "I believe," I said, "that he transmitted very much the same opinion to the B'nai B'rith."

There was a long, a very long, silence. It ended in one clipped and abrupt summation.

"Well, of course, anything Moses Jung approves." And he hung up.

With the sound of that click, Harry broke into rich and joyous laughter. He had been through five weeks of loud and insistent derogation. It was ended. We had a couple of double very dry martinis with our lunch.

SCHAFFNER: And what were your afterthoughts?

MINER: Anything but hilarious; sober rather, and often humbling. As we know, all prejudice is at a minimum in the theatre. Anti-Semitism is all but nonexistent; yet the roots of bigotry run deep. Too often our native prejudices are betrayed by some sin of omission, rather commission. Every man's history is a part of mine. We have an obligation to explore the legends of good and evil alike, of those we have reason to cherish, as well as those we have reason to shun.

SCHAFFNER: We're coming close to the end of your years at CBS. Is there any part of that experience you regret?

MINER: One thing. It was a matter of conduct. I became a tyrant, and it did not become me. It was against my nature and my intuition. I'd always sought to give an actor his head, to bring forth his hidden capacities, his smothered passions, his spontaneity, never imposing on him a rigid and inexorable pattern of performance. Many of my shows had been roasted, but seldom an actor. It took time, and it took patience, and these were luxuries that television could not afford.

The Storm is indicative, if excessive. As a director, I not only had to learn every shot to be used, I had to prepare the other two cameras for the shots that were coming up. It was a hideous chore. And, since I seldom stopped talking from the beginning of the show to the end, I was in the worst possible position to judge the delicacies and nuances of the actors' performances. The atmosphere was so tense, so lacking in professional calm, I knew I could not live with it, nor could any other director. The very next morning I created the role of Assistant Director, someone to set up the advance shots for all three cameras. So far as I know that function has remained constant at CBS ever since.

But the pressures on a director remained harrowing. With experience I learned to be far more flexible, to give the actors a great deal more freedom, but when the chips were down, an ironclad fist was again in demand. We still had but eight hours to put an hour-long dramatic show on camera, we still had too little time between Dress and Air -- two hours to give notes, make cuts, clean up video and audio foul-ups, and, if possible, engender a sense of excitement devoid of panic. It left no time for discussion, much less for courtesy. My first demand of a director was: "Be terse and be clear."

SCHAFFNER: But you were dictatorial at a much earlier stage than that.

MINER: Yes. Unhappily, yes. No one knew as much about every aspect of the medium as I did, electronic circuitry excepted. That is not an expression of conceit or vanity; it is simply a statement of fact. There were no other producers in the business who'd been allowed to handle every camera and lens available to us; no producer or director had spent three to four months working out a fast and effective lighting system to reduce time and improve mood; no one else had had the time to balance film and live. No one else had had fifteen years' experience in the Broadway theatre in which to learn how to spot talent among a mass of eager but untutored novices clamoring for a spot in the sun. I had no money to buy experience, and no experience to buy at any price. What untutored youngster would have dared to sink The Battleship Bismarck, or cover the struggle of two submarines in an Arctic storm?

And so, despite my innate distaste for such conduct, I began to adopt the intolerant manners of a dictator. I trod on many toes; I earned many enemies. Yet curiously enough those who worked closest to me, those whose feelings I had most often abused -- you, Franklin, are a case in point -- have remained my closest friends. I shall forever be grateful for your generosity and patience.

SCHAFFNER: How often were you right? How often wrong?

MINER: I was never wrong.

SCHAFFNER: (laughter) Naturally.

X

SCHAFFNER: It was still, I would guess, more than a little traumatic for you to leave CBS?

MINER: Far more than I had expected. They'd been so penny-wise and so damned graceless in their dealings with me, I thought I'd rather enjoy spitting in their eye. And so I might, if Pat Weaver hadn't been given the boot before we ever got down to trying out the ideas we'd tossed at each other. Fruition was always just around the corner; it never came to be. I hadn't realized how lonely a mind he was at NBC; once he was gone, there was nothing left but a mental void. When the only excitement a week holds forth is picking up the Friday paycheck, those extra zeroes are only symbols of the empty hours.

SCHAFFNER: What did you do for NBC -- aside from our ill-fated Unit Four?*

---

*Unit Four was a production company made up of Miner, Schaffner, George Roy Hill and Fielder Cook. It was ill-starred, and folded within a few months, thanks in large measure to the active enmity of Henry J. Kaiser of Kaiser Aluminum.

245

MINER: So little. They kept trying to sell a carbon copy of Studio One and failed. They couldn't seem to understand that it's not easy to sell a dry well. Eventually, to get some return on their lavish investment, they asked me to prepare a color presentation for the FCC. I did so, as I've said, and I did it well.

The compliments from the General were effusive, but I'd already been through all that for CBS back in 1941. It was for me a retrogression, a case of déjà vu.

Shortly thereafter I sold a half-hour dramatic series to RCA under the title Curtain Call. We presented some of the best half-hour shows television had seen up to that time, but in this case there were no compliments forthcoming. We were a summer replacement for Dennis Day. I should have realized that anyone whose taste could have selected Dennis Day could scarcely have found delight in thirteen weeks of Dostoevsky, John Cheever, John Collier, Henry James, and a delightful satire by Michael Dyne where the visitors to a zoo were animals and the caged animals were mortal men. Considering RCA's bewilderment and dismay, the only wonder is that we survived the summer.

Fortunately, well before its demise Ted Ashley had steered me to a script that won my heart. Despite my suspicions that it might be something less than a commercial smash I bought it, made a pilot and sold it to Dow Chemical. It was, of course --

SCHAFFNER: Medic?

MINER: Medic. Its one continuing character was an actor I had used once on Mr. I Magination, Dick Boone. The leads for the pilot were two equally unknown performers, Beverly Garland and Lee Marvin. The theme was a young girl trying to have a baby before dying of leukemia. Hot property, what? The pilot did, however, arouse enough enthusiasm to justify our belief we'd struck it rich.

And it might have been, it might so easily have been. But despite all its graces and virtues, Medic was born under an ill-fated star. It began with the fact that I neither liked, nor trusted, nor, in the end, respected, the author. This was scarcely eased by the fact that in our first contretemps I was in the wrong. I wanted to shoot it "live," using a mobile unit; the author and the director wanted to use film. I was not only wrong artistically and economically, but I was outnumbered. They disliked me quite as cordially as I disliked them.

This turned into a situation I found hard to credit, an advertising agency becoming my most trusted ally. I had learned so far to distrust the judgment and taste of McCann-Erickson and Westinghouse, it was startling to find McManus, John and Adams behaving with an intelligence and graciousness for which I was totally unprepared. Hank Fownes, as the account executive, was everything the breed is supposed not to be. He was bright and forthright and, if sleazy political sagacity were any part of his make-up, I never ran into it. For a beautiful, but brief, interlude, everything was coming up roses.

But our author lacked the stature and the solidarity to cope with success. Medic was never more than a razor's edge away from soap; nothing but his writing, and his best writing at that, placed it in a different and more adult category. Our author drunk was not our author at his best. At first this only cost us money; scripts began coming in late, overtime was horrendous. Sooner or later it was predictable that we would have no scripts whatever. It happened late in the first year. Faced with this reality, a second-rate crony was mustered into service to follow a detailed but uninspired outline.

Do I have to belabor the point? We struggled through two ugly and needlessly costly years, maintaining for the most part a semblance of the series' original quality -- for the most part, not invariably. During the second season there were more and more productions I could neither admire nor condone. We had won vast commendation, we had won the Sylvania Award; our ratings were reasonably high. We should have been a shoo-in for another season. That did not happen for a reason I could only applaud.

Hank Fownes and I bumped into each other one night in the bar of the Bel-Air; we'd both been living there for some time. He and Dow had been debating the pros and cons of a renewed agreement for the coming year.

"I was going to call you," he said. "I have some word for you from Dow."

He had a good poker face; I couldn't tell whether the word was fair or foul.

"Dow would like to renew. We're ready to go ahead, if -- "

It was a man-eating "if." "If it's that big you'd better let me have it straight."

"They want your guarantee that your partner will write thirteen of the twenty-six scripts, and personally supervise and edit the rest." What could I answer but "No"?

It was an unhappy evening; the association had been warm and diverting, and, God wot, rare. What a pity it could not have lasted a few more years.

SCHAFFNER: Where are we? 1955?

MINER: Right. That fall and the following spring I was doing another series, Frontier. As my life with Medic had been an unending disappointment, Frontier was, for as long as it lasted, a joyous adventure. My partners were two writers, Mort Fine and David Friedkin; our producer was Matthew Rapf; our associate producer was Bernie Kowalski and my personal assistant, Hal Polaire.

There was a quaint irony in the basic set-up; Mort and Dave had originally written Gunsmoke for radio. Their enthusiasm for the Frontier project was best expressed by Dave: "It's everything that Gunsmoke might have been."

Considering the fortune Gunsmoke amassed as compared with our one-season demise, this might be assessed as a
classic example of errant theatrical judgment. In point of fact,
there were some critical flaws in the structure of Frontier
that seriously curtailed its popular appeal, but they could have
been solved. The foundation was still solid.

One: As originally conceived, it was to be an hour-
long show. I allowed myself to be persuaded that this was not
essential to its success. I was wrong.

Two: By using historically true material, an audience
was asked to become involved with a new set of characters
each week while giving active attention to the development
and denouement of a new story. That would have been difficult
enough in an hour; again and again individual programs on
Frontier fell apart primarily because the guts of the script
ended on the cutting room floor. It was the old June Moon
syndrome. It was not just the appeal of James Arness that
captured the Gunsmoke audience's devoted attention; there was
Miss Kitty and Doc and Chester, each heartwarming enough to
hold a full hour on his own. Week after week our stories had
an authority, an interest, and often an emotional intensity far
above that of Gunsmoke, but what got on the air was skeletal.

Finally, we were up against Jack Benny. The best was
so good, and the potential so high, I feel no shame, only
regret, that our demise was so swift. Swift and stupid, a pithy
symbol of NBC management. You see, despite all the handicaps in our path, Reynolds Metals had been ready to renew, to
give us another year to cure our faults and capture an audience. NBC demurred. They insisted on replacing Frontier with
a kiddie show. The specific series they chose was Circus Boy,
a Jack Webb production. Webb had been the recent creator and
star of Dragnet. In NBC's eyes this made him another Irving
Thalberg; it was heresy in those days to point out that, aside
from Dragnet, Mr. Webb had had an astonishingly undistinguished career. Nonetheless they twisted Reynolds Metals' arm
sufficiently to force a cancellation of Frontier.

Circus Boy opened to lavish advance publicity; it
closed in something under ten weeks to no publicity whatever.
NBC not only lost the cost of all the Circus Boy episodes that

250

never reached the air, but lost Reynolds Metals as a client. I had heard without official confirmation that the entire transaction cost NBC something close to $4,500,000. I so hope it's true.

SCHAFFNER: (a laughs) I'm sure you do!

MINER: The reason for my relatively equable acceptance of Frontier's failure was strictly personal. I had by then been living on the Coast for close to four years. I had not prospered. Three months had been almost all of California I have ever been able to tolerate. My brain soon goes to wet cotton; I begin to find fault with my closest friends; I drink too much and I get fat. It was a glorious tonic to start East again.

But before I left I embarked on a venture rewarding enough to solace the waning days in Hollywood. I made a pilot for a new series called The Challenge, sponsored by Bob Hutchins and the Fund for the Republic. Bob and I had first got to know each other in the early twenties, even before his appointment to the presidency of the University of Chicago. I had followed his career, fully subscribing to his concept of a liberal education. After thirty-odd years we were able to establish a quick rapport. So many of our ideas, many of them out of favor with the Establishment of the fifties, won a welcome response from the other. The series I presented to him was designed to expose the widespread misconceptions respecting the intentions of our Constitution. Bob was enthusiastic about the idea.

For writers I had lined up Rod Serling and Reggie Rose; as a theme for the pilot I had chosen the loyalty oath. With the cancellation of Frontier and Medic we decided to shoot the pilot in New York. Reggie turned in a script with its focus on the driver of a school bus, his wife and son. Rod was supposed to write the last half of the program concerned with a meeting of the PTA, but Rod was loaded down with commitments and did not have the time he needed to do his homework. I ended up spending a week in the Law Library of UCLA, digging as deeply as I could into the background in both England and the United States of this delicate and still controversial subject. Much that I discovered was revelatory, all of it fascinating. If I could find the material that absorbing, I felt confident a respectable public could become our loyal and lasting audience.

It was, I believe, one of the best things I had contributed to the medium up to that time. This reaction was echoed by a large percentage of those who saw the pilot, critics included. And so -- (a laugh). You're ahead of me, I see.

SCHAFFNER: You could never find anyone to sponsor it.

MINER: They were petrified. In the words of Larry Hart, it was "much too good for the average monkey."

SCHAFFNER: Do you believe that?

MINER: No. I have too much belief in the native intelligence of "homo Americanus." That sums up, in fact, the raison d'être for my whole career in television, my hopes and aspirations alike. I wanted to give the isolated and underexposed portions of our population a chance to experience the best we had to offer. Only then, I believed, had we the right to expect them to know the difference between hogwash and magnificence. I respond in fury when I hear the sleazy and meretricious things we condone as proper fodder for a supposedly puerile public. But give us another thirty years. Who knows?

SCHAFFNER: What saved you from ending up a cynic?

MINER: No question, Play of the Week.

SCHAFFNER: Was it that much better than anything television had then produced?

MINER: Yes. Despite its many shortcomings, yes. Short-comings! To start with, it was in black-and-white, but when the lack of color was of least importance, its top productions, notably The Iceman Cometh, were able to challenge the medi-um's best. What meant far more to me was the fact that the finest of Play of the Week productions, three by my book, were as good, or better, than any production they had been given on Broadway.

SCHAFFNER: And the three were?

MINER: The Dybbuk, though the lack of color made it the most questionable. No Exit. In this case, the lack of color was no handicap; it was a distinct advantage. And The Iceman, undoubtedly the best of the three. I would remember it with untarnished pride, if the director's execrable taste had not befouled the show's final fade-out. He tacked on a cheap and nasty ending. It didn't become O'Neill.

SCHAFFNER: How much of the show's impact was due to Jason Robards' performance?

MINER: A lot. And his television performance was, by me, even more uncanny than his stage performance had been. But we had assembled quite a lot of other "uncannys": Myron McCormick, Jimmy Broderick, Bob Redford. They weren't Jasons, but they were pretty terrific in their own right.

SCHAFFNER: José Quintero had a genius for finding the proper actors for the most critical parts: Geraldine Page for Summer and Smoke, Jason for The Iceman, Colleen Dewhurst for A Moon for the Misbegotten. Or would you prefer me to say that you and he were both geniuses at casting?

MINER: I am no genius. Nor is José Quintero. The issue is muddied by a widely accepted but totally erroneous aphorism. "Genius is an infinite capacity for taking pains." This is a superb definition of the artist; genius is its complete antithesis. Mozart, Yehudi Menuhin, Gary Coleman were, and are, geniuses. Larry Olivier, Glenda Jackson, and Jason Robards are not; they are incomparable artists. The artist has to sweat, struggle and often fail in order to achieve the stature and subtlety genius is able to display without effort at five years of age. It's as unfair as inherited wealth. Up the revolution!

Genius does not necessarily create the greater artist, nor the finer man. The artist is still the product of grueling practice and elusive imagery. Baudelaire was a genius, but his most incomparable lyric phrases didn't stop his being a thoroughgoing son of a bitch. Great artists are often both human and humane; geniuses are too often neither.

SCHAFFNER: Your argument is persuasive. And now, where are we?

MINER: 1960. I spent the next three years making two pictures, one a fiasco, The Fool Killer with Tony Perkins and young Edward Albert (age twelve), and The Pawnbroker with Rod Steiger. It was a genuinely moving story needlessly cheapened at the end by the director's execrable taste -- the same director, I'm unhappy to say, who had so grievously diminished the finale of The Iceman.

SCHAFFNER: Sidney Lumet? Why did you use him a second time?

MINER: First, he was so good so much of the time. Second, he was only partially to blame.

SCHAFFNER: Who shares that blame?

MINER: The producer, Ely Landau. He was captivated by Sidney. He was a man with a genuine desire to enrich the

254

medium, to bring to television a taste for theatre at its best. But he lacked the toughness and the self-assurance to be true, all the way, to the properties he had chosen to do. He was so bedazzled by the names he could assemble on lighted marquees, he would utterly ignore the hurt they were doing to the production as a whole. He was self-destructive without ever meaning to be, without even knowing it. What a sad and wasted talent! If he'd only known whom to trust, himself above all, he could have been an important figure in our theatre. We quarreled bitterly, but, as we parted, I felt no rancor. I was too fond of what he might have been. And so I forgave, forgot and fled!

SCHAFFNER: What caused the final split between you?

MINER: Katie Hepburn.

SCHAFFNER: How?

MINER: I had secured for Ely the rights to <u>Long Day's Journey Into Night</u>. To be more exact, at the time I first persuaded Carlotta Monterey (Mrs. Eugene O'Neill) to sell the rights to <u>The Iceman Cometh</u> to <u>Play of the Week</u>, I began laying the foundations for securing television rights to anything of O'Neill's not already sold to pictures. Carlotta was so enthralled with the job we had done with <u>The Iceman</u>, and the job Jason had done with Hickey, she was amenable to almost anything I might suggest. Thus when Ely decided he wanted to do a picture version of <u>Long Day's Journey Into Night</u> with Jason playing Jamie, as he had on Broadway, I had little trouble persuading her to let Ely have the rights.

SCHAFFNER: What was her mental state at the time?

MINER: She was halfway to Ophelia a good share of the time. For some years she had been enamored of José Quintero, and so she should have been. He had given her beloved Gene two of the finest productions he'd ever received; they had solidified his claim to being America's foremost playwright. It was some years later that José added <u>Moon for the Misbegotten</u>. And so she had every reason to grant Quintero a claim on her gratitude, a very strong claim indeed.

This accounted for my apprehension when I first went to see her. My luck stemmed from discovering that we shared two enmities, a far, far stronger bond than a bushel basketfull of friendships can supply. Our venom was epoxy to our swift attachment. After my first visit she extended to me her trust in fullest measure. And so, when Ely evidenced a desire to give to <u>Long Day's Journey</u> the same loving care he had bestowed on <u>The Iceman</u>, she was putty in his hands.

At the same time it was taken for granted that I should be the producer. This lasted to the moment Ely became obsessed with the idea that Katie Hepburn was the one, and only one, to play Mary Tyrone, Gene's mother. My passionate opposition to this casting lasted a painfully long time. During our final arguments I wept, and I was no boy. I consider Katie Hepburn to be one of the truly formidable figures our theatre has produced in this century. As a person, her wit, her charm, her courage and authority are unique. As an actress, however, she has been a mercurial, unpredictable performer. When she's been right, as in <u>The Philadelphia Story</u>, <u>Woman of the Year</u>, <u>The African Queen</u> and <u>Coco</u>, she has been incomparable, a class unto herself. But when she's been wrong, she's been aggressively, monstrously bad. These performances, the crybaby performances, have generally been the ones for which she has received the highest commendations and awards -- <u>Morning Glory</u>, <u>Summertime</u>, or the characters she could neither appreciate nor fathom, <u>The Lion in Winter</u>, <u>The Madwoman of Chaillot</u>, and, most sadly, <u>Long Day's Journey Into Night</u>.

Ironically enough, in one scene from that play, the scene with Cathleen, the maid, she was at her most brilliant and intellectual best. But Mary Tyrone was not an intellectual; she was a plain Irish girl with a near-peasant mind, an infinite trust in the goodness of God and an intuitive faith in the hereafter. She could, indeed she should, have been a nun. She was not a super-sophisticate, guzzling heroin for kicks; she was a child who had unquestioningly put herself in the hands of a kindly but ignorant country doctor, who to assuage the ghoulish pains that beset her, had, out of the kindness of his heart, fed her that insidious poison. The image best suited to the anguish of the play was that of a high school girl in a white graduation dress. As Miss Hepburn played her, the image was that of a John Updike heroine, clothed in a sleek black sheath enroute to Studio 54.

Having her name to light up the marquee was a theatrical coup for Ely; having to endure her performance was a stab in the pit of the stomach for me. I had no part in the production. Ely and I had had our bone-naked fight over the lady; that afternoon I had emptied my desk and departed. I recovered, but never quite, my one-time fondness for Ely. It was "never quite" because I had been too deeply offended.

SCHAFFNER: But before that, why did <u>Play of the Week</u> close down?

MINER: There were no more rights to be had, no more exciting properties to be bought. That was the fatal flaw in the concept of the series from the start. Only scripts so controversial and so uncommercial as to be questionably popular had been our stockpile. By the spring of the second season, even those were running out; we were scraping the bottom of the barrel. None of us, Standard Oil included, had any stomach for keeping <u>Play of the Week</u> going merely to present a third-rate product to an indifferent public.

SCHAFFNER: So, what happened?

MINER: For a time I drifted. In the end it was the Academy.

SCHAFFNER: This was after <u>The Fool Killer</u> and <u>The Pawnbroker</u> then?

MINER: Yes. They were bitter and futile years.

SCHAFFNER: The Fool Killer intrigues me. I never heard of it.

MINER: And for a good reason. It never reached New York. That was a part of the bitterness, it was such a darlin' story.

SCHAFFNER: What happened?

MINER: Everything. Not by any plan, that's for certain. Call it coincidence. It began with Jack Dreyfus.

SCHAFFNER: The Dreyfus Fund?

MINER: The same, Polaroid and all that. Jack had had some money in NTA, I believe, the company that owned Play of the Week. In any case, he had fallen in love with a little book; he was, in fact, so enamored of it, he was ready to back it all the way, provided Ely would agree to produce it. That was the first mistake. It was never Ely's cup of tea.

SCHAFFNER: Why not?

MINER: Every decision he made was wrong. It started with his asking MacKinlay Kantor to write the script.

SCHAFFNER: Andersonville? Strange choice.

MINER: Was it not? But wait! There's more. At the same time, Ely had fallen in love with a young Mexican director named Servando Gonzales, who had just completed an artsy little picture called Yanco. This gave Ely an idea with a precedent behind it. When Ely was first putting Play of the Week together, he was lining up the people to do the Medea. His love affair at that time was with José Quintero. Jose had never been in pictures as far as I know. There was no way of knowing whether he could use a camera or not. To Ely, this seemed of no consequence. He was convinced that José was the man for the job.

A few weeks later a picture of José's opened. It was a catastrophe -- I can't even remember its name -- and the critics felt, almost to a man, that the principal fault lay in José's inept and clumsy camerawork. This came as a shocker to Ely; he'd already signed José for the Medea. His solution was bred of desperation. José was to be left in charge of the actors, while a television director was to be taken on to handle the cameras. Surprisingly enough, it had worked. Medea had given Play of the Week a whirlwind send-off.

So, why not again? As a result, for The Fool Killer he signed José Quintero as Director with the Mexican as Camera Consultant.

In the meantime I was in Florida with MacKinlay Kantor, and having a ball. The water was cool, the air warm and, as it turned out, Mac was a Cordon Bleu chef. I have seldom had better food anywhere. It would have been an altogether joyous occasion, had it not been for one lethal fly in the ointment. Mac had completed the outline for his adaptation well before I arrived in Pensacola. In addition he had roughed in the dialogue for some forty-five to fifty pages of script. It made for some lusty and vigorous reading. Indeed, it could have been cause for a champagne celebration, if it had born any resemblance whatever to the original story he'd been given. It had a dramatic line; it was rich in the sociological, physiological and historical background of the Florida littoral between Tampa Bay and Pensacola; its atmosphere was aglow with color and local appeal. Only one thing: The Fool Killer wasn't even laid in Florida.

When I got back to New York I attempted to forewarn
Ely and Jack Dreyfus that, although Kantor had taken a few
"liberties" with the story, he was a Pulitzer Prize-winning
writer with a marvelous sense of atmosphere and character.
This tentative warning in no way diminished their anger and
dismay, particularly Jack's. He made it eminently clear that
not a penny of Dreyfus money would go toward the filming of
this unfortunate travesty.

Needless to say the deal fell through. We were left
with two leading actors, two directors, and no script. It was
then that I suggested to Ely that we bring on Mort Fine and
David Friedkin, my two partners from Frontier. After reading
three or four of their scripts as samples, Ely agreed they were
worth a try. I had a great deal tougher time than I'd expected
persuading them to come to New York. The word regarding Ely
was out; he was anything but easy to work with. In the end,
however, I managed to con them into giving it a whirl. The
following day they were on the plane for New York.

Working closely with me on the outline and structure
of the screenplay, they turned out a first draft in about six
weeks. It was never substantially changed from that time on.
They had captured the atmosphere of the original so sensi-
tively and with such a wealth of gentle humor that even Jack
Dreyfus could find no carping fault with it. Only one hurdle --
José Quintero became so enamored of the script he began
demanding a greater and greater control over the direction of
the picture. Inevitably this meant a lesser and lesser role for
Servando. The air was heavy. Various other problems, unions
for the most part, began to bedevil Ely, causing delay after
delay before the picture could get under way. Weeks length-
ened into months before we were able to select an acceptable
location -- Knoxville, Tennessee -- and a starting date.

In the interim, Philip Langner, Lawrence's son, had
brought in a book he had bought --

SCHAFFNER: At last! This must have been The
Pawnbroker.

MINER: Right. Philip and his partner, Roger Lewis, had
had some sort of adaptation made in England. I thought it was
pitifully inadequate. So did Ely. Fortuitously Mort and Dave
had just completed their draft of The Fool Killer. As a result,
they were, for the moment, in high favor with Ely. As soon as
I said, "What about Mort and Dave?" Ely would consider no one
else for the job. Once again I found myself closeted with "the
boys," hammering out an outline for The Pawnbroker.

It was a far larger and more difficult job than The
Fool Killer, but after months of work, almost a year, they
brought forth a script in which I felt a genuine pride. It wasn't
a "big" production, no Gone With the Wind nor Apocalypse
Now; it was a small, but sparkling, gem. I had become so
wrapped up in it that, when Ely scheduled it to start one week
after The Fool Killer began, I was insistent on remaining in
New York. Let Jose and the others "do what they will" in
Knoxville.

Forewarnings of an impending storm reached New York
within forty-eight hours. Not only was the friction between
José and Servando disrupting morale, Quintero's rushes for the
first few days were so bad it was clear that they could never
be used. Within an hour I was on a plane to Knoxville; after
one day on location I was on the phone to Ely. Superb a
director as Quintero was for the theatre, he was at sea in
films. God had endowed him with no visual sense whatever.
Production, I suggested, should be stopped before wasting
another day.

Ely was realistic enough to offer no objection. But
then he made one of his tragic mistakes of judgment. Instead
of hiring another qualified director, he decided to go ahead
with Servando Gonzales in full command. His adulation of
Yanco was so exaggerated, he was blinded to Servando's crass
insensitivities, his lack of humor and his compelling sadism. All
Ely saw was that Yanco had been the story of a young boy
with a dream; The Fool Killer was the story of a young boy
with a dream; ergo, Servando was the one the gods intended to
bring The Fool Killer to life. There were two colossal hurdles,
however:

One: Servando would not, could not, speak comprehensible English, nor, it seemed, understand the little English he could read. If he had ever struggled through The Fool Killer script, which is doubtful, he had understood not a word. Its people were totally beyond his ken.

Two: Even had he read the script with full understanding, it would have made no difference. Servando was such an appalling egotist, he would have falsified The Fool Killer no matter what. As soon as shooting began it became evident that he was hell-bent on destroying the script; he was out to make a name for himself. Nothing the book had to say was to be allowed to obtrude.

By the time I was free enough to look at a rough cut of the film, what greeted me was so distorted I could scarcely sit through it. I spent close to a year trying to salvage this mutilated story; I redubbed every line spoken by either Tony Perkins or young Edward Albert; I re-cut every foot of the film; I transposed parts of scenes, even whole scenes; I brought some hint of cosmos out of utter chaos. It was not enough. After two or three pitiful efforts to release it, The Fool Killer was withdrawn from circulation. It remains interred within the locker of unhappy "might have beens." And it was such a darlin' script.

SCHAFFNER: And The Pawnbroker?

MINER: The Pawnbroker fared somewhat better. Lumet did such a sensitive and interesting job on eighty percent of it, it nearly concealed how gravely he had hurt the script as a whole by cheapening the end.

He had always been out of sympathy with what the book had to say. Thus he was forced to invent an entire new finale. Once he found a denouement to his liking, The Pawnbroker was left with an ultimate statement so meretricious and irrelevant that it became untenable. The one thing left was to recast the part of the woman through whom the pawnbroker was meant to find a new vista of life. In place of the large, maternal and unmistakably Nordic original, Sidney had selected Geraldine Fitzgerald. While a superb actress, Geraldine was so physically and temperamentally unsuited to the part, her every finest quality was hopelessly at war with everything the author and the script were trying to say. In self-defense Sidney rewrote her scenes to make his casting defensible. It also vitiated and demeaned an otherwise dignified story. Again Ely's native sensitivity was not strong enough to stand up to Sidney's insistence. The result? A modest success. It should have been, it could have been, a great deal more.

One final note, in part, at least, to balance the scales for Sidney. Some years later Ely offered him the chance to repeat on film the job he had done on tape with The Iceman, a job Sidney wanted so badly he could taste it. When Ely added the small proviso, however, that Lee Marvin should play Hickey in place of Jason Robards, Sidney's latent sense of integrity erupted. He refused. Ely's inability to resist the allure of a name in lights was, for once, stronger than his supine acceptance of anything Sidney demanded. Ely stood firm for Lee Marvin; Sidney did not do the picture. Sidney can forever count among his "finest hours" the knowledge that at this critical moment he could not be bought.

SCHAFFNER: According to my notes, The Pawnbroker marked a finale to your picture career. Is that true?

MINER: Substantially, yes.

SCHAFFNER: Why? Surely there was a place for you in pictures, even if you minimize the impact of The Pawnbroker.

MINER: I was up against something inexorable, and The Fool Killer and The Pawnbroker had done nothing to lessen its sobering validity. I was no longer in demand. Moreover, it would have taken too long for me to achieve once more a status commensurate with what I had known.

SCHAFFNER: Why?

MINER: I had no money of my own, and I had no one ready to give it to me without retaining final control. If I'd had the money, no one could have done to The Fool Killer, The Pawnbroker and, above all, to Long Day's Journey Into Night, what Ely and Sidney and Servando Gonzales had done. I had fought, and fought hard in each case, and I had lost each time. Had I been twenty-five I might have gone on bucking the system until I'd built up a solid enough record of success to tell the moneybags to go to hell. I'd been lucky, I'd been given more than my share of autonomy for the best part of thirty-five years. When I had fought, and God knows I had often and bruisingly, those with the money had repeatedly given me my way. Never before had my judgment and taste been ignored. I knew myself well enough to know I could never again live and breathe in this kind of atmosphere. Imagination would soon shrivel with so threatening a veto hanging over my head. To bring my own philosophy into play against myself, I'd had my quota of decades. I belonged to a generation that was gone; its one-time freshness was now stale.

SCHAFFNER: How old were you?

MINER: Roughly sixty-five. There may have been a flood of energy left, but I was growing tired of the emotional disappointments and disillusionments that had marked the latter part of my years in the business.

XI

MINER: Once again chance, or mischance, released me from writing my own epitaph in wasted days. In December of 1963 Fran and I were offered a house in Florida for the Christmas holidays. She had not been feeling well for some weeks; both of us felt that a warming sun and a few lazy days might soon set her on her feet once more. Thus we accepted the offer, arriving in Pompano Beach a week to ten days before Christmas.

Forty-eight hours later, a day when a southern sun lifted the thermometer to a temperate 80 degrees Fahrenheit and a mellow breeze came in from the Caribbean, Fran awoke with a hacking cough and a fever of 102. By afternoon she was in the hospital with what the doctors called a "threat of TB." Further tests over the next few days did not, we were told, support those dreary predictions. And so, on Christmas Eve she was allowed to come home.

We stayed on until just after the New Year, 1964. By then her condition had so evidently worsened, we decided to desert the balmy Florida sunlight and head for New York, frostbitten though it might be. We were blessed with one stroke of fortune. Fran's doctor of many years standing turned out to be the foremost authority on tuberculosis to be found. His name was Carl Muschenheim and he saved her life. But this took a weary time, early January to late July.

SCHAFFNER: You've said Fran's TB started you on a whole new career.

MINER: A simple, yet nearly tragic, accident. By late
April the final dubbing on <u>The Pawnbroker</u> was completed. My
mood was sullen, even despondent. I was in no rush to make up
my mind about the future course of my life. Any move that
deferred such a decision was enticing to me. The idea of
dropping in on the the American Academy (where Fran was
president) for a week or so to check on its instructors and
directors was just such a transient prospect. The renovations
on the Stanford White home acquired for the Academy's new
location on Madison Avenue were nearing completion; we had
assumed occupancy a week or two earlier. I also looked forward to the opportunity of checking on the final selections of
color for the paint and carpeting, particularly for the hallways
and the two reconstructed theatres. And so on a Monday
morning in early May I arrived in Fran's office with the sole
intention of visiting the classrooms and theatres where a
schedule of Senior Class plays was in rehearsal.

My first report was glowing. There was excitement in
the classrooms. A large share of the directors was thoroughly
professional, often stimulating. It was a relief to let Fran
know that everything at 120 Madison was healthy and sound.
There were soft spots, of course. There were some students
who should never have been invited back for the senior year;
there were some directors whose handling of comedy left much
to be desired. Overall, however, the word was "Go!"

It was a bare two weeks before the hidden rot was
exposed. I arrived that morning to find the school's Business
Administrator waiting on my doorstep. He had just received in
that morning's mail a bill from the City of New York for
overdue taxes, plus interest, of $17,000. A few questions
revealed that this was due to an inexcusable oversight on the
part of our then-legal counsel. To make matters even stickier,
he was also a member of the Board of Trustees. His tenure
dated back to the days of Franklin Haven Sargent, the Academy's founder, who had died in 1924. While I could gladly have
cut his legal throat, I was relatively unconcerned about the
immediate problem. Fran, I knew, had left the Academy with
enough reserve funds to take care of such a contingency.

"Don't look so unhappy," I said. "The school's not going
to collapse. We're tax exempt, you know. Besides -- "

"That I know," he said, "but we weren't then. Our lawyer goofed. It could have been avoided, but it wasn't. So -- where are we now?"

"What do you mean, 'where are we now?'"

"We don't have $17,000."

Little by little the facts began to spill forth. Not only did we not have the $17,000, we had already invaded our advance tuition by $42,000. The brutal truth was we were bankrupt.

I had served as a Trustee of the Academy since 1948; Fran had been its President and Director since 1954. She had pulled it out of a threatening bankruptcy then and left it with a reserve fund of $185,000 when she entered the hospital. I was not about to let that Herculean effort go down the drain without a struggle. I made up my mind then and there that I would not leave the Academy before the school was once again healthy and financially secure.

SCHAFFNER: So where did you start?

MINER: Fran came up with the first coherent suggestion. A year before she had had the foresight to arm herself against a possible cost overrun on renovations. Even though the estimate was only $135,000 against a cash reserve of $185,000, she had gone to the bank and secured a guaranteed loan agreement. . . .

Precisely because the Academy's situation appeared desperate, if not impossible, it awakened the quickening excitement and the stubbornness of one more pioneering adventure. It was the overture to my third and final career.

Fran dreamed of leaving the Academy with a home of its own. That she accomplished in the first ten years, 1954-1964. To establish the Academy as a truly national institution, operating in both of our major production centers took another ten years. The American Academy West enrolled its first student body in September '73. What remained was my pledge, silent and to myself alone, to stick with the school until it had at last established financial security.

SCHAFFNER: But I thought it was thriving.

MINER: Relatively true. When Fran took over in 1954 there were a mere 143 students in the school, and a projected deficit of $57,000. By 1963 enrollment had increased to over 1,000, and the Academy was the owner of that beautiful Stanford White building.

SCHAFFNER: At a cost of?

MINER: One dollar.

SCHAFFNER: You stole it?

MINER: You'd like that, wouldn't you?

SCHAFFNER: I wouldn't go that far, but I certainly wouldn't put it beyond you.

MINER: It was free enterprise at its best. Fran and I had gone to look over the building two years earlier. We had known at once that it was ideal, but the asking price at that time was $750,000 down against a purchase price of $1,200,000.

One lucky happenstance -- we had Roger Stevens on our Board at that time. He hadn't yet taken over Kennedy Center. It gave us an inside track in the field of real estate in the City of New York. Two years later Fran got a call from Roger, letting her know that the following week 120 Madison Avenue was coming up for a bankruptcy sale. We could probably get it for one dollar by taking over a first and second mortgage totalling $515,000 at six percent constant, roughly $36,000 a year including amortization. Since we were by then paying something over $52,000 per annum in rent for thoroughly inadequate space in the ANTA Theatre Building, along with scattered rooms outside, there was little opposition from the Board. We bought. But with Fran in the hospital and the renovation of the building under way, we got into trouble, and only evaded catastrophe by a combination of luck, timing, and fundraising.

My first appeal was to CBS via Ralph Colin. I got nowhere; CBS had, he told me, recently established a policy precluding its support of any theatrical training school. It was thoroughly justified; if it backed one, why not all? I wrote NBC, but with no luck whatever; they didn't even grant me the courtesy of a response. Last, and least likely, was ABC. As I sat down to write the letter, a long-ago and hazy memory kept nudging at my mind. You probably remember that Fran's uncle was Jimmy (James F.) Byrnes. I kept recalling an evening we'd had during the brief time he'd served as Czar of the Motion Picture Industry. He had described for Fran and me a meeting with all the best-known moguls of the day. One young man, Leonard Goldenson, had particularly attracted Jim's attention. While obviously a figure of lesser importance, Jim was impressed by his clarity of mind.

While I had never met Len, his name was, of course, known to me. Why not? I thought. A little flattery was never amiss. I started my letter by recalling this incident. From there I went on to call his attention to the fact, almost certainly unknown to him, that nine of the most popular series on the ABC network were headed by graduates of one school, the American Academy of Dramatic Arts.

My specific proposal was that ABC organize a nationwide set of auditions by eight regional stations to select sixteen qualified scholarship students to enroll in the American Academy in the fall of 1965, and, we fondly hoped, in each fall thereafter. His response came through in the form of a telephone call requesting that Fran and I meet with him.

We arrived a few minutes early to be escorted at once to Len's office where he, Tom Moore and Jim Hagerty were already assembled. Not only was everyone uncommonly cordial, but all three seemed eager to get things moving as fast as possible. I don't think it was more than five minutes before Len turned to me and said:

"How much do you need? Not just these auditions, we're sold on them already. How much do you need to get your heads above water?"

I was too stunned to give a thoughtful response. I merely grinned. "Oh, I don't know," I said. "Half a million?" I was, of course, joking. It was outrageous.

Without blinking he turned to Tom Moore. "I think that ought to be all right, don't you Tom?" Tom nodded.

"Jim, can you get together with Tony this week? I'd like to get this thing rolling."

Jim grinned. "As long as you don't sick too many goddamned lawyers on my tail, yes."

There was no champagne, but the mood was bubbly. The first ABC scholarship student was Cleavon Little. The agreement lasted three years before ABC fell on hard times and had to cut it off. It's one of the few times I've ever heard "regretfully" uttered with genuine feeling. It had been a warm and rewarding venture on both sides, and it had been enough to rescue the Academy. It had supplied the impetus, as well as the dollars, we needed. By 1969 not only had the school paid off its second mortgage, but all its other debts had been liquidated as well. Just a month ago our surplus reached $1,000,000.

SCHAFFNER: You became a financial wunderkind!

MINER: (a laugh) I've been no wizard. Let's call it unconventional. And I'm delighted to find so many of my gambits working out against all predictions. Even at the time, I knew what I was accomplishing did not greatly matter to me as a person. It was as though I had found out I could juggle. It brought an instant, but evanescent, satisfaction. It mattered for the Academy, and that was good, but it never, even for a moment, enthralled me. I belong with the grease paint and, despite any help I may have been to the Academy and its economic survival, my happiest moments have come with the direction of the few productions I have taken on at the school, and with the solidification in my own mind of those principles of acting that have stood up against the test of years.

SCHAFFNER: Sounds as though you had begun to think deeply about acting only after you were no longer an active part of the theatre.

MINER: If that's a castigation, I must accept it. But the truth is not quite that simple. In the thirties I had become dedicated to certain principles and practices that appeared to me most productive and enduring. I was a loner; I was never a joiner. From this vantage point I observed the Group from its inception; many of its members were, as I have said, favorites of mine. We worked well together. We argued, of course. We argued long hours. The parts of Stanislavsky I revered, the disciplines, were often the parts of Stanislavsky they dismissed. I could never quite understand it; they had all in fact been through a rigorous amount of training, a training they insisted on denigrating in theory. The best of them, the Adlers, Luther and Stella, Joe Bromberg, Morris Carnovsky, Franchot Tone, Lee J. Cobb, won swift recognition. Even some of the lesser members, Julie Garfield, Bobby Lewis, Sandy Meisner, etc., were aided by the intensification of their emotional responses.   But the younger people, Alexander Kirkland, as a prize example, suffered from their technical clumsiness, from their failure to exercise the controls, physical and mental, that derive from professional discipline.

The Group got away with it for a time; so many were topnotch actors even before they were taken into the Junior Theatre Guild. Indeed, it was why they were taken in. The grievous flaw in their philosophy was only exposed as the Studio tried to expand from an Elysée for proven actors, a place where they could take refresher courses or work on expanding their range, into a school of basic training. Then began the adulation of instinct over training, of street-language over articulate speech, of meretricious mannerisims over honest characterization. And so, when a truly fine talent like Marlon Brando began to mumble, half the actors from coast to coast began to mumble too, and, quite unforgivably, the great majority of critics applauded. Fine actors like Lee Cobb and John Garfield survived, but too many, far too many, fell into habits as spurious as the old ham's handkerchief. Otherwise good actors began picking grubs out of the wood-work, or using naked toes to attract attention. A whole generation learned to give dazzling performances for the first six rows in the orchestra; from the seventh row back they offered little more than inaudible mush.

SCHAFFNER: And what were the principles you learned after you moved into the Academy?

MINER: I learned that what I had advocated and prac-ticed for some forty years of theatre and television had been advocated and practiced at the Academy under Charles Jehlinger for close to sixty years, a couple of decades before An Actor Prepares reached these shores. The transition from television to the Academy opened few new windows for my mind, but finding the things I had believed articulated with such sympathy and cohesion aroused my deep and persistent admiration.

What did astound me was the fact that the Academy had been, since its inception, far more than a school of dramatic training. It had represented a radical and remarkably sensitive approach to the basic principles of education itself. Franklin Haven Sargent had rebelled against the stuffy and inflexible pedagogy of the post-Civil War era at Harvard. He proclaimed that teaching in American universities stopped at the exact point where true teaching should begin. It was not enough, he asserted, to cram knowledge into a young person's head; the teacher had a moral obligation to help that young person to translate that knowledge into creative thought and creative action. It was not just a two- to four-year concept; it was a lifetime principle.

All of this fitted in with Bob Hutchins's belief that a liberal arts education was not designed to teach a trade -- law, banking, art or carpentry -- but to teach a young person how to think. The Academy supplied for me a stronger mental and intellectual stimulus than I had known for many a year.

Concurrently Berkeley was bursting into flame and the catchword most loudly proclaimed by an angry youth was "irrelevant." God in heaven, can you think of anything more relevant to those tortured young minds than the history of Athens in the 5th Century B.C.? Even more disheartening to me was the craven conduct of the teaching community, so many of whom sold out their integrity for a dollop of popularity with the student body. . . .

We found we could still, even in the sixties and seventies, teach with the insights of the Academy's former great leader, Charles Jehlinger. "To become an actor," he said, "a young person must possess the soul of a child and the hide of a rhinoceros." And then, after a pause, "The sad part is that in acquiring the hide of a rhinoceros, so many lose the soul of the child."

But Jehli never wrote anything. There's one little pamphlet we pass around to everyone in the school, and to other interested parties, called "Jehli in Rehearsal." It's nothing but a collection of notes taken down by a student in 1918-19. It doesn't define a coherent theory, nor lay out a course of study. It merely records the type of things Jehli would say again and again and again to students in the classroom.

SCHAFFNER: Such as?

MINER: "Don't talk. Converse!" -- "Stop acting. Become!" -- "Don't declaim. Converse!" -- "Never change thought, theme or mood, until something happens to change them." -- "Don't shout. Converse!" -- "Never be untrue to the character. But always be as attractive as the character will allow." -- "Don't rant -- !"

SCHAFFNER: " -- Converse!" And if I were to ask: "What is acting?" how would he have responded?

MINER: No one but Jehli should answer that, and I'm sure he would have had an answer we'd remember. The best I can hypothesize is: "Listen. Understand. And respond."

SCHAFFNER: But good as it is, I have a feeling it wasn't all.

MINER: You're right, it wasn't all. There remained all the unspoken parts, the parts that were still carried forward from an earlier tradition. When Jehli said: "Respond," the voice of the Academy was adding: "And let it be heard in the last seat of the house." And the voice of Sargent would add: "And let it be spoke in its proper accents, not in distorted remnants of Hillbilly, Cockney or Georgian vernacular." When he said "understand," the voice would add, "Let nothing mundane nor ugly impede an audience's or a fellow actor's swift comprehension of the words being spoke."

SCHAFFNER: What I'm not sure I grasp is the essence of what you teach at the Academy. What makes it so different?

MINER: One simple declarative sentence: "The mind comes first."

SCHAFFNER: So?

MINER: Now add: "For an actor."

SCHAFFNER: For an actor the mind comes first.

MINER: But think how many would insist that "the emo-tions come first," or "the heart comes first," or "the body comes first" -- including voice, speech and physical grace. But for Charles Jehlinger and Franklin Haven Sargent it was unequivocably "the mind." "The mind comes first" is the rock on which the Academy is founded.

SCHAFFNER: Why is it that the Academy is so often accused of being old-fashioned?

MINER: Because we are. We're the oldest school of act-ing in the English-speaking world.

SCHAFFNER: Older than the Royal Academy?

MINER: By close to twenty years. We opened our doors for the first time in 1884 -- October, to be precise. We're also the inheritors of some profound truths about acting. So long as no more profound truths are unearthed, we prefer to stick with what we have. But the popular sweep in recent years has given little weight to truth. Its demand has been for something new. "Innovative" has become the catchword, and a most unattrac-tive word it is.

XII

SCHAFFNER: Tony, what are you?

MINER: I'm impatient and I'm intolerant, and age doesn't seem to have softened me one damn bit. I'm intolerant of stupidity.

In the thirties I foresaw the war with Hitler and I abhorred it. But I also foresaw, and with no qualifying doubts, that we were going to win out. Today, unlike 1937, we are living on the brink of annihilation. No matter how unspoken, the Bomb is every person's nightmare. Because of this obscenity I view the closing days of this 20th century with haunting apprehension. I still know with a kind of illogical and indefensible assurance that we are going to survive. Our industrial plant is less invincible, our armed forces are in greater disarray and our political establishment is infested with greed. But none of this, including the Bomb itself, will be as bad as we now expect it to be. We will survive, but at such a cost that the rejoicing will be reserved for our children's children.

How could anyone have predicted the course or the culmination of this swirling century? It, and I, began with sleigh bells, buckboards and firecrackers on the Fourth of July. Our nation was a composite of thousands and thousands of "Our Town's" -- our hopes were high, but the pace was drowsy. It began with pride and a quiet dignity; it is ending with shame -- the shame of Hiroshima, the shame of My Lai, the shame of 'Nam. We've come too far too fast. We are ending by invading space, by exploring the planets, by setting our watches by light-years. We have out-raced our mind's capacity to adjust, to digest, or to comprehend.

275

SCHAFFNER: Where are we going?

MINER: We are the serfs and servitors of a Supreme and Magnificent Illogic. It is both arrogant and unapologetic. That's why I am still so hopeful for our tomorrow. The search remains a glorious adventure and a grail. (a laugh) I can see this is all too simplistic and roseate for you.

SCHAFFNER: Is this a long-lasting belief of yours?

MINER: Not so very. Oh, all of us enjoy the search for Truth with a capital "T"; it's a teenage syndrome. But this sophomoric earnestness is soon dispelled by the pragmatic struggle to break away from home, to make it on our own, to love and be unloved, to succeed and to fail.

SCHAFFNER: Abandoning faith when we need it most.

MINER: Out of misplaced shame. I was ashamed, so hideously ashamed, of my need for faith. It lasted damn near thirty years. I ridiculed the "Hound of Heaven" in the futile hope it would start pursuing someone else. But, because Fran was a Catholic, I found myself having to articulate what I believed, and what I did not believe. Echoes of childhood began to intrude. With me it was still the First Chapter of Genesis. It was there I had taught myself to read, and, curiously enough, to believe without ever really asking myself what it was I accepted, what I rejected. I only knew that this part of the Bible was, for me, an evocative symbol of inexpressible beauty and ineluctable wonder. I began to steep myself in all I could unearth on the subject. It became, at least intermittently, an obsession. I had to find for myself, if for no one else, an answer I could accept. Late one night I tried to describe the quest and the hold it had taken.

SCHAFFNER: You mean you put something down on paper?

MINER: Yes.

SCHAFFNER: Can you remember it?

MINER: I think so. It's not long.

    "Two travelers met on a dark and raging night.
Against the storm one cried out:
    'Where are we going? Dost thou know?'
    Said the Other: 'If I knew better whence I had
come, I might a better answer give.'
    They were brothers and knew it not.
    So goes the legend."

SCHAFFNER: Finis?

MINER: Finis. What better way can you think of than to
end with a question?

SCHAFFNER: What you have achieved in your lifetime
matters. Do you agree?

MINER: I do indeed.

SCHAFFNER: Then why do I get the persistent feeling
that what you're trying to say is that your life is no more than
an entry marked: "Forgettable"?

MINER: Isn't it? Provided, of course, you're talking about
my so-called "career." Why else am I here talking to you now
except to capture a fragment of immortality? Immortality for
what I have done and the ideas I have had. I am not a Hank
Fonda nor an Alan Alda whose achievements have been
recorded on film or tape. Thereby some immortality is for
them foretold. What I face is more endemic to Mankind. Given

a decade, two at the most, and all I've accomplished, every idea I've nurtured will be as forgotten as Colley Cibber. If that had made me bitter, I long since would have put a bullet through my head.

SCHAFFNER: Then what accounts for the solemn mood?

MINER: Because, for me, it is solemn. I find it hard to chuckle over an infinity of light-years. Eternity has made anything I've accomplished in the theatre or television seem relatively trivial. What I have contributed as a human being has become, to my mind, of immeasurably greater importance. And something I could never have predicted. I have discovered from working with the young, that as each acquires stature as a Man so each acquires stature as an artist.

My apparent digressions into a more philosophic turn of thought have proven to be unexpectedly relevant to a summary of my years. A soberer and wiser set of values was not, I found, tangential to a Man's brief interlude on earth. Those values could indeed contribute to both his stature and his success.

SCHAFFNER: Is that your ultimate conclusion?

MINER: There remains a sequitur. Once I had accepted the existence of a Creator, it became impossible for me to believe that our vast universe had been conceived without purpose. As I could not accept that all the laws holding our galaxy together were merely accidental, nor that a Big Bang could have occurred without there having been something there ahead of time to go "bang" with, so it defied credence that this could have happened without intent. But intention implies that, up until now, our universe is both incomplete and imperfect. It never has been anything else. Here the Bible and I come to a parting of the ways.

The Bible says that the Lord looked on the light "and saw that it was good." In other words, up until Eden all

Creation was perfect. Only later, and through the evil handiwork of Satan, Beelzebub, Lilith and Eve, that perfection was
destroyed, meaning, or so the orthodox insist, that Man is now
granted a lifetime of struggle and temptation for which the
highest reward he can hope to achieve is a return to the same
perfection that had been his at conception.

What a stinking deal! And, if Heaven is to be the home
of the Just for eternity, it better have a few more attractions
to offer than either God, the Bible or the Church has yet
revealed. A wholesale supply of harps is paltry reward for a
lifetime of suffering, pain and self-denial.

SCHAFFNER: You have not always been popular, have
you?

MINER: Signally unpopular for a large part of my lifetime. I have learned to keep my private life private. It's been
far from easy. We disrespect the needy, we shatter the silent,
we buffet the still. . . .

SCHAFFNER: And to what do you cling?

MINER: I cling to the idea that God has created an
imperfect world. I cling to the belief that God is less than
almighty, that perfection, His kind of perfection, is not yet
within His grasp. I believe that we were created for a purpose,
and that, while the existence of life at some other point in the
universe is still possible, it becomes less and less probable as
we bore more deeply into space.

My ultimate belief is that God has nowhere else to
turn, that we are needed, and that the balance we leave of
good or evil becomes the reserve on which God in some final
cataclysmic moment may have to draw for the power He needs
to complete the dream. We who hold this belief must accept
the enormity of our responsibility for our earthly conduct.
This, I assert, gives to life a meaning it has never had, an
eternal partnership with the universal God-head.

280

SCHAFFNER: And that is the essence?

MINER: That is everything I have to leave, a small balance of good, I hope, over evil. All the rest, my name included, will be forgotten.

SCHAFFNER: Tony, thank you.

MINER: Adieu.

286